MW00770385

Unsettling the University

CRITICAL UNIVERSITY STUDIES
Jeffrey J. Williams and Christopher Newfield, Series Editors

Unsettling the University

Confronting the Colonial Foundations
of US Higher Education

Sharon Stein

JOHNS HOPKINS UNIVERSITY PRESS   BALTIMORE

Johns Hopkins University Press
2715 North Charles Street
Baltimore, Maryland 21218
www.press.jhu.edu

Library of Congress Cataloging-in-Publication Data

Names: Stein, Sharon, 1986– author.
Title: Unsettling the university : confronting the colonial
    foundations of US higher education / Sharon Stein.
Description: Baltimore : Johns Hopkins University Press, 2022. |
    Series: Critical university studies | Includes bibliographical
    references and index.
Identifiers: LCCN 2022005888 | ISBN 9781421445045 (hardcover) |
    ISBN 9781421445052 (ebook)
Subjects: LCSH: Education, Higher—United States—History. |
    Universities and colleges—United States—History. |
    Violence—United States—History.
Classification: LCC LA226 .S687 2022 | DDC 378.73—dc23/
    eng/20220315
LC record available at https://lccn.loc.gov/2022005888

A catalog record for this book is available from the British Library.

*Special discounts are available for bulk purchases of this book. For more
information, please contact Special Sales at specialsales@jh.edu.*

For Sarah R.
and all those fighting for decolonial futures

Contents

Unsettling the University

Introduction

Colleges and universities are historical institutions. They may suffer amnesia, or have selective recall, but ultimately heritage is the lifeblood of our campuses.

—John Thelin, 2004, p. xiii

Settler colonialism pervades almost every aspect of institutional memory and life. Let us not forget that what seemed to be "barren and desolate" actually held centuries of connections to plants, medicines, creation stories, and other meaningful connections that are forgotten in the told stories of higher education institutions.

—Robin Starr Zape-tah-hol-ah Minthorn & Chris Nelson, 2018, p. 85

American colleges were not innocent or passive beneficiaries of conquest and colonial slavery. The European invasion of the Americas and the modern slave trade pulled peoples throughout the Atlantic world into each others' lives, and colleges were among the colonial institutions that braided their histories and rendered their fates dependent and antagonistic.

—Craig Steven Wilder, 2013, p. 11

On September 18, 2019, New Mexico announced plans to offer free public higher education for all state residents, funded largely by increased revenue from oil production in the state.

Just a day earlier, the University of California announced that it would divest its endowment funds of fossil fuel stocks. In an op-ed piece for the *Los Angeles Times*, the university's chief investment officer–treasurer and chairman of the board of regents' investments committee noted, "The reason we sold some $150 million in fossil fuel assets from our endowment was the reason we sell other assets: They posed a long-term risk to generating strong returns for UC's diversified portfolios.... We have chosen to *invest* for a better planet, and reap the financial rewards for UC, rather than simply *divest* for a headline" (Baccher & Sherman, 2019). Viewed together, these two announcements offer a glimpse into the possible futures for public higher education that are deemed imaginable and desirable in what is currently known as the United States. In one case, a state planned to boost public funding through profits made from the extraction and sale of fossil fuels, while in the other, one of the country's largest public university systems justified its divestment from fossil fuels out of concern for future profits.

Beyond illustrating some of the contradictions and convergences that circulate within current popular horizons of hope about the future of US higher education, when viewed from a decolonial perspective, these two announcements expose the ethical and ecological limits of these horizons. Throughout this book, I use "decolonial" to refer to analyses and practices that (1) critique ways of knowing, being, and relating that are premised on systemic and ongoing colonial violence, and that (2) gesture toward possible futures in which these colonial patterns of knowledge, existence, and relationship are interrupted and redressed. I describe my approach to decolonial critique further in chapter 1. Despite their differences, in both announcements the future of public higher education is predicated on the continuity of a political economic system that requires endless growth, extraction, and consumption and that can therefore hold little regard for its negative impacts on the human and other-than-human beings who pay the price for this expansion. In this way, both of these proposed funding models reproduce the colonial architectures of accumulation that form the foundations of US higher education.

I use the phrase "colonial foundations of US higher education" to point to the fact that while entrenched patterns of institutional violence do have specific starting points, they are not relegated to the past. Rather, they have continued to shape all subsequent higher education developments—never in a deterministic way but nonetheless in a way that suggests different higher education futures will not be possible if we do not first untangle and reckon with these historical and ongoing colonial foundations. I trace the origins of these foundations, consider how the harms of colonization and slavery continue to seep through these foundations into the present, and question the structural integrity of a future that rests on these foundations, especially if we fail to confront their disavowed costs for people and the planet.

Situating This Book's Intervention

Scholars have addressed the immense contemporary challenges of US higher education from numerous theoretical and methodological perspectives. Yet across these different perspectives one finds a common rhetorical strategy (echoed in the popular media) that compares the current state of higher education to an idealized higher education past and uses that past as a guide for imagining an idealized higher education future.

There is an alternative means of engaging with contemporary US higher education that problematizes the naively hopeful narratives of US higher education futurity that presume seamless continuity and progress, as well as the selectively nostalgic narratives of US higher education history that invisibilize (make absent) colleges' and universities' structural complicity in racial, colonial, and ecological violence. In doing so, this book intervenes in what are by now fairly prolific and increasingly mainstream conversations across the fields of critical university studies and higher education studies about the privatization and marketization of higher education. The book engages this literature but also stretches it by bringing a decolonial lens to the fore using a historiographic method of analysis.

By examining the colonial foundations of US higher education with a view to their implications for the present and future, I suggest that contemporary forms of academic capitalism in the neoliberal university should be seen not as entirely novel but as rooted in a long-standing architecture of dispossession and accumulation that has formed the template for US higher education from the very beginning. Although this book does not address in great detail pressing contemporary challenges, such as surging student debt, precarious academic labor, and contentious questions about increasingly diverse campuses and curriculum reform, it suggests that if we engage these issues with the underlying colonial template of US higher education in mind, we are likely to arrive at very different conclusions about both the root causes of these problems and ethical modes of responding to them.

In this sense, *Unsettling the University* resonates with the work of a small but growing number of scholars and activists who have drawn attention to how US colleges and universities have been consistently implicated in the reproduction and naturalization of social and ecological harm, particularly by serving as "*an arm of the settler state*—a site where the logics of elimination, capital accumulation, and dispossession are reconstituted" (Grande, 2018, p. 47 [emphasis in original];

see also Andreotti et al., 2015; Boggs et al., 2019; Boggs & Mitchell, 2018; Boidin, Cohen, & Grosfoguel, 2012; Chatterjee & Maira, 2014; Daigle, 2019; Hailu & Tachine, 2021; S. Hunt, 2014; La Paperson, 2017; Meyerhoff, 2019; Minthorn & Nelson, 2018; Minthorn & Shotton, 2018; Patel, 2021; Rodríguez, 2012; Stewart-Ambo & Yang, 2021; Wilder, 2013). Many of these scholars are situated not in higher education studies or critical university studies but rather in Black, Indigenous, or other critical ethnic studies, women and gender studies, and related interdisciplinary fields (Stein, 2021), some of them organized under the heading of abolitionist university studies (Boggs et al., 2019). Despite their internal diversity, these critiques share a diagnosis that the fundamental harm inflicted by US higher education institutions is not only that they *exclude* historically and systemically marginalized communities but also that they were founded and continue to operate at the *expense* of those communities.

Drawing on this basic decolonial insight, this book offers an invitation to rethink inherited assumptions about the relationship between the past and the present of US higher education so that we might pluralize the available imaginaries for the future (Barnett, 2012, 2014; Stein, 2019). To pluralize possible higher education futures requires first interrupting the hegemony of the currently dominant vision for the future, which is rooted in three primary promises: (1) that higher education should exemplify and enable *continuous progress* within its own walls and society at large; (2) that higher education is, in its truest form, a benevolent *public good*; and (3) that a primary purpose of higher education is to enable *socioeconomic mobility*. These promises, which I unpack in more detail in chapter 1 and illustrate throughout this volume, shape the terms of both scholarly and popular conversations about higher education, including the questions that we ask about the predicament we currently face and, thus, the responses we are able to imagine and desire.

These promises have such a hold on the collective imagination about higher education that nearly all of the available theories, frames, grammars, and vocabularies for thinking about or enacting justice and change in higher education fail or falter when confronted with decolonial analyses that challenge their orienting assumptions and investments. As a result, many people—including scholars, administrators, students, staff, and the public as a whole—lack a frame of reference for substantively engaging with decolonial critiques and considering their implications for research, teaching, and practice in higher education. Further, even once people start to see the value of these critiques, they often decontextualize them, selectively extract from them, or graft them back into mainstream frames and practices in ways, whether intentional or not, that align with and therefore do not interrupt existing individual advantages and institutional agendas (Ahenakew, 2016; Spivak, 1988; Tuck & Yang, 2012).

Thus, one reason that decolonial critiques are often misunderstood or misused in higher education contexts is that preexisting intellectual scaffolding is not in place that would support rigorous, reflexive decolonial inquiry. But another reason is that many of us lack the capacities to hold space for the affective difficulties and discomforts inevitably involved in facing the depth, complexity, and magnitude of problems that have no immediate, feel-good solutions. Such difficulties and discomforts are further amplified when decolonial critiques ask us to question our investments in the benevolence and futurity of the institutions that helped to create these problems in the first place and, further, to accept responsibility for our own role in reproducing those problems. To confront these difficulties and discomforts in generative ways would require us to go beyond mere critique in order to develop stamina for the difficult, long-term work of confronting the violence that underwrites modern institutions of higher education, the study of higher education itself, and thus our livelihoods as scholars, practitioners, and students. It would also require us to develop capacities for redressing and repairing these violences within the contemporary context of volatility, uncertainty, complexity, and ambiguity. This, in turn, has significant political and economic implications, as it would require those who currently benefit from systemic injustice to give up their accumulated power and wealth. Mobilizing these kinds of decolonial changes at both individual and institutional levels is beyond what can be accomplished in this or any scholarly text, especially because it requires more than just intellectual work; however, I gesture toward some possible pathways forward.

While there remains a serious question as to whether higher education institutions can "right the wrongs that brought them into being" (Belcourt, 2018), this book is primarily intended for those who are most invested in the promises offered by US colleges and universities, which tend to be those of us who work and study within them. However, the aim here is not to convince people to adopt or embrace decolonial critiques of higher education. Instead, I invite those concerned about the current state and future of US higher education to "pause" (Patel, 2015) long enough to open themselves up to being surprised and unsettled by what decolonial critiques might teach us—including insight into the underlying costs of the promises our institutions offer. This will require interrupting the temptation to selectively "consume" decolonial critiques in ways that circularly affirm existing colonial assumptions, investments, and desires, in particular desires for virtue, purity, progress, and futurity (Jimmy, Andreotti, & Stein in Ahenakew, 2019; Shotwell, 2016; Stein et al., 2020; Tuck & Yang, 2012).

The book therefore offers no simplistic, universal, or feel-good solutions but rather emphasizes the challenges, complexities, conflicts, failures, and contradictions involved in trying to interrupt colonial patterns.

Although decolonial critiques offer no universal prescription for action, they can make it more difficult to avoid what many of us would rather not see and would prefer to turn our backs to. Facing this reality is vital in a time when it is increasingly difficult to ignore calls to reckon with the ongoing colonial legacies of our campuses. Thus, whether or not they ultimately agree with the decolonial critiques that orient this book, those who accept the invitation to pause might find that it enables them to ask previously unthinkable questions about the past, present, and future of US higher education, and about our subsequent responsibilities as scholars, practitioners, and students, without immediately demanding solutions or seeking absolution.

Addressing Unthought Questions

This book seeks to make tangible what remains largely "unthought" (Hartman & Wilderson, 2003) in both scholarly and mainstream conversations about US higher education. In particular, it seeks to interrogate the socially sanctioned ignorance (Spivak, 1988) about higher education's colonial foundations, so that we might identify and interrupt the reproduction of colonial logics and practices in the present. To do this, the book offers a thorough examination of what Kevin Bruyneel (2017) calls "settler memory" in narratives about US higher education. As Bruyneel notes, "When we fight about the meaning of the past, we are not fighting over history, we are fighting over memory, specifically the collective memories that purport to bind and define a people's sense of who they are from past to present and on into the future" (p. 36).

Settler memory refuses to attend to the implications of colonization in the present, even when evidence of those implications is readily available. I suggest that collective investment in the continuity of the shiny promises offered by US higher education, as well as collective disavowal of the role of racial, colonial, and ecological violence in enabling those promises, shapes the settler memory that contributes to the reproduction of higher education's romantic foundational myths and organizational sagas (Clark, 1972; Meyerhoff, 2019). Approaching the foundations of US higher education from a decolonial angle challenges the common framing through which people resist (admittedly troubling) contemporary institutional economic formations and imperatives by pining for a return to "better days."

As Abigail Boggs and Nick Mitchell (2018) note, this romanticism about the past "repeats the forgetting of the dispossession at the university's origins while simultaneously drumming up a sense of crisis regarding the potential consequences of its downfall" (p. 441; see also Boggs et al., 2019; Stein & Andreotti, 2017). In contrast to this wilful ignorance about the past and the ways it shapes the present, I invite readers to take up Jodi Byrd's (2011) question "*How might the terms of current academic and political debates change if the responsibilities of that very real lived condition of colonialism were prioritized as a condition of possibility?*" (p. xx [emphasis added]).

I supplement this question with another, which is implied by Byrd's but is nonetheless worth articulating, given the risk that critiques of colonialism will become anthropocentric and overlook the effects of colonization on other-than-human beings. That is: *How might the terms of current academic and political debates change if we also prioritized our reciprocal responsibilities to the earth as a living entity, rather than as a property or*

resource that can be commodified, owned, and even "made sustain-
able" for continued extractive purposes?

In bringing these two questions together, I am drawing on the work of decolonial, especially Indigenous, scholars and activists who have for a long time drawn connections between colonialism, capitalism, and climate change (Davis & Todd, 2017; Whyte, 2020). These connections point to the close relationship between (1) the systemic, historical, and ongoing racial-colonial violence that enables the US socioeconomic system and the comforts and securities it promises its citizens (especially white citizens) and (2) the inherent ecological unsustainability of a socioeconomic system that is premised on infinite extraction, growth, and accumulation, given that we inhabit a finite planet. This book seeks to integrate these two, often-siloed concerns, and consider their combined implications for higher education.

Many of the colonial dynamics, dispositions, and patterns that I address here have relevance beyond the US context. In particular, the book might resonate with the foundations of higher education in other settler colonial contexts, especially such Anglo-settler nations as Canada, Australia, and New Zealand. However, one thing decolonial thinking teaches is that the specificity of our social and geographical locations matter a great deal in the production of knowledge. There is no universal, objective "view from nowhere." Thus, before I offer my decolonial analysis, it is important to clarify the locus of enunciation from where I speak. In this introduction, I situate my approach to this project based on my own social and geographical location as a white settler US citizen living and studying higher education in what is currently known as Canada. I also address possible responses to the book, articulate some of the questions that orient the book, and then outline each of the forthcoming chapters.

Colonial Foundations across the 49th Parallel:
The View from Canada

Unsettling the University is about the colonial foundations of higher education in what is currently known as the United States, but it was largely written in what is currently known as Canada. I say "what is currently known as" in order to remind us that while settler colonization is an ongoing structure, its continuation is certainly not inevitable. Indeed, it is important to remember that "compared to the thousands and thousands of years of history and relationships that Indigenous nations have with these lands and waters," the Canadian nation-state is very young (Corrina Sparrow, personal communication, November 3, 2021). In this section, I focus on the Canadian context not only because it helps situate me as the author but also because some have suggested that institutions of higher education in Canada are more "advanced" in their conversations about settler colonialism. This perspective is often supported by a narrative, repeated on both sides of the US-Canada border, that positions Canada as more progressive and less racist than its southern neighbor (Shaker, 2010). Among other factors, this framing helps to perpetuate narratives of Canadian exceptionalism and to minimize the violences perpetrated and sanctioned by the Canadian state (Thobani, 2007). Thus, rather than frame Canadian higher education as an exemplary "model" for how to engage decolonizing work, we can ask what it might teach those in the United States about the complexities, challenges, circularities, failures, and possibilities that are involved in institutional efforts to address systemic colonial violence.

As Michael Marker (2011) notes, the US-Canada border is a colonial fiction, a relatively recent construct that has nonetheless arbitrarily, forcibly, and violently divided Indigenous communities and other-than-human beings in the service of securing settler state sovereignties along with capitalist profits. Over time, the nation-states on either side of the border have developed their own particular brands of colonial governance (Thobani, 2018). It was on the Canadian side that I learned to think deeply about what it means to be a white settler-occupier on dispossessed Indigenous lands. And on that side of the border is where this book was mostly written, specifically, on the traditional, ancestral, and unceded lands of the hənq̓əminəm̓-speaking xʷməθkʷəy̓əm (Musqueam) Nation, which is currently situated within the boundaries of what is currently known as Vancouver, British Columbia. More precisely, I wrote this book largely from my office in what is today the Vancouver (Point Grey) campus of the University of British Columbia (UBC) and my rented apartment in Wesbrook Village, on land that is "owned," managed, and made extremely profitable by UBC.

To avoid reproducing colonial notions of universality and placelessness, efforts to address enduring colonial relations in higher education should be highly attuned to the specific histories, landscapes, and contemporary social contexts of each institution. At the same time, the case of UBC, its colonial foundations, and contemporary efforts to address those foundations, illustrate larger systemic patterns that characterize the coloniality of higher education across both Canada and the United States—and in many other settler colonial contexts as well.

As Corrina Sparrow, a Two Spirit member and leader within the Musqueam Nation, points out, "UBC and essentially all academic institutions have situated their campuses on ancestral Indigenous lands without local Indigenous nations' consent" (personal communication, January 29, 2021). Before colonization, what is now the UBC Point Grey campus in Vancouver was a forest that fed and educated the Musqueam Nation and played a central role in their spiritual and social life (Grant, 2018). Sparrow notes, "According to Musqueam cultural knowledge, our Nation has occupied and cared for these lands and waters in our ancestral territories since the last Ice Age, and we have resided in the 'Point Grey' area (we have our own hən̓q̓əmin̓əm̓ names for these places and the villages we have established here), for the past 3,000 years, as far as we know" (personal communication, November 3, 2021). Today, Musqueam continue to assert their presence as the original and ongoing inhabitants and caretakers of this place. So how did UBC come to occupy these lands, especially given that, as is the case with most lands in what is currently known as the province of British Columbia, the Musqueam Nation never signed a treaty to share it with settlers, let alone surrender it? In addressing this question, I first introduce how "whitestream" higher education institutions have sought to displace and replace Indigenous peoples and their knowledges. "Whitestream" refers to a context that is not only dominated by white people "but also principally structured on the basis of white, middle-class experience, serving their ethnopolitical interests and capital investments" (Grande, 2004, p. 125).

Settler Replacement and the Universalization of Western Universities

Western universities claim universal relevance as if they were synonymous with higher education itself, despite being rooted in the particularities of medieval Christian Europe and later of the European Enlightenment and industrial capitalist society. However, if we define higher education as the pursuit of specialized learning, then arguably every society has its own form of higher education (Perkin, 2007; Stonechild, 2006). Blair Stonechild (2006) reminds us that long before

European colonization and the establishment of settler colonial colleges and universities, Indigenous peoples "had traditional concepts of 'higher education' in which they undertook lifelong pursuit of specialized knowledge in order to become hunters, warriors, political leaders, or herbalists" (p. 2).

One way of de-universalizing the institutionalized modern university as the only viable model of higher education is therefore to suggest that "higher education" is not reducible to the modern university, much in the same way that K–12 scholars have established that "education" is not reducible to "modern schooling" (Calderon, 2014). In this framing, "education" refers broadly to learning oriented toward ends that different societies determine differently, whereas schooling is just one possible, Western industrial–style mode of education that specifically happens in classrooms according to a particular set of rules and norms (Andreotti & Ahenakew, 2013). Some have suggested that the term "higher education" itself presupposes and reproduces harmful hierarchies of value, given the implied contrast with "lower education" (Meyerhoff, 2019); in response to this concern, we might propose an alternative term, such as "deeper education," which avoids an assumption of vertical ascent or mastery. Regardless of the terminology we choose, the basic fact remains that many different forms of education preexisted modern schools, colleges, and universities and continue to persist beyond their walls.

Although not universal, the European mode of higher education was exported throughout the world and asserted as universal largely through processes of both settler and exploitation colonialism (Grosfoguel, 2013; Smith, 2012; Wilder, 2013). As Tamson Pietsch (2016) notes, "The most significant legacy of empire [in higher education] is the dominance of the university itself as the pre-eminent institution for higher education" (p. 34). This dominance of the Western university significantly narrows which (and whose) knowledges, experiences, and forms of education are perceived to be legitimate and worthy of study, and this narrow range of possibilities is repeated in most mainstream US higher education history texts.

For instance, non-Western educational histories tend to be erased when we discuss the history of whitestream institutions. Yet as Robin Starr Minthorn and Chris Nelson (2018) write, whitestream institutions in the United States were not founded on empty spaces or terra nullius, waiting to be filled by Western people and knowledge. Instead, they "held centuries of connections to plants, medicines, creation stories, and other meaningful connections that are forgotten in the told stories of higher education institutions" (p. 85). The construction on Indigenous lands of an institution dedicated to Western learning is one tactic within the larger settler colonial strategy of seeking to permanently sever Indigenous relationships to place and thereby interrupt Indigenous political, economic, and ecological organization.

As Timothy Stanley (2009) notes, "How the European cultural institution of the University came to be located on the West Coast of what is today Canada is very much a matter of a history of colonization by people of European, and principally British, origins" (p. 148). In the case of what would become the UBC Point Grey campus, this process of colonization began decades before the institution was established and physically built in the early twentieth century (UBC, n.d.). At UBC, and at all universities in what is currently known as North America, colonial forces "remade the cultural landscape of the territory, imposing their disciplinary practices and ways of knowing on the territory and its inhabitants, effectively steamrollering [sic] the systems of cultural representations and the meanings already in place" (Stanley, 2009, p. 143). The intention was to remake the material landscape in ways that erased Indigenous presence, relationships, names, and governing authority and naturalized white European settlers' presence, ownership, authority, and institutions.

Violence against Indigenous peoples went hand in hand with violence against the land itself. As Heather Davis and Zoe Todd (2017) note regarding the ecological impacts of colonization, "In actively shaping the territories where colonizers invaded, they [the colonizers] refused to see what was in front of them; instead forcing a landscape, climate, flora, and fauna into an idealized version of the world modelled on sameness and replication of the homeland" (p. 769). In the name of settler ownership, sovereignty, and futurity, many Indigenous peoples were and continue to be forcibly displaced from much or all of their traditional territories through violent means, and thereby alienated from ancestral webs of reciprocal connections between humans and other-than-humans (Tuck & Yang, 2012). This "disruption of Indigenous relationships to lands represents a profound epistemic, ontological, cosmological violence" that is not just historical but also ongoing (Tuck & Yang, 2012, p. 5). As Justin Farrell and colleagues (2021) note, "Land dispossession and forced migration created the groundwork for contemporary conditions in which Indigenous peoples in the United States today face greater vulnerabilities to their health and food security, lack access to culturally appropriate education, and have heightened exposures to contaminants."

What I have learned during my time in Canadian higher education, first as a graduate student and now as a faculty member, is that institutionally sanctioned efforts to address historical and ongoing colonial relations tend to involve not only the selective recognition of Indigenous presence, rights, and sovereignty, and the conditional inclusion of Indigenous peoples and knowledges, but also the mobilization of these efforts, paradoxically, to reassert the benevolence of the institution and legitimize its continued presence on Indigenous land (Ahmed, 2012; Daigle, 2019). These efforts are framed as part of an institutional commitment to continuous improvement and progress in ways that conveniently situate harms as done largely in the past or as at least gradually receding into a distant memory through the passage of time. The effect is both to ignore or minimize ongoing harm in the present and to foreclose further consideration of different possible—especially decolonial—futures. Thus, institutional efforts to reflect on examples of injustice can serve as an opportunity to demonstrate a commitment to justice and rehabilitate an institutional reputation, while leaving largely in place the continuation of colonial "business as usual" (Jimmy, Andreotti, & Stein, 2019). Such efforts do little to deepen settler responsibilities, enact repair for harms done, or support Indigenous resurgence.

There is a parallel danger in scholarship as well: that descriptive accounts and critiques of injustice authored by white settlers like myself may serve primarily as opportunities to demonstrate our own innocence and righteousness. The challenge is to instead invite ourselves and others into generative spaces of discomfort and deep learning and unlearning by decentering and disarming ourselves enough for the knowledge of our complicity to sink in, and for us to truly hear the call to responsibility that has always been there but long been denied.

We can consider that there are at least three different but interrelated dimensions of responsibility, based on a framework developed by the Gesturing Towards Decolonial Futures arts and research collective of which I am a part: (1) *attributability*, or recognition that the privileges and benefits one enjoys are rooted in historical and ongoing colonial and ecological harm; (2) *answerability*, or recognition of one's role in the systemic dimensions of harm; and (3) *accountability*, or recognition

that one is both systemically culpable and individually complicit in harm, and thus there are both an individual and a collective obligation to not only interrupt the reproduction of
harm but also enact restitution for harms already done.

In higher education, the process of accepting all three layers
of responsibility would require that we identify, denaturalize,
interrupt, and seek to repair the harm caused by the enduring
colonial modes of existence that are taken for granted within
Western higher education in settler colonial contexts and
within the societies in which they are embedded (Andreotti
et al., 2015; Shotwell, 2016; Stein, 2019, 2020; Stein et al., 2021).
In the following section, I consider the colonial origins of my
own institution to illustrate a more generalized set of patterns.

The Colonial Foundations of UBC

While the initial idea for a university in British Columbia
(BC) emerged in the late 1870s, UBC was not established until
1908. Between 1906 and 1915, a private institution—the McGill
University College of British Columbia—offered courses toward
a degree at McGill University, located in Montreal, Quebec, on
the other side of the continent from British Columbia (MacK-
enzie, 1958). While the institution was short-lived, as rosalind
hampton (2020) notes, this history indicates "the roles of universities in the westward expanding Canadian Dominion" by
"symbolizing and propagating European civilization and
Western knowledge" (p. 18). As UBC's first chancellor (and
former McGill University College of British Columbia chancellor) Francis Carter-Cotton wrote in the early twentieth
century to express his appreciation for the interprovincial
connection to McGill, "[British Columbia's] sense of unity
with other parts of the Dominion and with the Empire as a
whole, and of the possession of common ideals of citizenship
and culture has been deepened" (MacKenzie, 1958, p. 4). It is

also worth noting that McGill has its own histories of racial and colonial violence: James McGill, who bequeathed funds to establish what would become McGill University, was a co-lonial merchant and trader in and owner of enslaved persons (hampton, 2020).

UBC itself was first funded through the University Endowment Act of 1907, in which the BC provincial government granted lands in what is now central and northern British Columbia to be sold to fund a provincial university. In 1910, 175 acres of land at Point Grey, in the Musqueam Nation's territory, were identified as the future site of the university. The university was formally established through the University Act of 1908. From its earliest days, UBC presented itself as a purveyor of Canadian national progress, development, and enlightenment via higher education in the face of "ignorance" and "in-competence." Frank Fairchild Wesbrook, the university's first president, said in 1913: "The people's University must meet all the needs of all the people. We must therefore proceed with care to the erection of those Workshops where we may design and fashion the tools needed in the building of a nation and from which we can survey and lay out paths of enlightenment, tunnel the mountains of ignorance and bridge the chasms of incompetence." The choice of metaphors here that celebrate the violent and rationalistic mapping and transformation of landscapes as a universal good that "meets the needs of all the people" attests to the colonial processes involved in building higher education institutions, processes that were both natu-ralized and invisibilized in sanctioned accounts of the institu-tion's history. This meant not only that Musqueam people were excluded from the early institution of UBC but also that the institution's presence at Point Grey was enabled at their expense. Thus, the claim that the university must meet the "needs of all the people" suggests that certain communities, especially Indigenous communities, either were not counted among "the people" who mattered or were otherwise paternalistically perceived to lack the authority and the ability to determine their communities' own needs. In this way, non-Indigenous people were and continue to be prioritized over the Indigenous peoples of this place.

In 1914, the forests at Point Grey were cleared with dynamite (Metcalfe, 2019). In 1920, lands originally granted by the province in 1907 to fund the university were swapped for 3,000 acres of land near the campus. The "development" of these endowment lands was meant to finance the university instead. The permanent UBC campus was not opened until 1925, thanks in no small part to the efforts of students who were frustrated at the stalled construction. Their "Build the University" campaign culminated in what came to be known as the "Pilgrimage" and, later the "Great Trek," in which UBC students marched from the university's temporary location in downtown Vancouver to the Point Grey campus location. In doing so, the students were in many ways embodying the university's motto, *Tuum Est*, "It is yours," taking what they believed to be rightfully theirs—in this case, Musqueam lands at Point Grey.

Since then, the Great Trek has been widely celebrated as a turning point in the university's "organizational saga." As Burton Clark (1972) noted, "An organizational saga presents some rational explanation of how certain means led to certain ends, but it also includes affect that turns a formal place into a beloved institution, to which participants may be passionately devoted" (p. 178). These sagas, which may be understood as the product of selective, officially sanctioned institutional memory, have both internal and external purposes. Internally, these sagas help facilitate a shared identity and investment in the institution by its various members and stakeholders; externally, they tell a positive story about the institution in a way that legitimates its existence and social purpose by linking the institution to a proud tradition, often in relation to the overcoming of some kind of adversity. In UBC's organizational saga, the Great Trek is presented as evidence of a university tradition of student engagement and advocacy on behalf of the institution (Metcalfe, 2012).

Noticeably absent from the sanctioned narrative of this organizational saga is any discussion of the Musqueam Nation's consent or sovereignty (Sparrow, personal communication, November 3, 2021). It likely never occurred to early UBC students that the lands at Point Grey were not theirs to claim and occupy. The norms of white settler Canadian society at the time certainly supported assumptions about settler ownership and entitlement to Indigenous lands. Yet the notion that it is wrong to judge past racist and colonial actions according to contemporary ideas of justice implicitly centers white perspectives; Indigenous peoples at the time certainly did not perceive their dispossession as just. For instance, in 1906, around the time of UBC's inception, several Indigenous leaders from nations whose territories make up British Columbia petitioned the king of England for recognition of their claims to the land (Carlson, 2005).

The idea that we should not judge the past according to the norms of the present can be understood as a means of absolving settlers today of their complicity in historical and ongoing racialized violence and the theft of Indigenous lands and resources. It also dubiously implies that the colonial norms of settler societies and institutions have significantly shifted with the passage of time. Certainly, much has changed at UBC and in Canadian higher education in general since their founding moments. In particular, many things have shifted in the wake of the 2015 release of the final report of the Truth and Reconciliation Commission of Canada (2015), which reckoned

with Canada's history of forcibly placing over 150,000 Indigenous youth in residential schools for over one hundred years.
However, the underlying colonial template and governing
logics of higher education largely remain in place. As a result,
as Marker (2019) notes, "Universities are in increasingly para-
doxical positions as they ostensibly invite Indigenous expres-
sion, but resist the undoing of hierarchies that maintain hegemonic equilibrium" (p. 502).

This paradox can be attributed in part to the persistence
and power of (white) settler memory. As Bruyneel (2017)
notes, settler memory is characterized by both acknowledging *and* disavowing "the history and contemporary implications of genocidal violence toward Indigenous people and the
accompanying land dispossession that serve as the fundamental bases for creating settler colonial nations-states" (p. 37).
To be oriented by settler memory is not necessarily to be an
outright supporter of colonization or to be entirely ignorant
of the colonial past, but rather to leave "unthought" how
deeply colonization shapes the present, including the current
position and systemic advantages of settler citizens. Allowing
the enduring impacts of colonization to remain unthought in
turn limits the kinds of futures, practices, and solidarities that
are imaginable, often resulting in uncritical desires for settler
futurity.

Settler Futurities in Higher Education

The UBC Vancouver campus now includes street signs written in both the English and the Musqueam language and prom-
inently displays the Musqueam flag alongside the UBC and provincial flags. Most official university events now begin with a
land acknowledgment, recognizing that the university is located
on the "traditional, ancestral, and unceded territory of the Mus-

queam people."* Many visitors, both international and Canadian, have remarked to me how impressed they are with UBC's commitment to Indigenization. However, as Michelle Daigle (2019) notes, on many Canadian university campuses, "white settler futurities, including university futurities, remain unchallenged despite good-feeling and albeit good intentioned reconciliation mandates" (p. 709). White settler futurities are rooted in desires for the seamless continuity of a colonial society that affirms white peoples' unrestricted autonomy, authority, and right to arbitrate justice. This does not mean that alternative futurities and desires are not posed by Indigenous peoples and others, including some settlers; indeed they are, and from a range of different perspectives. However, generally only approaches to Indigenization and decolonization that do not pose a substantive challenge to settler futurities are endorsed or tolerated in whitestream higher education institutions.

Perhaps nowhere is the presumption of settler university futurities more evident at UBC than in the example of Wesbrook Village, which lies just south of the Point Grey campus, where I lived for nearly two years. According to its official website, Wesbrook Village is "a collection of shops and residences on Vancouver's West Side. Located on a spectacular peninsula known for its ocean views, old-growth forest, outdoor recreation and the tier-one University of British Columbia (UBC), Wesbrook is an ideal starting point for an hour of excitement or a lifetime of enrichment."

In March 2019, the headline of an article in the *Vancouver Sun* about Wesbrook Village declared, "UBC turns land into a river

* For critical discussions of the limits and possibilities of land acknowledgments as decolonial gestures, see the work of Chelsea Vowel (2016), Lou Cornum (2019), Joe Wark (2021), and Theresa Stewart-Ambo and K. Wayne Yang (2021).

of gold" (Ryan, 2019). The title of the story illustrates how Indigenous land is framed within the settler imaginary as a permanent possession and an ongoing source of profit, rather than a living entity embedded in reciprocal relationships. In this framing, UBC itself is also celebrated for the ingenuity of this colonial act of commodification. The story reports on the vision of UBC alum and businessman Robert H. Lee, who proposed to use a portion of the UBC campus lands to build housing and to invest the profits in the university's endowment fund. Lee attributed the university's rise in status and reputation over the past thirty years primarily to its landholdings (Business in Vancouver, 2016). According to the article, as of 2019 the housing developments have generated $1.6 billion in profit. Legally, the university cannot spend the endowment funds, but it can spend the interest they generate. Most notably from the perspective of decolonial critique, none of these profits are shared with the Musqueam Nation.

In the article, UBC's associate vice president of campus and community planning said, "Universities plan for 1,000 years, they don't plan for 50, so there is perpetual benefit through the generations." This statement articulates a clear image of what Daigle (2019) calls university futurities: the endowment land is presumed to be unproblematically and unquestionably the property of UBC in perpetuity (or at least "for 1,000 years"). Thus, the continued colonial-capitalist transformation of land into a particular profitable, Eurocentric iteration of human-centered property and legacy is celebrated as an ingenious pathway toward generating revenue for the university "for generations"—particularly given the notoriously high value of Vancouver real estate. In this sense, Musqueam elder Larry Grant's (2018) rhetorical question is extremely poignant: "You know who the biggest benefactor of UBC is? It's not Koerner, it's not Barber, it's not Allard [the names of big institutional donors]—it's Musqueam!" The big difference, of course, is that those institutional donors gave their wealth to UBC willingly, whereas with Musqueam land, this was hardly the case: it was not a donation but an act of dispossession. Indeed, Grant draws attention to "the billions of dollars of real estate that have been appropriated, that Metro Vancouver and UBC sit on." Sparrow notes that while UBC has made cautious institutional acknowledgments of this history over the past few years, "no plans have been made to make adequate/comparable repair, or to rematriate these lands back to xʷməθkʷəy̓əm Nation, despite this knowing" (personal communication, November 3, 2021).

UBC and Musqueam first signed a memorandum of affiliation (MOA) in 2006. It outlined some guiding dimensions of their relationship, including affirming "the importance of building a long-term relationship between the parties," an intention to "facilitate cooperation" between the two entities, and a commitment from UBC to ensure more opportunities for students from Musqueam to access UBC. A revised memorandum has been in the works for many years. As Sparrow observes, the 2006 MOA "does not mention anything about the land sovereignty of the xʷməθkʷəy̓əm Nation, and the fact that we are a significant (if not the most significant) institutional partner, and how the university plans to rectify its illegal occupation of our ancestral lands for its own profit" (personal communication, November 3).

In 2020, UBC debuted its Indigenous Strategic Plan and accompanying self-assessment and action tools. The plan is framed as a response to the United Nations Declaration on the Rights of Indigenous Peoples, the Calls for Justice of the National Inquiry into Missing and Murdered Indigenous Women and Girls, and the Truth and Reconciliation Commission's Calls to Action. Many of the goals outlined within the plan specifically mention relationships and partnerships with Musqueam as well as with the Okanagan Nation, whose lands UBC's Okanagan campus occupies. The plan acknowledges that "the University of British Columbia has been, and continues to be, in many respects, a colonial institution" and that "for many Indigenous students, faculty and staff, colonialism is a daily reality at UBC" (UBC, 2020, p. 8). While these kinds of institutional acknowledgments and plans can be an important starting point for further action, as Sparrow emphasizes, universities have a long way to go in order to operate from a genuine commitment to reciprocity and "being in good relation" with local Indigenous nations (personal communication, November 3, 2021). She observes, for instance, that the UBC Indigenous Strategic Plan "does not acknowledge historic land dispossession fully, nor does it make actionable recommendations for how to give land back to the Nation, or how to specifically and equitably share university resources with the xʷməθkʷəy̓əm Nation. It only speaks about supports offered to xʷməθkʷəy̓əm members/Indigenous people who want to become students or faculty within the university."

It is important to note that Indigenous peoples have varied responses to institutional Indigenization and reconciliation efforts. It is not my place as a settler to speak on Indigenous peoples' behalf, nor is it possible within these pages to include all of the complex and heterogeneous desires and strategies that different Indigenous people have for engagement with UBC and other higher education institutions. Nevertheless, many questions remain about whether the recent expansion of institutional commitments at places like UBC will lead to a shift away from simply offering more conditional inclusion of Indigenous peoples and knowledges and toward redressing the ways that higher education has historically operated, and in many ways continues to operate, at the expense of Indigenous peoples. Such a shift would require going beyond institutional acknowledgements and apologies toward not just the redistribution of power and resources but also, ultimately, reparation for harms done.

At UBC, some have identified Wesbrook Village as a crass example of the contemporary corporatization of higher education, and of the movement away from education itself as the primary purpose of universities. However, Wesbrook Village may also be understood as a novel iteration of an enduring colonial pattern of property that was first established with the original University Endowment Act, a pattern whereby Indigenous lands are continuously transformed into new forms of institutional wealth. In this way, the initial "accumulation" and ongoing occupation of Indigenous lands by UBC enabled future processes of accumulation. The case of Wesbrook Village also makes clear that universities' complicity in Indigenous dispossession and environmental destruction was not a one-time, exceptional event that can be comfortably relegated to the past, but rather an ongoing structural condition and set of social and ecological practices that enable universities to continue to exist, thrive, and expand. As Amy Scott Metcalfe (2019) notes, "Signage announces the 'Brand New UBC Faculty & Staff Rentals' in buildings named 'Pine House' and 'Cypress House' that are '100% Leased.' The replacement of a forest with apartments named after trees is done without irony or apology" (p. 88).

Further, it is generally presumed (if rarely stated outright) that this dispossession will continue, as the land at Wesbrook Village is framed as UBC's property to dispose of as it sees fit (and, in particular, in the most profitable way), always with its public and educational mandate somewhere in mind. Thus, the university's statement of "long-term commitment to the Musqueam Indian Band and our vision of solidarity moving forward" (*University News*, 2019) seems to fall away when it comes to certain dimensions of officially sanctioned university futurities. Rauna Kuokkanen's (2004) observation, made well before the Truth and Reconciliation Commission, continues to be relevant: "The Musqueam are recognized when it is convenient for the university but ignored, neglected, and pushed aside on other occasions, particularly when the university wants to represent itself—walk on the spotlights—as the sovereign master to the outside world" (p. 222).

Sparrow argues that although Musqueam have "made some headway in reclaiming our rights as a sovereign Nation within the university," there is much work that UBC still needs to do in order to enact true accountability in its relationships with the Musqueam and other local Indigenous Nations. "We can imagine all sorts of ways to right and repair these colonial histories and relations between universities and local Nations in a good way," she notes, but to do this requires "a tangible university commitment to make larger changes within its own infrastructure and ways of relating with local Nations as true university partners and benefactors long term" (personal communication, November 3, 2021).

An Invitation to Start—and Stay—with Complicity

Decolonial critiques contest the notion that there exists any universally true knowledge that can be formulated from a neutral "view from nowhere." They emphasize instead that the ____ le, partial, contested ways to see and sense the wor____ these different ways of seeing and sensing the world also shape how we identify, understand, and respond to an issue or a problem of concern. As a white, middle-class, cisgender US citizen who moves across the US-Canadian border with relative ease, by securing first a student visa, then a post-graduation work permit, and now permanent residency status,

I am acutely aware of how deeply I am implicated in the structural problems that I seek to make visible. And while indispensable, this awareness in itself is deeply insufficient and does not absolve me of my complicity in various systems of ongoing social and ecological harm.

For instance, not only did I benefit from the excellent scholars, comparatively plush resources, and "world-class" reputation of UBC as a student, but also then, as now, the university paid my bills. When I lived in Wesbrook Village, I benefited from a modest staff-faculty subsidy that the university offers in a subset of housing there. Having been born into a white middle-class family, I benefited from numerous structural advantages that granted me access to high-quality public education for my whole life and that ultimately allowed me to secure a tenure-track faculty position that places me near the top of the academic hierarchy within a highly unequal system of academic labor.

These "advantages" are not simply benefits or privileges from which others have been excluded and that can therefore theoretically be expanded and extended outward until they are all but universal. Rather, these advantages are directly and indirectly subsidized by harmful and unsustainable colonial processes rooted in the ongoing exploitation, expropriation, and extraction of both human and other-than-human beings "at home" and "abroad." If people like me are to even begin the lifelong work of attempting to interrupt these colonial processes and disinvest from the colonial promises they enable, then we would need to honestly confront "how [our] own position is implicated in producing the problem" (Meyerhoff, 2019, p. 5).

Colonialism is not only what prompted me to write this book but also, paradoxically, what enabled me to write it. Apart from the aforementioned material comforts and securities it affords me, in order to critique higher education institutions,

I am mobilizing Indigenous, Black, and other de-/anti-/post-colonial critiques that are largely directed at the systems that structurally advantage people like me. White scholars have been rightfully critiqued for selectively engaging and instrumentalizing these critiques to serve our own ends, particularly for the accumulation of economic and moral capital. As Eve Tuck and K. Wayne Yang (2012) note, "Settler scholars may gain professional kudos or a boost in their reputations for being so sensitive or self-aware" (p. 10). Meanwhile, my Black, Indigenous, and racialized colleagues are frequently either ignored or punished for raising similar critiques, especially if they do so in ways perceived as "unproductive" (i.e., focused on something other than "moving on") or as insufficiently sensitive to white peoples' feelings. Sara Ahmed (2012, 2019) describes how, when racialized and Indigenous staff and faculty *name the problem*, they are perceived to *become the problem*. Although this experience at times happens to me as well, the backlash is rarely as intense or virulent, and it is just as likely I will be rewarded for being a "champion" of justice.

I offer these reflections on my own structural complicity not as a navel-gazing confession or self-flagellation in search of absolution or as a blanket mea culpa that excuses me from attending to these issues as I proceed. Rather, I use them as a means to both situate and provincialize what I offer in this book, and also to invite a broader and deeper conversation about responsibility for complicity in relation to the colonial past and present of higher education. My understanding of complicity is informed by incisive theorists of colonialism and especially of colonial desires, including Eve Tuck and K. Wayne Yang (2012), Gayatri Spivak (1988, 2004), David Jefferess (2012), Alexis Shotwell (2016), and Ilan Kapoor (2004, 2014).

The Impossibility of Innocence, and Uneven Implication in Harm

Complicity in harm is primarily shaped by our structural positions in relation to social, political, and economic systems, rather than by the effect of individual willed choices—meaning we cannot simply "opt out" of complicity or be excused from it just because we critique or disidentify with those systems. Particularly in relation to the question of complicity, I am conscious about my use of "we" and "our" throughout this book. Just as there is no universal individual subject, there is no universal "we." The use of "we" and "our" by white authors often recenters the supposedly neutral white collective.

I strive to be as specific as possible when referring to a particular group of people, but there is inevitably some slippage. One reason is that our membership in groups is slippery, and contested; it is not singular but multiple, contextual, and relational. However, often when I say "we," I am speaking broadly about those who study and work in universities in settler colonial states. This is already a considerable flattening of social positions and individual circumstances. Nonetheless, the choice of "we" also speaks to the fact that the university is a place of privilege and thus of structural complicity in harm—even as, of course, this complicity is not distributed evenly.

As Tiffany Lethabo King (2019) puts it, "'Innocence' does not exist within the lifeways of this hemisphere or the modern world" (p. xi). Speaking of complicity in higher education more specifically, Nick Mitchell (2015) writes, "There is nothing about our position in the academy, however marginal, that is innocent of power, nor is there any practice that will afford us an exteriority to the historical determinations of the place from which we speak, write, research, teach, organize, and learn" (p. 91). None of this means that we are "equally responsible" or "equally called to respond" (Shotwell, 2016, p. 7) to the systemic violence perpetuated by the institutions that we inhabit. But it does suggest we are all implicated in that violence in some way, even when we are critical of it, even when we desire something different, and even if it has been enacted against us as well. Suriamurthee Moonsamy Maistry (2019) describes "a state of complicity by default," a phrase she uses to suggest that "western Eurocentric academics (of all races) are in a sense complicit in perpetuating coloniality as this is the theoretical home in which they have been raised and continue to build" (p. 181). This colonial home that we inhabit—albeit for some with great discomfort and a sense of being "out of place"—is not just theoretical; it is also deeply material. Furthermore, intellectually critiquing this "home" is not always necessarily accompanied by an affective desire or a practical ability to live outside its walls, especially if we have never known any other kind of shelter. That is, we can intellectually question a colonial habit-of-being without necessarily wanting to break the habit and enact restitution for its harmful impacts. Ultimately it is up to readers to decide for themselves whether or not to be interpolated by my use of "we" throughout the text.

To accept that we inhabit a colonial present that is inherently violent and unsustainable, and that our complicity in that violence and unsustainability is structural and systemic rather than individual, suggests that one cannot simply choose whether, when, or how to be complicit or not. Instead, one can choose only how one responds to the fact of complicity and the subsequent responsibilities that derive from it. This includes attending to the fact that the desire to address one's complicity, while extremely important, can quickly take the shape of a non-generative desire for innocence and absolution.

Once we can no longer get away with pretending "that we don't need to tell or hear the painful stories of the actions that created the world we live in" (Shotwell, 2016, p. 38), we often seek to quickly address that harm so that we can move on without the weight of history following us around, but without having to give anything up, either (Jefferess, 2012; Tuck & Yang, 2012). As Shotwell (2016) argues regarding white people in particular, "That feeling, of wanting to be people unmoored from history, of endorsing the pretence that we have nothing to do with the past that constitutes our material conditions and our most intimate subjectivities, is a feeling that defines us" (p. 39). This feeling drives efforts to address complicity in a transactional way that seeks to shore up, rather than interrupt, a sense of security, purpose, exceptionalism, innocence, and worthiness, a sense possible only within a colonial system ordered by colonial hierarchies of value. This transactional approach often emerges when one tries to address complicity from a sense of guilt or shame. While there are important discussions to be had about the potential of both guilt and shame for mobilizing action (Snelgrove, Dhamoon, & Corntassel, 2014), without further processing of these responses, both tend to circularly recenter the complicit party. Actions driven by guilt or shame are often motivated by a search for redemption that would allow for a return to enjoying socially sanctioned perceived entitlements to feeling "good" and being seen as doing "good." Conversely, my intention in this book is not for people to feel "bad" about their complicity. Instead, I emphasize activating or amplifying a sense of responsibility—including the different layers of attributability, answerability, and accountability reviewed at the beginning of this chapter.

Focusing on complicity can be risky. Attending to the deconstruction of dominant myths of higher education, for instance, can be understood as recentering white settler memories and futurities. This presents an interesting paradox: in order to decenter something, do we have to first center it so as to then denaturalize it, deconstruct it, disinvest from it, and ultimately clear space for something else? Boggs and colleagues (2019) observe that one way "to refuse and replace narratives of university history conditioned by white settler memory" is to "highlight counter-memories from the perspectives of people, such as Native Americans and African Americans, who have been involved in worldmaking projects alternative to liberal-capitalist modernity, and whose perspectives have been obscured or elided in the dominant narratives" (p. 12). This is absolutely necessary work. Yet, if we do not simultaneously identify and interrupt the conscious and unconscious effects of white settler memory, white settlers like myself risk letting mainstream narratives and colonial investments continue to implicitly frame how we read other histories and to haunt the possible futures that we can imagine.

Anticipating Possible Responses

By centering higher education's entanglement with racial, colonial, and ecological violence, this book necessarily decenters other questions and conversations, but it does not dismiss them or suggest they are no longer useful or important. As historian of higher education John Thelin (2004) notes, "My interpretation is admittedly selective" (p. xxii); I admit the same about my own interpretation. This selectivity is inevitable in the crafting of any narrative, academic or otherwise. I do not argue that colonization is the *only* "condition of possibility" for US higher education—indeed, there are many. Rather, I emphasize the need to make this particular condition visible where it is currently invisibilized or is engaged with insufficient depth. I seek to offer neither a replacement account of the problems of higher education in the present nor a comprehensive "alternative history" of higher education. As Thelin also notes, "No author can succeed at narrating a wholly comprehensive chronology of American higher education in a single, concise volume" (p. xxii). One primary violence of colonialism is not simply that it asserts the universality of Western knowledge in particular but that it asserts the possibility of universal, totalizing knowledge in general.

To bypass the imperial tendency to compete for a position of universal epistemic authority, we would need to foster an ecology of narratives about higher education, rather than a single story. At the same time, to crack the currently hegemonic narrative, we need to attend to the uneven epistemic and social power of different narratives by both drawing attention to the harmful impacts of this hegemony and creating more space for alternative narratives to be engaged in nontokenistic ways. Following Roland Sintos Coloma's (2013) suggestion that "the analytic of empire can enable new questions to be asked and persistent problems to be addressed differently" (p. 640), my intention in offering a decolonial reading of higher education history is not to replace dominant narratives and create a new hegemony but rather to clear pathways for more complex, difficult, self-implicating questions and conversations about the colonial foundations of our institutions, about how these foundations shape present challenges, and about how we understand and address those challenges.

Those who are suspicious of the overarching premise of the book—that racial, colonial, and ecological violence are underlying conditions of possibility for US higher education—are unlikely to read it in the first place. But to those who nonetheless do, rather than approaching the book with the intention to either agree or disagree with the analysis offered, I invite you to instead ask what you might learn through your own engagement with the text (including what you might be taught by your resistance to it). To those who might suggest that I give insufficient attention or credit to (white) institutions or (white) individuals who mobilized higher education toward doing "good" or who resisted or reformed mainstream practices of violence, I would direct you to a considerable body of higher education literature that already offers these more celebratory narratives. I focus on the mundane, systemic patterns through which white settler individuals and institutions reproduce and benefit from harm, rather than on stories of those who committed either "exceptionally bad" acts of violence or "exceptionally good" acts of challenging that violence. In doing so, I also seek to bring attention to the fact that this violence is painfully ordinary—which makes it easier for white settlers not to see.

As I note earlier in this introduction, some might dismiss my decolonial readings of universities' histories for being "presentist." These responses maintain that the implicated individuals and institutions were simply acting according to the (racist and colonial) social mores of their time and, therefore, they should not be judged against the now-reformed, more progressive morals of the present (e.g., Davenport, 2015). Yet these responses effectively recenter dominant white perspectives from the past while ignoring the fact that Indigenous and Black people were, at the very same time, actively critiquing and resisting their own subjugation through various means (Patel, 2021; Mustaffa, 2017; Stonechild, 2006; Wright, 1991). These responses also in many ways ignore the fact that racist, colonial social mores are still very much alive and thriving today, albeit often in revised forms.

At the same time, this book is not intended to "trash" US higher education; indeed, US colleges and universities have offered many benefits that have been extensively catalogued and recounted in mainstream literature and thus need not be repeated here. However, I invite readers to consider the hidden costs of these benefits and whether higher education might take other, less harmful forms. This book is also not meant to dismiss other accounts of US higher education history, including those that I review with a decolonial lens. Rather, like Thelin, I suggest the need to consider that all historical accounts of higher education (including this one) emerge from particular contexts and situated perspectives that shape the production of knowledge itself. Provincializing and contextualizing these accounts is crucial if we seek to engage and produce knowledge about higher education in more socially relevant and socially accountable ways.

It is not only those who are skeptical of this book's premise who might be frustrated by what it does or does not do. For instance, this book will likely disappoint those who support decolonization in higher education but are looking for concrete solutions or how-to guides for immediate change. Such proposals are extremely important, and many are being put forward by various groups and collectives, including students making demands on their own institutions, as well as social movements not formally rooted in or affiliated with higher education institutions. What I offer in this book is meant not to replace or supersede those proposals but rather to supplement them. The urgency of ongoing systemic violence demands immediate responses that can reduce harm and push the boundaries of what is currently possible within existing institutions. At the same time, there is also an imperative to preserve spaces for sitting with the full depth, magnitude, and complexity of how enduring colonial patterns and structures continue to shape higher education institutions, the individuals who work and study within them, and, to a large extent, the resistance that can be intelligible and actionable within them. In rushing to translate our analyses into action, we might overlook the need to address the complexities, contradictions, and circularities often involved in efforts to interrupt, unlearn, and disinvest from colonial promises and to create

and practice more generative ways of knowing, being, and relating. This work of pausing (Patel, 2015) is crucial for those invested in transforming higher education, whether from within
or outside existing institutions. We will need to learn how to do
this work of pausing alongside the practice of systemic change
in ways that do not treat pausing as an excuse to perpetually
defer this practical work, and in ways that do not treat this practical work as if it makes the former irrelevant or unimportant.

For those who expect this text to offer clear promises of
"hope" and who might therefore interpret it as propagating
cynicism or pessimism in its refusal to offer easy solutions or
alternatives, I suggest that this is only a further indication of
the need to develop deeper capacities to address the complexities involved in decolonizing work, including the possibility
that our institutions might be "beyond reform." These are issues that many students in our institutions are already raising,
and we owe it to them to create spaces where we can sit with
these possibilities without seeking immediate resolution.

This book might also frustrate those who are seeking a
more comprehensive account of how racism and colonialism
have shaped US higher education across time. In particular,
some might take issue with my rather exclusive focus on the
violence that has been enacted toward and resisted by Black
and Indigenous communities. This choice of focus is not to
suggest by any means that the violence experienced by other
racialized communities, including Latinx, Asian American,
and Middle Eastern communities, is somehow less important. This focus is also not intended to erase the fact that there
are individuals and whole communities that fall into multiple
groups (such as Black or Indigenous peoples from Latin America, or people who are both Black and Indigenous). Rather, I
recognize the impossibility of addressing within a single text
the foundational legacies of anti-Black and anti-Indigenous vio-

lence, and Black and Indigenous resistance to that violence, in higher education, while also doing justice to the important histories of anti-Latinx, anti-Asian, and anti–Middle Eastern violence and resistance to that violence.

Indigenous, Black, and other racialized students, scholars, and activists in both Canada and the United States have pointed out the pressing need to address the complex, entangled relationships between the historical and ongoing legacies of settler colonialism, slavery and anti-Blackness, anti-Asian racism, Islamophobia, xenophobia, border imperialism, and the extraction of wealth and resources across the Global South (e.g. Day, 2015; Diabo, 2019; hampton, 2020; King, 2019; Patel, 2016; Simpson, 2016; Thobani, 2007; Tuck & Yang, 2012; Walcott, 2019; Walia, 2013). These thinkers have pointed to the importance of linking these overlapping and often mutually reinforcing systemic violences (in higher education and beyond), without collapsing important differences between these multiple violences, and between the experiences of different communities that are subject to and resist these violences. They also note the importance of not assuming that there is solidarity between communities just because they are all harmed by white dominance, and emphasize the need to recognize that marginalized peoples are not immune from complicity in the oppression of others. Although it is impossible for me to do justice to these complex entanglements in this book, consideration of their implications must be deepened in conversations about the possibility of alternative futures in higher education.

Finally, this book might frustrate those who are looking for a text that approaches social, political, and institutional change based on the "Five E's": exceptionalism, exaltedness, entitlement, empowerment of the ego, and externalization of culpability (Andreotti, Jimmy, & Calhoun, 2021). Overall, an approach to change that is rooted in the Five E's tends to rest on the romanticization and idealization of a virtuous and in-fallible leader, movement, or community that is held as the highest measure of humanity. Different theories of change tend to elevate different groups. For instance, in whitestream aca-demic culture, the Five E's tend to be applied in ways that re-produce white and Western supremacy by elevating white and Western scholars. In other cases, often in an effort to contest that presumed white or Western supremacy, it is marginalized people or communities that are romanticized and idealized with the Five E's.

While the harm of applying the Five E's to white individu-als or communities might be obvious given that they already enjoy many systemic advantages, applying the Five E's to sys-temically marginalized communities has in many cases served as an effective way to counter narratives that pathologize or deficit-theorize these communities. The mobilization of the Five E's by these communities has served as a source of internal belonging, community, strength, and well-being and has also enabled important forms of social and organizational change (especially increased representation of and redistribution to those communities) within institutions in which the Five E's are the most intelligible and accepted forms of politics. However, romanticization of marginalized communities is not necessarily a sustainable alternative to pathologization in the long run. In general, it creates a dynamic in which support for marginalized peoples' struggles and commitments to redress historical and ongoing harms done to them are contingent upon their living up to a nearly impossible ideal, disallowing space for their com-plex personhood, and creating the conditions under which soli-darity can be easily withdrawn (Kelley & Moten, 2017).

Although I seek to challenge the Five E's throughout this book, this is a failed experiment; undoubtedly, I have reproduced them at various points. This is due both to my own limitations and to the limitations of the frames of reference and intelligibility that organize most critical scholarship. Rather than view this failure as a problem, I view it as an important reminder that decolonizing work is difficult, complex, and at times seemingly impossible. This reminder also underscores the need for those engaged in decolonizing work to develop greater stamina and deeper intellectual, affective, and relational capacities and dispositions that can allow us to face not only the challenges, discomforts, tensions, and failures that inevitably arise in the work of decolonization in practice, but also the uncertainty, complexity, and volatility that characterize the contemporary moment.

Just as colonization is an ongoing practice rather than a singular event, so is decolonization. If decolonization is not a predefined destination, then perhaps it can be a compass that continuously reorients us away from reproducing further harm and toward enacting redress and repair for harms already done, as well as toward more generative possible futures that are collaboratively woven in ways that support collective well-being for current and future generations. In this process, we will stumble and make mistakes along the way, and we must hold ourselves accountable for our failures, including by learning from them so that we do not repeat them. This requires us to develop maturity, comfort with uncertainty, and a mode of engagement driven not by guilt, shame, or a desire for "goodness" but by a sense of humility, hyper-self-reflexivity, and accountability that comes "before will" (Spivak, 2004).

Orienting Questions and Directions

Addressing higher education's historical and ongoing complicity in systemic racial, colonial, and ecological violence entails raising a number of difficult questions, a few of which

I include below. To engage these questions with the depth they warrant requires rethinking some of the most cherished ideas about US higher education, and its promises. Many contemporary critiques of higher education are rooted in a concern that these promises have been broken and thus need to be repaired and even expanded. This book takes a different starting point, arguing that the fulfilment of these promises has always been subsidized by racialized exploitation, expropriation, and ecological destruction; it also suggests that the perpetuation of these promises may no longer be tenable, at least in the long-term. In turn, this approach challenges the illusion that we can—or should—hope for a return or restoration of an earlier, more innocent era of higher education. Instead, it gestures toward the difficult, long-haul work of both interrupting enduring colonial modes of existence and imagining higher education otherwise.

This book seeks to lay the contextual and conceptual groundwork necessary to even *ask* the following questions; for the most part, it does not presume to *answer* them or to offer prescriptive reforms or prefabricated alternatives to the higher education we have inherited.

- How have US universities benefited from exploitation, expropriation, destitution, dispossession, displacement, ecocides, genocides, and epistemicides? How are those of us who work and study in universities also complicit in this systemic, historical, and ongoing harm?
- Why do we remain so deeply attached to a higher education system premised on racial, colonial, and ecological violence? Why do we often deny that this violence is harmful and unsustainable, even when we have plenty of research that proves that this is the case?
- How has our higher education system set us in the direction of exceptionalism, entitlement, and individual-

ism? What other kinds of knowledges and educational practices might interrupt these patterns and reorient us toward responsibility and interdependence? How can those of us educated outside these knowledges and practices engage them without reenacting colonial patterns of extraction, appropriation, or romanticization?

- How can we interrupt and unlearn harmful ways of thinking, feeling, doing, relating, knowing, and being? What would we have to give up in order to do this work and to enable other ways of thinking, feeling, doing, relating, knowing, and being to become viable?

- What will it take for us to actually do the difficult and uncomfortable work of restitution and reparation for racial, colonial, and ecological violence that needs to be done without expecting it to be easy, to feel good, or to make us look good to other people?

- Why is it so difficult to imagine higher education otherwise, even when we are faced with the limits of dominant imaginaries? What could prepare us to face the many challenges ahead, accept our responsibility for contributing to the creation of those challenges, and shoulder our responsibility to address them in ways that do not create further harm?

In the book's concluding chapter, I return to and supplement these questions in an effort to indicate that our inquiry about these issues needs to be continually deepened and nuanced.

How to Read This Book

While this book is primarily an intellectual endeavor, it also addresses some of the limitations of undertaking decolonizing work solely in the intellectual realm. This tendency to intellectualize to the exclusion of other forms of engagement is reflected in Melissa Phruksachart's (2020) observation that "there is a long tradition of white people thinking they can read their way out of trouble." In turn, this tendency is rooted in what Bruyneel (2013) describes as a "liberal rationalist approach" to violence in which, "if only we all knew better, had all the facts, then these historic injustices would be resolved, or at least we would be on our way to addressing them" (p. 238). From this perspective, white settlers' collective failure to accept accountability for complicity in harm and responsibility for repair can be painted as a product of *ignorance about colonialism* rather than a product of *investment in colonialism*. This approach also effectively erases the place of injustice in the ordering grammar of modern systems and institutions, which require the continuation of violence for the continuation of their existence.

By contrast, this book addresses the ways the enduring coloniality of US higher education is not only the result of ignorance that can be solved with more information. Certainly, this lack of information is part of the problem, but it is not the whole story. Coloniality also endures because of a denial of individual and collective responsibilities, and an investment in the continuity and expansion of the "American Dream" and its associated promises, pleasures, comforts, and securities without being accountable to the "Colonial Nightmare" that is its underside (TallBear, 2019). As such, one can "know better" on one level while denying the implications and responsibilities of that knowing at another level.

Further, at least some of these investments and desires are unconscious, meaning that bringing individuals' conscious attention to the violence required for their fulfilment may not necessarily lead to different investments and desires. Thus, I argue that the general lack of engagement with colonial violence in higher education can also be understood as a product of denial, disavowal, and desire, rather than a lack of information. In that case, what is required in response is not only intellectual critique but also an ongoing affective and relational practice of disinvesting from the harmful desires projected onto higher education, and investing in remaking our collective existence in ways that honor our responsibilities to one another and indeed all beings on a shared, finite, living planet. Toward this end, I invite readers not only to engage and reflect on this book in intellectual ways but also to observe their visceral and embodied responses to an uncomfortable reality that many would rather not confront: the foundational and ongoing complicity of US higher education in genocides, ecocides, and epistemicides and, thus, the true social and ecological costs of higher education's shiny promises. This is one possible way forward for reimagining higher education.

Structure of the Book

I begin chapter 1 by arguing for the importance of addressing the colonial foundations of US higher education. I introduce the decolonial historiographic methodology I employ in chapters 2, 3, and 4 in order to examine these foundations in different eras, and offer a synthesis of the decolonial critiques that inform my reading method. I establish the need for a decolonial approach by considering which questions and concerns are centered in mainstream historical accounts of US higher education and which questions and concerns are absent. In doing so, I also describe how decolonial analyses differ from analyses that center on legacies of exclusion. As well, I address how presumptions of exceptionalism shape US society and higher education and then review the three specific promises of US higher education, which I revisit throughout the book.

In chapter 2, I consider how most mainstream accounts of the beginnings of US higher education (starting before the United States itself existed) naturalize the establishment of early colonial universities. These accounts further tend to center white men as the subjects of higher education history and presume that readers will identify with these protagonists. I first review these accounts and read them through a decolonial analysis in order to denaturalize how they frame the founding of universities in the colonies as part of the natural progression of a settler society, and to emphasize the racial, colonial, and ecological violence that subsidized these institutions. I then review the ways that early institutions of higher education were implicated in and actively supported and benefited from settler colonialism and slavery. I conclude the chapter by considering how continuities between the past and present of US higher education offer new openings from which to examine contemporary challenges but also to reimagine possible futures, a theme I return to throughout the book.

In chapter 3, I address the Indigenous dispossession that is at the root of land-grant colleges and universities. In mainstream higher education scholarship, as well as in more popular discourses, land-grant institutions serve as a powerful metonym for the public good promises of US higher education. In this function, land-grant legacies are periodically evoked in efforts to reinvigorate public higher education (Sorber & Geiger, 2014). I argue that if indeed land-grant institutions are the model for US public higher education, then our vision of the public good has always depended on colonial expansion and, thus, on ecocidal and genocidal modes of capital accumulation. Land-grant institutions were made possible through the colonial enclosure of Indigenous lands, which were accumulated by the federal government through processes of removal and dispossession and then sold as private property to pay for the schools. By establishing stolen Indigenous lands as the ongoing material base of the public land-grant university, the Morrill Act helped produce a colonial "template" of the public good that reemerges in new forms in the context of contemporary higher education privatization.

In chapter 4, I address the most celebrated era of US higher education, the post–World War II and Cold War "golden age," from the 1940s to the 1970s. During this time, there was a promise of expanded access to the American Dream. A booming economy and pressure to represent US capitalism in a positive light vis-à-vis socialism resulted in the creation of new opportunities for social mobility by way of higher education. As access to higher education expanded, Simon Marginson (2016) suggests, it was "widely agreed that the fairest and best means of sorting the continuing competition for social position and success were higher education and the nexus between education and professional occupations" (p. 15). However, the expansion of access to higher education and the accompanying promise of merit-based social mobility were facilitated through conditional forms of inclusion, and historically high levels of public funding depended on a commitment to positioning the US as a global military and economic hegemon (Labaree, 2016). Thus, the shine of the "golden age" relied on the shadows of US imperialism and on the domestic promise of formal equality of opportunity that functioned to "explain (away) the inequalities of a still-racialized capitalism" (Melamed, 2006, p. 9).

In chapter 5, I address the recent trend in universities' institutional responses to these histories of violence. I argue that these responses tend to be articulated through liberal frames of justice that relegate institutional complicity to a regrettable but discrete historical moment in ways that disavow universities' active participation in ongoing structures of colonial violence. I also consider how these responses often become opportunities for institutions to reassert their own relevance, benevolence, and underlying character of institutional "goodness." Thus, the very moment in which the existence of an institution is revealed to be a by-product of violence paradoxically becomes a moment in which the institution justifies its existence and importance and exemplifies its commitment to the promise of "continuous progress." Framed within a "hermeneutic of reconciliation" (Hunt, 2018), these institutional efforts narrowly circumscribe the kinds of justice it is possible to demand and desire. I also consider alternative approaches to addressing these ongoing legacies of institutional violence, emphasizing the importance of a horizon of change oriented by a commitment to interrupt and repair colonial harms.

In chapter 6, I consider some of the contemporary implications of the colonial narratives that the previous chapters examine. Decolonial engagements with both the past and present of higher education can interrupt satisfaction with the currently imaginable higher education futures. I therefore ask how the colonial histories reviewed in previous chapters might shift commonsense understandings about the contemporary challenges that we face. I reemphasize that my intention with the book is neither to describe an alternative history nor to prescribe a particular future, but rather to rethink how we frame the problems of the present and their relationship to the past so that we might pluralize the available horizons of hope and futurity (Scott, 2004). Thus, rather than put forward any particular alternative vision of higher education, I emphasize the importance of nurturing the "possibility of possibilities" from which different futures and formations of higher education might emerge (Barnett, 2014)—while enabling the important work of immediate harm reduction in the institutional spaces in which we find ourselves. Finally, I suggest that it might be possible to imagine higher education otherwise only once we confront the possibility of the end of higher education as we know it, and move away from a mode of existence rooted in entitlement, exceptionalism, and innocence, and toward modes of knowing, being, and relating rooted in humility, generosity, and responsibility.

Chapter One

A Colonial History of the Higher Education Present

From the sixteenth century onward race and gender divided humans into three categories: owning property, becoming propertyless, and being property.

—Aileen Moreton-Robinson, 2015, pp. xxiii–xxiv

We need to learn again how five centuries of studying, classifying, and ordering humanity within an imperial context gave rise to peculiar and powerful ideas of race, culture, and nation that were, in effect, conceptual instruments that the West used both to divide up and to educate the world.

—John Willinsky, 1998, pp. 2–3

The crisis that American and European universities suffer today [is] not only the result of pressures created by neoliberalism, the financial crisis and global capitalism. . . . This crisis also originates in the exhaustion of the present academic model with its origins in the universalism of the Enlightenment.

—Capucine Boidin, James Cohen, & Ramón Grosfoguel, 2012, p. 2

The decolonial framework that I employ in this book emphasizes the relationship between modern promises and the colonial processes that subsidize them. From this perspective, colonialism, racism, and environmental extractivism are not the result of the failures or shortcomings of modern institutions to fulfill their promise of extending their universal benevolent gifts to all. Instead, these harmful practices are primary *conditions of possibility* for the (re)production of modern infrastructures and subjectivities. This interdependent relationship between modern promises and colonial processes can be understood through the concept of "modernity/coloniality," developed by Latin American scholars including Anibal Quijano, Walter Mignolo, Nelson Maldonado-Torres, Ramón Grosfoguel, and Maria Lugones, which suggests that "modernity and coloniality are two sides of the same coin" (Mignolo, 2007, p. 42).

Within the dynamic of modernity/coloniality, violence is the constitutive underside (the "shadow") that makes possible modernity's "shiny" achievements—including social mobility, political stability, economic growth and development, legal equality, and public goods. These achievements have been guaranteed for some people at the expense of other people, as well as other-than-human beings, who are subject to genocide, dispossession, enslavement, displacement, segregation, incarceration, exploitation, militarization, ecological degradation, destitution, and cognitive imperialism. Modernity/coloniality is broadly made up of a relational system organized to ensure unrestricted and unaccountable autonomy, a political system organized by nation-states, an economic system organized by racial capitalism, and a knowledge system organized by supposedly "universal" reason. In this chapter, I present my approach to decolonial critique by reviewing the basic elements of these systems, and then describe how they shape the historiographic reading of US higher education that I offer in this book.

Before I proceed, I should note that the mainstream historical narratives analyzed here come predominantly from overview texts that are often used in courses about the history of higher education. The general trends and trajectories synthesized by their authors and analyzed by me are not equally relevant for all institutions or institutional types at all times, and are most relevant for the four-year institutions (public or private) that can be understood as historically white colleges and universities (HWCUs)—meaning institutions that were historically founded and developed primarily to educate white students, serve the interests of white people, and reproduce and naturalize white middle- and upper-class social, economic, and intellectual norms. These institutions have different histories than historically Black colleges and universities (HBCUs), tribal colleges and universities (TCUs), and community colleges. However, the histories of all these institutional types are also quite intertwined and are deeply, though differently, shaped by the colonial logics and practices that I review in this book. Thus, although the general systemic patterns described in this book are present to varied extents across different institutional types and different individual institutions, further analyses of how these patterns have shaped these specific institutions and different institutional types, and how these patterns have been negotiated and resisted within them, are certainly warranted.

In this chapter, I briefly introduce the importance of critically engaging the colonial foundations of US higher education before introducing my approach to decolonial historiography. I then review the decolonial critiques that inform this approach before using it to consider dominant ("whitestream") narratives of US higher education history. From here, I consider how a decolonial analysis of the foundations of US higher education differs from analyses that focus on exclusion. Next, I address how presumptions of exceptionalism, entitlement, and innocence shape US society in general and higher education specifically, and then conclude by reviewing three primary promises of higher education that both rest on and reproduce these presumptions.

"The Past That Is Not Past"

As Lindsey Walters (2017) notes, most "universities pay constant homage to aspects of their pasts, while simultaneously 'forgetting' those histories that are difficult, embarrassing, or shameful to remember" (p. 727). However, US higher education institutions are increasingly coming to terms with their violent foundations, often in response to pressure from students and community activists. These responses have included formal apologies, sponsored reports on institutions' racial and colonial histories, and subsequent commitments that often take the form of commemoration and a promise to mobilize the research and educational missions of the institution toward further analysis and understanding of these shameful pasts.

In the United States, most efforts to address higher education institutions' complicity in systemic, historical, and ongoing violence have focused on slavery and, to some extent, segregation and other forms of anti-Black racism that endured after the Civil War. Less work has been done to address institutional complicity with settler colonialism or global imperialism, though this too is shifting. Some of the first examples of addressing complicity in settler colonialism were the University of Denver's and Northwestern University's investigations of the role of shared founder John Evans in the Sand Creek Massacre, a mass murder of hundreds of Cheyenne and Arapaho people, a majority of whom were women and children, by US soldiers in 1864 (Stratton, 2017).

As I argue in more detail in chapter 5, even when higher education institutions' historical entanglements with racial and colonial violence are addressed, these entanglements are often framed as separate or distinct from histories of pride, benevolence, and accomplishment—rather than as the hidden cost of those accomplishments. There is also a common temporal separation of violence between past and present. That is, not only are the "good things" understood to be entirely separate from the "bad things," but the "bad things" are also understood to shape the present only marginally, at most, as they recede ever further into the past with the passage of time. When legacies of violence are framed as if they are contained within discrete and exceptional moments, they can be safely addressed and left in the past, creating the illusion of a clean break between the present and earlier transgressions. Meanwhile, "proud" moments of early institutional history are framed as the kernel of a continued, inevitable evolution toward ever greater and more democratic forms of inclusion and universalism. In reality, as I argue throughout this book, violence is foundational to US higher education's structure and organization, and it is an ongoing condition of possibility for its contemporary existence—that is, violence is in the marrow of the bones of contemporary institutions.

The wealth that was expropriated from Black and Indigenous peoples through enslavement and colonization and then donated or granted to various institutions of higher education in the seventeenth, eighteenth, and nineteenth centuries continues to circulate and produce more wealth for these institutions (Boggs et al., 2019; La Paperson, 2017; Lee & Ahtone, 2020; Stein, 2020; Wilder, 2013). Universities have trained, and continue to train, graduates for all kinds of jobs that require them, both directly and indirectly, to extend extractive practices and relationships in both the public and the private sector. Meanwhile, the underlying imperative of perpetual capital accumulation continues to propel much of the research and teaching at US universities and to leave social and ecological destruction in its wake.

This book specifically seeks to make visible the disavowed colonial conditions of possibility for three celebrated eras of US higher education: the initial "colonial era" of early institutions in the seventeenth and eighteenth centuries; the land-grant era in the mid- to late nineteenth century; and the post–World War II era in the mid-twentieth century.

Scholars of US settler colonialism find that it forms an ongoing structural relation that organizes everyday life in US society. Thus, "it cannot be reduced to, as many nationalist ideologies would have it, the merely unfortunate birth pangs of its establishment that remain in the distant past" (Arvin, Tuck, & Morrill, 2013, p. 12). Similarly, scholars of anti-Black violence describe how US society and modern global society more generally continue to be structured by anti-Blackness in ways that were first established through chattel slavery and that continue to be perpetuated through what Saidiya Hartman (2008) calls "the afterlife of slavery," in which "black lives are still imperiled and devalued by a racist calculus and a political arithmetic that were entrenched centuries ago" (p. 6).

Thus, to single out three specific eras of history is just one possible way of storying the foundations of US higher education, one that mirrors but also speaks back to current historical "common sense" rooted in settler memory. Theoretically, one could write a continuous history of the racial-colonial entanglements of US higher education from the seventeenth century to the present. Or one could read this history in a nonlinear fashion that traces recurrent colonial patterns across time.

However, the fact that settler colonialism and anti-Blackness cannot be reduced to a single event or era of history does not mean that specific historical events are unimportant. Rather, as Bruyneel (2013) suggests, "we need to see events as productive and reproductive of contemporary structures and structural relations" (p. 315). Hence, by unpacking narratives of particular historical moments or eras, especially those that are highly celebrated, we can better understand how the racial and colonial structures of US society and its institutions are naturalized and reproduced, including institutions of higher education.

A Decolonial Historiography of US Higher Education History

Inspired by Christina Sharpe (2016), I undertake decolonial historiography as "a method of encountering a past that is not past." To do so, I primarily read secondary sources, as well as some primary sources, "along the grain" while also offering parallel accounts of the invisibilized violence that subsidized celebrated moments of US higher education history. I also point to how these histories inform the present. This approach challenges the common organizing desire of white settler memory to "move past" these histories in order to "move on" or "move forward," instead suggesting that we cannot move past what is not actually past and continues to shape US society. Referring to museums, Sharpe asks: "How does one, in the words so often used by such institutions, 'come to terms with' (which usually means move past) ongoing and quotidian atrocity?" (2016, p. 13). Increasingly, universities, too, are trying to move past the colonial relations that continue to make the campus possible in the first place and that the campus also continues to make possible.

Rather than understand the current moment as the outcome of linear historical developments from "here" to "there," or presume that we can cleanly separate formations of US higher education between "then" and "now," this method recognizes that "attending to the present moment implies, necessarily, understanding that the present we move through . . . is a reliquary of the past, holding traces of everything that has happened and everything that has been erased" (Shotwell, 2016, p. 77).

If the entanglement of US higher education in genocidal and ecocidal violence is acknowledged at all in mainstream history texts, the presumption of linear progress generally frames it in the past tense. In this framing, that violence can now be acknowledged but also neatly relegated to history, safely integrated into white settler memory in a way that allows us to move past it and thus cease to be accountable for it. This book questions the assumption of linear progress, even as it proceeds in a fairly typical linear fashion through three eras of history.

To situate my decolonial historiographic reading of the foundations of US higher education, in the following section I briefly synthesize the analyses offered by decolonial critiques.

Decolonial Critiques

Within the decolonial analyses that inform this book, modernity/coloniality is not understood as a single event, or even a distinct historical era; rather, it is taken as a contested and constantly shifting but enduring global system. Decolonial scholars date the origins of this system to the fifteenth century when Europe first initiated the colonization of the Americas and the transatlantic slave trade. They suggest that, since that time, in the United States and elsewhere, this system has shape-shifted and transformed, often as a means of adapting to resistance to its violence. Through these shape-shifting efforts, the global colonial system has continued to affect the ongoing dispossession (exploitation and expropriation), destitution, and premature death of Indigenous, Black, and other racialized communities both "at home" and "abroad." In addition to racial and colonial violence, this system also affects ecological violence through the objectification of nature and the extraction and consumption of so-called natural resources.

The theoretical framework that I employ is informed by several genealogies of decolonial theory and practice that have challenged this violence and sustained the possibilities of other modes of existence. These include Black studies, Indigenous studies, postcolonial studies, modernity/coloniality studies, and queer and feminist studies. The decolonial lens I employ is also deeply informed by my work as a founding member of the Gesturing Towards Decolonial Futures arts and research collective and by our collaborations with Indigenous communities in Canada, Peru, and Brazil. I position my theoretical framework as being "inspired by" these genealogies because it is not possible to articulate a definitive decolonial critique or to do justice to the internal diversity, depth, and complexity of each genealogy. Thus, my theoretical framework is situated and partial, as all frameworks inevitably are. This is particularly important to emphasize given my position as a white settler author and the risk that my analyses will be privileged over Indigenous, Black, and racialized peoples' analyses because of the colonial politics of knowledge that naturalize white epistemic authority (Cusicanqui, 2012; King, 2019). Engagements with decolonial theories and practices must attend to the intellectual, political, and other labor of the above-mentioned and many other communities that have developed these critiques in the context of high-intensity struggles to protect their lives and livelihoods. Apart from merely crediting these communities for this labor, we need to ask what our ongoing accountabilities to them are in the context of higher education and beyond.

Below I summarize my approach to decolonial critique by reviewing four primary systems that sustain a modern/colonial mode of existence: relational, political, economic, and

Table 1. Modern promises and the colonial process that makes them possible

	Modern promise	Colonial process
Relational system: Separability	Independence, individualism, and unrestricted autonomy (for certain [white] people); accountability and responsibility are optional choices	Denial of interdependence and refusal of its related responsibilities; creation and maintenance of racialized and gendered hierarchies of existence
Political system: Nation-states	Security, order, progress; protection of (certain) people and property; national homogeneity	State and state-sanctioned violence (e.g., policing, prisons, occupation, dispossession, borders, militarism, imperialism)
Economic system: Global capitalism	Continuous economic growth, consumption, and wealth accumulation	Expropriation and exploitation of humans and other-than-human beings; ecological destruction
Epistemological system: Western universalism	A single, totalizing knowledge system that offers certainty, predictability, and consensus	Suppression and attempted obliteration of other knowledges; knowledge used to index, control, and engineer the world

epistemological. Each of these systems has significantly shaped US higher education and how we understand its history and imagine its possible futures. These critiques make connections between the modern promises made by each system and the colonial processes that enable those promises (summarized in table 1). Although higher education predates the modern university and has taken many forms throughout time, today it is extremely difficult to imagine a form of US higher education that would effectively operate outside even just one of the systems reviewed below, let alone all four of them.

Relational System: Separability

Decolonial critiques emphasize that modern modes of existence are established through a colonial relational system that promises unrestricted and unaccountable autonomy through an organizing principle of separation. Scholars identify slavery and colonialism as foundational moments of this separation, which resulted in a denial of responsibility to and interdependence with not only other humans but also with other-than-human beings and the earth itself (e.g., Ahenakew, 2019; Alexander, 2005; Silva, 2014; Whyte, 2018, 2020). Davis and Todd (2017) argue that colonization and slavery affected "a severing of relations between humans and the soil, between plants and animals, between minerals and our bones" (p. 770). According to decolonial scholars, this initial fantasy of separation created the necessary conditions for the subsequent creation of colonial categories of being and "deadly hierarchies of life" (TallBear, 2019, p. 26) that rank purportedly separate beings according to their perceived value (Alexander, 2005; King, 2019; Silva, 2014; Wynter, 2003). The resulting hierarchies both naturalize human exceptionalism in relation to other living beings and claim racial or cultural exceptionalisms within humanity itself. As a result of this relational system, Black and Indigenous peoples, as well as "nature," are systemically treated as possessable, exploitable, and expendable for the sake of "progress" and the fulfillment of modern promises that are offered primarily to white people, who in turn are structurally positioned as the rightful leaders of humanity.

Political System: The Nation-State

Higher education institutions are significantly shaped by, and in many cases expected to serve, the political systems in which they are embedded. The modern political system is organized by nation-states. Mainstream narratives imagine this system to be the result of a social contract in which rational individuals decided to give up certain freedoms for the promise that the state will ensure order and protect their life, liberty, and property (Mills, 2015; Silva, 2016). In contrast, many decolonial critiques suggest that this promise is actually kept through colonial processes of state and state-sanctioned violence against "othered" communities (Byrd, 2011; Hong, 2014; Wynter, 2003). These processes include various forms of removal, confinement, occupation, incarceration, enslavement, and outright state or state-sanctioned murder; domestic policing as well as policing of nation-state borders; and the export of state violence through global militarism and various forms of political and economic intervention abroad (Walia, 2013).

Decolonial scholars argue that the nation-state protects only those it deems "worthy"—generally, white and wealthy people. Thus, these critiques tend to challenge mainstream horizons of hope and change that define justice as democratized inclusion into the state. Decolonial critiques do not suggest that efforts to expand access to civil rights and public services are unimportant, but rather that there is also a need to simultaneously imagine entirely different modes of political organization outside the nation-state (Aikau, 2015; Arvin, Tuck, & Morrill, 2013; Byrd, 2011; TallBear, 2019; Trask, 2004; Wilderson, 2010).

Economic System: Global Capitalism

Higher education institutions are also deeply shaped by the economic system in which they are embedded and operate. The modern economic system of capitalism offers the promises of perpetual growth and wealth accumulation. Even as some have sought to harmonize capitalism with meritocratic promises of a prosperous and diverse middle class, decolonial critiques conclude that capitalism continues to require unequal outcomes, premised as it is on profits made from exploitation, expropriation, and ecological destruction (Coulthard, 2014; Silva, 2014; Whyte, 2018). Here, "expropriation" refers to the appropriation of the entire value of land, labor, or "natural resources," and "exploitation" refers to underpaying for land, labor, or "natural resources"

Decolonial scholars suggest that the wealth that was expropriated through slavery and colonialism continues to form the basis of global capitalism (Coulthard, 2014; Robinson, 2000; Silva, 2014). They note that while most white people are themselves exploited by the capitalist system, this system nonetheless offers them security and prosperity at the expense of other people and other-than-human beings. W. E. B. Du Bois argued that even when white individuals are poor, they are advantaged in their relative social and political position, being "compensated in part by a sort of public and psychological wage" that promises superiority, entitlement, and exceptionalism (as quoted by Nopper, 2011, p. 19). Beyond access to public services and institutions—including higher education—these "wages of whiteness" foster white people's allegiance to the dominant political and economic order.

Epistemological System: Western Universalism

It perhaps goes without saying that the epistemological system of higher education institutions significantly shapes the form, content, and direction of the education offered by those institutions. These institutions serve as primary sites where this epistemological system is reproduced and naturalized, though this role is increasingly being challenged. Decolonial analyses argue that this epistemological system promises that there is only one, universally relevant truth and way of knowing, which can be used to describe, make predictions about, and engineer outcomes in the world. Although this "truth" is continually revised, there is a consistent investment in the idea that it will be found within Western knowledge (Maldonado-Torres,

2007). Boaventura de Sousa Santos (2007) observes that the colonial cost of the modern promise of universal epistemic relevance has been denial of the value and even the existence of other knowledge systems. These other knowledge systems have been ignored, repressed, and in some cases entirely eradicated. Decolonial analyses argue that historically modern universities have sought to contain the challenge that other knowledges and ways of knowing pose to the supposed universalism of the modern Western episteme and its ordering of the world, given that these other knowledges signal the limits of mastery and totalizing truths and continue to hold possibilities for otherwise worlds (Hong, 2008; Silva, 2014; Wynter, 2003).

Contesting Whitestream US Higher Education History

Especially in the analysis of early US higher education in chapter 2, I focus my decolonial historiographic reading on four higher education history books: John R. Thelin's *A History of American Higher Education* (2004), Arthur M. Cohen and Carrie B. Kisker's *The Shaping of American Higher Education* (2010), Christopher J. Lucas's *American Higher Education: A History* (2006), and Roger L. Geiger's *The History of American Higher Education* (2014).

I chose these books because they are commonly assigned as key texts in courses about the history of US higher education. Thus, for many scholars and practitioners of higher education, this literature provides some of the only exposure to higher education history that they have unless their own research, practice, or personal interest inspires deeper engagement. While Lawrence Veysey's *The Emergence of the American University* (1965) and Frederick Rudolph's *The American College and University* (1962) are also considered classic works in this area, I focus my analysis on more recent texts.

One way to begin a decolonial engagement with historical narratives is to ask a few basic questions: From whose perspective is this history told? Whose experiences are centered in the narrative? Which events are considered significant, which are given passing mention, and which are ignored?

~~I~~ ~~se~~ of most mainstream higher education history ~~narratives~~ implicitly center the stories and experi- ~~white~~, middle- and upper-class, property-owning men. In certain ways, this choice feels logical, as these are the people for whom and in whose image US higher education was largely developed, particularly in its earliest eras. Further, even to the extent that these institutions were intended to serve "society" or "the public," the imagined constituencies and their inter- ests were narrowly defined by and in the service of the white male elite. Yet, while the earliest institutions of higher educa- tion were white and male supremacist to their core, rarely are they explicitly framed as such, and rarely is their role in both producing and upholding the raced and gendered hierarchies of early colonial society thoroughly examined. Our under- standing of racism, colonialism, and sexism in the present will be less rigorous if we lack a solid account of how these sys- tems of domination shaped our institutions from the start.

While it is inevitably acknowledged at some point in most contemporary texts that the staff and student body in early higher education were largely white and male, little attention is paid to the implications of this fact for how higher education developed, how we understand the challenges of present, and what kinds of futures we imagine as desirable and possible.

Although accounts focused on the racial and colonial foun- dations of US higher education are still relatively few, there is scholarship that documents marginalized peoples' exclusion from, subjugation within, resistance to, and transformation of whitestream colleges and universities. Yet these histories of marginalized communities are also marginalized histories, in that even when considered, they are rarely understood as formative or definitive of US higher education as a whole (Chambers & Freeman, 2017; Patton, 2016). As a result, what are presented as universal, neutral "view from nowhere" histories (Maldonado-Torres, 2011) are largely histories of white, male, middle- and upper-class higher education.

Beyond what and whose stories are told in historical narratives are other questions: How should we address or adjust existing narratives such that the absence of invisibilized narratives can be noticed? Why were these other histories invisibilized for so long, and what did their absence enable and foreclose? How can we make what is absent present in ways that do not become tokenistic or additive and thereby leave systemically marginalized histories at the margins, while the colonial center remains unexamined and untouched (Ahenakew, 2016)? After all, the history of dominant groups is deeply entangled with, and often directly dependent on, the subjugation and conditional inclusion of marginalized communities (Wilder, 2013). This entanglement includes the ways that the resistance of marginalized communities has prompted various institutional changes over time.

Craig Steven Wilder (2013) describes the life of Henry Watson, a white early Harvard graduate who was trained in scientific racism at his alma mater and eventually became a plantation owner and enslaver. According to Wilder, Watson "likely never appreciated the intimacy of his connections to Native and African peoples—the ways that their lives unfolded into his hands and his into theirs, but his choices reflect that reality" (p. 8). Watson's "career as master of a 'degraded race' forced to work the lands of a 'vanished people' embodies central themes in the history of the American college" (p. 8). Like Watson, many of us—especially white people—who work and study in US colleges and universities also fail to realize the intimacy of our own, unevenly distributed entanglements with social and institutional violence, or the implications of those entanglements for our responsibilities in the present.

According to Jana Nidiffer (1999), "Historical treatments of the poor and higher education" (p. 324) generally fall within one of five categories, or some combination of these: "traditional/omission, increased inclusion, center of analysis, issue specific, and broader social analysis" (p. 323). Nidiffer's typology is useful for analyzing historical treatments of marginalized communities in higher education more generally. Most popular, contemporary higher education historical survey texts have adopted an "increased inclusion" approach. These reference, at various points, the experiences of Black, Indigenous, and other racialized peoples, poor people, and (primarily white middle- and upper-class) women, but these experiences and the structures that shape them are not centered or placed in the context of broader social analyses (Mustaffa, 2017; Nicolazzo & Marine, 2016). Further, when they are referenced, these experiences are generally framed as the product of exclusion from white, middle-class, and male-dominated institutions. In the following section, I consider possibilities for thinking about US higher education history beyond the common frames of "exclusion" and "inclusion."

Beyond Inclusion and Exclusion

As Justin Leroy (2016) notes, when thinking through the constitutive role of slavery and colonization in the United States, "the hinge of inclusion/exclusion both misnames that violence and narrows any sense of possibility for how it can be redressed" (para. 3). This book does not primarily provide a history of exclusion from US higher education, though it contains some elements of this history. Rather, it draws attention to the systemic, historical, and ongoing racial, colonial, and ecological violence that has subsidized US higher education over time. More specifically, it offers an account of how mainstream narratives tend to reproduce white settler memory by disavowing universities' complicity in that violence.

This focus on violence risks reproducing what Tuck (2009) describes as "damage-centered" narratives that take "a pathologizing approach in which the oppression singularly defines a community" as part of an effort to document "harm or injury in order to achieve reparation" (p. 411). Damage-centred research frames marginalized, especially Indigenous, Black, and racialized communities as if they were defined by the violence that has been committed against them by white settler individuals and institutions. Tuck suggests that an antidote to this tendency is for marginalized communities to instead create "desire-based research" that is "concerned with understanding complexity, contradiction, and the self-determination of lived lives" (p. 416). Jalil Mustaffa (2017) models a version of this desire-based approach to research by reading anti-Black violence and Black life-making practices and resistance alongside each other throughout US higher education history. He describes practices of Black life-making as "creative spaces of possibility and freedom Black people produce when practicing self-definition, self-care, and resistance" (p. 712).

Resistance to violence is not just a refusal of what is but also an insistence that it can be otherwise. Insisting on other educational futures continues in contemporary efforts that seek to reform, transform, or even abolish higher education institutions. In this book, I deconstruct the foundations of US higher education in order to discern the significance of these foundations for both the present and the future. But while I do attend to resistance at various points throughout the book, this book is not a history of Black and Indigenous resistance in and to higher education. I do hope, however, that this text will encourage others to seek out accounts that offer a deeper focus on the histories and complexities of anticolonial and antiracist resistance in higher education where they already exist and to create them where they remain to be written. Such accounts include Roderick Ferguson's *The Reorder of Things* (2012), Nick Mitchell's *Discipline and Surplus: Black Studies, Women's Studies, and the Dawn of Neoliberalism* (forthcoming), Robin Starr Zape-tah-hol-ah Minthorn and Heather Shotton's edited volume *Reclaiming Indigenous Research in Higher Education* (2018), Leigh Patel's *No Study without Struggle: Confronting the Legacy of Settler Colonialism in Higher Education* (2021), Ibram X. Kendi's *The Black Campus Movement* (2012), Eddie Cole's *The Campus Color Line: College Presidents and the Struggle for Black Freedom* (2020), rosalind hampton's *Black Racialization and Resistance at an Elite University* (2020), and La Paperson's *A Third University Is Possible* (2017).

I have chosen to focus here on the colonial structures and subjectivities that make up the foundations of US higher education, rather than resistance to these structures and subjectivities, in part because I do not think I am the right person to write the latter book. As Leigh Patel (2015) writes, before embarking on research, one should ask the question "Why me?" alongside the questions "Why this?" and "Why now?/ Why here?" She suggests that these questions "should prompt a humble pause and reflection on the specific of individuals' experiences that make them appropriately able to craft, contribute, and even question knowledges" (p. 58). As a white settler, I may be unable to do justice to the full depth, complexity, and texture of nonwhite peoples' educational experiences and resistance. I am also wary of reproducing the pattern whereby white people celebrate and even romanticize racialized and Indigenous peoples' resistance to systemic violence in order to deflect attention from their own complicity in that violence.

In an effort to interrupt this pattern, I read mainstream narratives of US higher education history along the grain. Ann Stoler (2009) distinguishes between reading *against the grain* and reading *along the grain*. She notes that in many cases, critical engagements with colonial archives position themselves against the grain, seeking to renarrate history "from the bottom up" and emphasizing the agency and resistance of oppressed and dispossessed peoples. However, at times efforts to read against the grain assume that the colonial narrative of history— "the grain"—is already adequately understood and accounted for. "Assuming we know those scripts," Stoler cautions, "rests too comfortably on predictable stories with familiar plots" (p. 50). She suggests adopting a humbler stance. She argues for the value of also rereading colonial narratives in ways that examine how these narratives are constructed and naturalized. It is this approach that I adopt in this book, while recognizing the importance of both forms of reading for the larger project of decolonizing higher education.

By bringing mainstream narratives about celebrated higher education accomplishments into conversation with the racial and colonial conditions of possibility for those accomplishments to occur, I seek to denaturalize and problematize the whitestream narrative arc of US higher education history that posits the inevitability of linear movement across time (of growth, democratization, and inclusion) and expansion across space (from East to West, and now globally). In particular, this method enables me to identify how narratives of US higher education history that are steeped in settler memory are mobilized in response to challenges of the present in ways that obscure the ongoing impacts of racial and colonial violence.

As Mark Lewis Taylor (2020) notes, "None of us, especially in US higher education, is free from being entangled in the webs that slavery and white supremacy have spun" (p. 309). To focus on the violence that US higher education institutions actively participated in and benefited from is to turn the gaze toward those institutions and toward the individuals who continue to benefit from the institutions' entanglements with slavery and colonization—including myself.

Kyle Whyte (2018) argues, "There's just no way to imagine an alternative where the US is exactly what it is today economically, culturally, and politically without the commission of genocide, unwarranted killing, sexual violence, forced assimilation, child abuse, and economic injustice" (p. 284). This framing, which emphasizes the deep dependence of the US and its white settler citizens on genocide, ecocide, and epistemicide, contrasts with the common assumption that the white citizen is independent, self-made, and self-determined (Silva, 2007). This framing suggests, instead, that white settler subjectivities are largely constituted through their structural complicity in systemic state and state-sanctioned violence (Flowers, 2015). Indeed, decolonial analyses suggest that many of the accomplishments and advantages that white people enjoy are a product not of their hard work and natural abilities but of a colonial system. This may in fact be part of the reason why these analyses are often perceived as threatening and destabilizing to white people. These decolonial analyses are not intended to suggest that people who are white are solely defined by the violence in which we are complicit. However, they do suggest that white people are accountable for interrupting and enacting restitution and reparation for the ways that violence continues to subsidize our lives and livelihoods.

By reading along the grain, this book offers, if anything, a "damage-centered" narrative of whitestream higher education itself. While merely flipping inherited scripts of damage will not necessarily lead to transformation, it can be a first step in denaturalizing and identifying the limits of those scripts and gesturing toward the possibility and necessity of entirely different ones. By emphasizing the colonial constitution of mainstream institutions of higher education, I also consider the limits of efforts to decolonize higher education history that simply incorporate marginalized groups into mainstream historical narratives as temporarily excluded parties. In these narratives, it is assumed that the inclusion of these groups will be achieved with the passage of time, as higher education delivers on its promises of continuous progress and intrinsic benevolence, and that this is the only viable path forward. I consider how these narratives of inclusion and exclusion naturalize both the emergence *and* presumed continuity of white settler colonial dominance, both in higher education and in general.

To bring attention to the dependence of whitestream US higher education institutions on violence is to challenge presumptions of the exceptionalism, entitlement, and innocence of white people, the United States as a whole, and US higher education specifically.

Undoing Presumptions of Exceptionalism, Entitlement, and Innocence

One way that white supremacy is sustained in higher education is through narratives that reproduce white exceptionalism. White people often convince ourselves that we have earned all of our advantages and achievements through our individual talent, merit, and hard work. In this way, white people come to believe that we are the rightful leaders of society and, indeed, humanity as a whole. In other words, we use our presumed exceptionalism to rationalize our socially sanctioned entitlement to a range of promises offered by dominant systems—including the promise of moral and political authority, epistemic certainty, unrestricted autonomy, and material (economic) security. This presumed exceptionalism also tends to extend to a sense of our own innocence of wrongdoing, which makes it very difficult to draw white peoples' attention to their complicity in structural domination without activating significant resistance (Ahmed, 2012; DiAngelo, 2011; Shotwell, 2016; L. Taylor, 2013; Tuck & Yang, 2012).

To remind white people of the specificities of our position, and specifically of how that position is subsidized through colonial violence and ecological destruction, is to interrupt our presumed innocence as well as the presumption that we have rightfully earned our structural advantages. Even when white settlers critique settler colonialism, it is often difficult for us to confront just how deeply we are shaped by it (Kotef, 2020). And even those of us who critique structural white supremacy do not necessarily see our own self-images of exceptionalism, entitlement, and deservingness as an extension of that white supremacy—in part because we still tend to think of ourselves as unique, objective, independent individuals, rather than consider the ways we are embedded and socialized into larger structures of domination.

Beyond the presumed exceptionalism inherent in white supremacy, in order to address colonial violence in US higher education, it is important to confront the characteristics of American exceptionalism.* As Donald Pease (2009) notes, "A vast complex of ideas, policies, and actions is comprehended

---

* Throughout this book, I avoid referring to the United States as "America," or US higher education as "American higher education," given that "America" can also refer to two entire continents (North and South America). However, I do reference "American exceptionalism" and the "American Dream," given that these terms have a particular socio-historical meaning within the US context. In some cases, quoted sources also use "America" to refer to the United States.

under the phrase American exceptionalism, and the disparate significations of this complex are neither compatible [with] nor derived from a shared semantic source" (p. 23). Broadly speaking, however, American exceptionalism paints the US nation-state as both an exemplar and a defender of freedom, and in so doing rationalizes its right to make war to protect that freedom, both on the continent (through Indigenous dispossession framed as Manifest Destiny) and abroad (beginning with the Spanish-American War and continuing to this day).

Natsu Taylor Saito argues that the narrative of American exceptionalism "presumes that human history is best understood as a linear progression toward higher stages of civilisation, that western civilization represents the apex of this history, and that the United States embodies the best and most advanced stage of western civilisation and therefore, human history to date" (as cited by Sirvent & Haiphong, 2019, pp. xx–xxi). In this way, American exceptionalism is rooted in a broader narrative of Western civilizational supremacy that is premised on a racist hierarchy of humanity and a Eurocentric imaginary of progress and development that have been used to justify anti-Black and anti-Indigenous violence for more than five centuries.

Among other consequences, narratives of American exceptionalism reproduce ideas of innocence that disavow the historical and ongoing genocidal and ecocidal violences that are performed and sanctioned by the US state. US higher education is deeply entangled in the reproduction of these narratives and, in many cases, in the reproduction of their material manifestations. Piya Chatterjee and Sunaina Maira (2014) observe, "As in all imperial and colonial nations, intellectuals and scholarship play an important role—directly or indirectly, willingly or unwittingly—in legitimizing American exceptionalism and rationalizing U.S. expansionism and repression, domestically and globally" (pp. 6–7).

US exceptionalism is also tightly linked to the promises of the American Dream. The term "American Dream" is likely a twentieth-century coinage by James Adams in his 1931 book *The Epic of America*, in which he described it as "that dream of a land in which life should be better and richer and fuller for every man, with opportunity for each according to his ability or achievement" (Adams, 2017, p. 404) However, the underlying ideas of the American Dream have been around in some form for all of US history (Cullen, 2003), ideas made particularly visible in Frederick Jackson Turner's "frontier thesis" in the late nineteenth century (see chapter 3). The Dream has several interrelated varieties, which have shifted over time, but most rest on ideals of individual freedom and security and require a stable social order. Common elements across many varieties of the American Dream include upward social and economic mobility; (formal) equality of opportunity; home ownership; personal fulfillment; and a comfortable retirement (Cullen, 2003; McNamee & Miller, 2009). While white people have historically had greatest access to the American Dream, it is not exclusively white people who have sought to achieve it, as its access is promised to anyone who "earns" it.

Higher education is today often understood as a central pathway or engine for achieving the American Dream. According to Martin Trow (2000), "This sense of society with limitless possibilities for all, largely (though not exclusively) through higher education, is what is usually meant by 'the American dream'" (p. 312). Several recent books reiterate this association, primarily as a means to critique recent political economic shifts toward privatization and marketization in higher education, changes perceived to have compromised higher education's central role in providing a pathway to the American Dream. This includes Suzanne Mettler's *Degrees of Inequality: How the Politics of Higher Education Sabotaged the American Dream*

(2014) and Sara Goldrick-Rab's *Paying the Price: College Costs, Financial Aid, and the Betrayal of the American Dream* (2016).

However, decolonial analyses of the American Dream offer a different perspective. From a decolonial perspective, the promises of the American Dream have always depended on a disavowed underside of racial, colonial, and ecological violence (TallBear, 2019). In this analysis, the issue is not primarily that certain subjugated communities have been and are still being excluded from the promises of the American Dream, but that it is through the subjugation of those communities that the Dream is realized for other communities (especially white communities). Thus, current economic inequities and insecurities are understood not as a betrayal of the American Dream but rather as a product of its continued operation and expansion. I expand on this argument further in chapter 4.

Much in the same way that narratives of US exceptionalism are often embedded within a larger presumed exceptionalism of Western civilization, narratives of *higher education exceptionalism* are also embedded within the US and Western civilizational exceptionalisms. By higher education exceptionalism, I mean the ways that US institutions of higher education are framed as moral and intellectual leaders of society and, thus, as sites of social progress, in a way that other institutions are often not. Eli Meyerhoff (2019) describes the "romance" of (higher) education, which promises both individual and national uplift. It is partly due to the prevalence of these exceptionalist narratives that the entanglements of higher education with racial, colonial, and ecological violence have been overlooked for so long. And even when this violence is acknowledged, as is increasingly the case today, it is generally assumed that "universities are especially able to facilitate meaningful apologies and engage their history regardless of its emotional or political valence" (Clarke & Fine, 2010, p. 107).

However, it is questionable whether institutions can honestly confront and redress the impacts of their histories of violence while also restoring the promises that underscore claims of US higher education exceptionalism, including (1) the promise of continuous progress, (2) the promise of a benevolent public good, and (3) the promise of social mobility. These promises are common within whitestream narratives of US higher education history and are still widely held today. In the following section, I offer a brief decolonial reading of each of these promises, and in following chapters I read historical narratives along the grain in an effort to trace the origins, development, and continued investments in these promises, as well as the colonial processes that subsidize them.

The Promise of Continuous Progress

A teleological and progress-oriented history shapes most narratives about higher education, including critiques of the present (Boggs et al., 2019; Stein, 2018). These narratives presume that higher education reached its zenith in the post–World War II "Golden Age" but was interrupted by the rise of neoliberalism over the past several decades (Boggs & Mitchell, 2018). This historical narrative is often mobilized to assert an underlying imperative to redeem institutions and restore the derailed path of progress.

In their 2015 article, "The Public University: Recalling Higher Education's Democratic Purpose," Michael Benson and Hal Boyd offer what is by now a familiar narrative: the history and development of US higher education was premised on commitments to "fostering more fulsome democratic engagement, raising the country's global reputation, cultivating goodwill between states and nations, and expanding opportunities for more Americans" (p. 70). According to this narrative, contemporary developments toward the economization, privatization, commercialization, and marketization of higher education threaten this proud legacy, and it is therefore necessary to return to the promises of an earlier era and thereby "recapture the democratic purpose of higher education in America" (p. 79). Their critique of the contemporary moment is relatively mild, but others offer more passionate invectives about how these developments threaten the proud legacies of public US higher education and, in effect, the integrity and futurity of the American Dream itself (see chapter 4).

This "progress, interrupted" narrative has a broad appeal that brings together concerned academics with a range of disciplinary—and to some extent, political—affiliations, ranging from Benson and Boyd's fairly measured contribution to books with such dramatic titles as *The Fall of the Faculty*, *The Last Professors*, and *Zombies in the Academy*. Boggs and Mitchell (2018) diagnose the genre of responses that romanticize histories of higher education as part of "the crisis consensus." They write, "With the glossy patina of an ostensibly progressive liberal humanism, the crisis consensus invokes the university as the protector of time-honored and -tested values, one whose defense requires a temporality characterized simultaneously by urgency and nostalgia" (p. 434). This narrative has taken on the role of an organizational saga of US higher education writ large (Kimball & Ryder, 2014) and is commonly evoked in arguments for varied proposed higher education reforms.

From decolonial perspectives, however, the notion of progress itself imperialistically presumes a single valid "forward" direction for all and often rationalizes the sacrifice of any people and other-than-human beings who are perceived to be barriers to that progress (Smith, 2012; TallBear, 2019). Indeed, the expansion of higher education has always come at the expense of marginalized peoples. This includes, to different degrees, both those who are conditionally "included" in existing institutions (Ahmed, 2012) and those who are excluded from these institutions and pay the highest price for systemic expansion. However, because notions of progress tend to "have a teleological bent, presuming that society is meliorative—gradually moving toward perfection—through incremental reforms of social action" (Seamster & Ray, 2018, p. 316), it can be difficult to identify these continuities of violence. Colonial promises of continuous progress shape how we understand the history of higher education, as well as how we understand possible responses to contemporary challenges and crises.

The Promise of a Benevolent Public Good

Adriana Kezar (2004) outlines the different elements of higher education's "traditional" public good role, including "educating citizens for democratic engagement, supporting local and regional communities, preserving knowledge and making it available to the community, working in concert with other social institutions such as government or health-care agencies to foster their missions, advancing knowledge through research, developing the arts and humanities, broadening access to ensure a diverse democracy, developing the intellectual talents of students, and creating leaders for various areas of the public sector" (p. 431). Several critiques of neoliberalization express concern that these public good roles of higher education have been compromised (Marginson, 2016; Newfield, 2016; Pusser, 2014). Others have brought attention to how certain communities have historically been systemically excluded from the category of "the public." Yet, whether one believes that higher education ever in fact fulfilled these promises or that these promises remain an orienting compass for change, there is a broad consensus in public discourse as well as scholarship that US higher education both *should* and *can* be a benevolent institution that serves the public good. This is a form of higher education exceptionalism that presumes higher education is "a good in itself, as an institution defined ultimately by the progressive nature at its core" (Boggs & Mitchell, 2018, p. 434).

Decolonial critiques raise questions about what constitutes the "good" and "the public" in common notions of "the public good"—including questions about who decides what is good, in whose name, for whose benefit, to what end, and at whose expense. However, these critiques also draw attention to the ways many "public goods" were and are accumulated through racialized processes of exploitation and expropriation, and ecological extraction, in much the same way that "private goods" were and are. Thus, while many decolonial critiques challenge contemporary patterns of neoliberalization and privatization, they also question the assumptions that are naturalized through the very notion of public goods, and whether institutions so deeply rooted in violence can ever be made "benevolent." Further, these critiques draw attention to how the assumption of benevolence might lead to a narrowing of horizons, including the foreclosure of futures in which life is organized in another way than through the inherited categories of public versus private that are naturalized by the modern/colonial political economic system.

The Promise of Social Mobility

According to Trow (2000), "Through its role in fostering social mobility and the belief in a society open to talents, American higher education legitimates the social and political system, and thus is a central element in the society as it is nowhere else" (pp. 312–313). The promise of higher education as a means to access social mobility is premised on meritocracy, that is, the presumption that "those who are the most talented, the hardest working, and the most virtuous get and should get the most rewards" (McNamee & Miller, 2009, p. 4). The existence of socioeconomic classes in the United States is partly justified through the promise of accessible pathways for mobility between classes based on merit, which today is largely assessed through educational sorting.

Many critiques point to the failure of higher education to live up to its promise and potential as a pathway to social mobility. Evidence for this failure includes the facts that the rising cost of college bars access for many low-income students (especially access to more elite institutions); that the universities which enable the most social mobility tend to be the least accessible (Reber & Sinclair, 2020); and that dominant ways of operationalizing merit often serve to rationalize and facilitate the persistence of existing inequities, rather than to interrupt those inequities (Guinier, 2015). Other critiques point to the ways that opportunities for social mobility are often made available only to those who are willing and able to approximate or align with white middle- and upper-class norms and values (Jimmy, Andreotti, & Stein, 2019).

Notwithstanding the important concerns raised by these critiques, they are somewhat distinct from a decolonial critique of social mobility that challenges the framework of mobility altogether, as this frame implicitly assumes the continuity of a hierarchical capitalist system in which there is an unequal distribution of resources and power, and thus unequal socioeconomic "positions" (classes) within which one can be mobile, or not (Ahenakew et al., 2014; Paradies, 2020). Beyond its inherently hierarchical nature, this framework implicitly presumes the continuity of ongoing capitalist accumulation that is, according to decolonial critiques, structurally dependent on racialized and gendered forms of exploitation, expropriation, and ecological destruction. The promise of an ever-expanding middle class thereby naturalizes the continued exploitation of the classes below it, and the outright expropriation of lands and labor from the most marginalized, both domestically and abroad. Middle- and upper-class lifestyles are also ecologically unsustainable and burden the earth itself. For instance, if everyone in the world consumed resources at the same rate as the average person in the United States, we would need about five earths to sustain us (Global Footprint Network, n.d.).

In our current context, in which there is more competition for fewer secure middle-class positions, many nonetheless believe that higher education is a means through which to distribute social positions fairly (Boggs & Mitchell, 2018). Furthermore, when the promise of social mobility is unfulfilled, it is framed as a *broken* promise that requires repair (Goldrick-Rab, 2016). The inevitability of the enduring hierarchies within which one is or is not mobile is rarely questioned, and increased access to mobility is treated as the primary horizon of justice, hope, and change. A decolonial reading suggests instead that for many people the promise of social mobility has always been impossible and that, to the extent it has been possible for some, it has always come at the expense of others. A decolonial approach to social mobility would never shame or discourage low-income students from seeking mobility by pursuing higher education. If the only options are a classed system with no or low mobility or a classed system with some possibility for mobility, then the latter is clearly preferable. But these critiques invite us to ask how and why we have come to accept these as the only two possible options, as well as to consider what other modes of social organization might be possible and why is it so difficult for many people to imagine, let alone create, these other possibilities.

The Limits of Higher Education's Promises

In this chapter, I review the promises offered by modern relational, political, economic, and epistemological systems, and the related promises offered by modern institutions of higher education. I also consider the colonial processes that subsidize the fulfilment of these promises. These promises tend to be fulfilled most widely during times of abundance, and less so during times of scarcity. In the current context, these promises are increasingly going unfulfilled as we face the biophysical limits of a finite planet and the sedimentation of a state-enabled financialized capitalism with few redistributive imperatives. One possible response is to double down on demands that modern promises be met, hoping they can be reinvigorated and even expanded to new communities and contexts. However, this book offers an alternative approach, one in which we intellectually grapple with the ethical and practical limits and costs of these promises themselves, so that we might affectively and relationally untangle and disinvest our hopes and desires from those promises. In this way, we might gesture toward horizons of hope that open up the possibility of less harmful, more sustainable higher education futures that are viable but currently unfathomable.

Chapter Two

The Violent Origins of US Higher Education in the Colonial and Antebellum Eras

An institution of higher learning distinguished a civilized community from an unlettered settlement in the wilderness.

—Arthur Cohen and Carrie Kisker, 2010, p. 55

The American liberal myths of the self-made man, of the liberal individual, and of American exceptionalism all rely upon a disavowed relationship to the constitutive role of settler colonization in the foundation, development and structure of the USA.

—Kevin Bruyneel, 2013, p. 311

The fundamental problem is not that some are excluded from the hegemonic centers of the academy but that the university (as a specific institutional site) and academy (as a shifting material network) themselves cannot be disentangled from the long historical apparatuses of genocidal and protogenocidal social organization.

—Dylan Rodríguez, 2012, p. 812

Although the earliest period of US higher education is commonly referred to as the colonial era, the role of colonization in shaping higher education history, alongside the role of slavery, has long been ignored while "hiding in plain sight" (Harris, Campbell, & Brophy, 2019, p. 4). Mirroring the periodization of mainstream narratives, I define the colonial era as extending roughly from the early seventeenth century until the Revolutionary War, during which time the first institutions of higher education were founded in what would later become the United States. In this chapter, I examine how colonization and slavery were entangled with the emergence of US higher education. I also reference some developments in the first half of the nineteenth century—that is, between the Revolutionary War and the Civil War—as slavery and colonialization still played a central role in the development of higher education at this time.

The earliest higher education institutions in the British colonies that became the United States were active participants in deeply racialized efforts to accumulate capital and develop a white settler society to replace Indigenous societies (Wilder, 2013). Institutions acquired wealth in the form of money, enslaved persons, and land for themselves. But they also served as vectors of wealth extraction and accumulation for the upper classes and for the wider emerging US society. Boggs and Mitchell (2018) coined the useful term "accumulation by education," refracting and repurposing David Harvey's (2005) concept of "accumulation by dispossession," in order to capture the specific ways that US (higher) education has throughout its history served as both a direct and indirect means of, and justification for, capital accumulation.

Not only were early colleges complicit in the material expropriation and accumulation of Indigenous lands and Black lives through colonization and slavery, but they also provided the intellectual defense of these practices in the name of white peoples' presumed natural superiority and entitlements. For instance, Wilder (2013) notes, "in a 1783 sermon celebrating the American Revolution, Yale president Ezra Stiles lauded the rise of the 'Whites' whose numerical growth alone proved divine favoritism toward the children of Europe," and argued that "any remaining social injustices would disappear with Native Americans and Africans, whose decline seemed inevitable" (p. 177).

White supremacy, racial science, and the presumed inferiority and inevitable disappearance of Indigenous and Black peoples were not limited to presidential speeches; they also shaped higher education curricula. The entanglement of higher education with colonialism, anti-Black racism, and white supremacy only intensified following the Revolutionary War, as the United States' "founding fathers" looked west to expand the young nation-state. During this time, Wilder (2013) notes, "the academy refined and legitimated the social ideas that supported territorial expansion, a process that transformed the people of the new nation from revolutionaries to imperialists" (p. 182). A decolonial reading of history emphasizes that the new nation was in fact imperialist all along and that, as Wilder documents, the early colleges supported the socialization of their students into colonial modes of knowing, being, and relating that justified white male settler supremacy, colonization, and racial domination.

I argue that mainstream historical narratives that are told about the colonial era of US higher education (and, to an extent, the era between the Revolutionary War and the Civil War) are ordered by "white settler memory" (Boggs et al., 2019; Bruyneel, 2017), which is implicitly linked to assumptions about the inevitability of US expansionism and investment in a "white settler futurity" (Daigle, 2019). While this white settler memory remains hegemonic, today some people—especially students and community organizers—are seeking institutional acknowledgments, redress, and reparations for the initial colonial entanglements of what would become US higher education. I examine some of these efforts in chapter 5.

Mainstream Narratives of the Colonial Era of US Higher Education

Many narratives about the early history of US higher education emphasize that the institutions were often connected to religious orders but were "not so much religious as educative, founded to produce learned people" (Cohen & Kisker, 2010, p. 23). This aim was premised on a particular notion of "learned" rooted in the knowledges and religious and social mores of the European-descended settler merchant and planter classes. Modeled on European higher education institutions, but developing their own unique style, these institutions focused on preparing men to serve as clergymen as well as public servants for colonial society (Thelin, 2004). Many graduates were both, particularly given the close relationship between the church and state at the time (Lucas, 2006). Most came from wealthy families and stood to "inherit family commercial enterprises in shipping and selling" (Thelin, 2004, p. 24).

Although Thelin does not say it, many of these "commercial enterprises" were entangled with the triangular transatlantic slave trade, which transported enslaved peoples, crops, and manufactured goods between Africa, the Americas, and Europe (Wilder, 2013). Many college students were also the children of plantation owners from the southern colonies and the British West Indies. Although the children of these wealthy families did not necessarily need a degree in order to inherit their parents' social position and wealth, by preparing clergymen and public servants from these families, early colleges "ratified and perpetuated an elite that would inherit positions of influence in communities" (Thelin, 2004, p. 25) and also "provided an insurance policy guaranteeing that these favored young men would acquire not only literacy but also a sense of leadership and service" (p. 26).

The early colleges were therefore central institutions in naturalizing and reproducing the colonial social order. According to Trow, motivation for establishing these institutions included "the idea of perpetuating a civilized society in frontier communities; the growing need for better-trained people not only in law, medicine, and theology but also in commerce and navigation; community pride; and idealism and philanthropy on the part of community leaders" (as cited by Cohen and Kisker, 2010, p. 23). Alongside this mix of public and private interests, early colleges were also shaped by a mix of public and private control (Cohen & Kisker, 2010). David Labaree (2016) argues that these colleges were private nonprofit institutions. Yet what we now understand as standard distinctions between public and private institutions were not yet clearly established—and would not be clarified until the famous *Dartmouth* case (*Dartmouth College v. Woodward*, 1819). In any case, funding for early institutions was made up of a combination of donations, legislative appropriations, and some student tuition fees (Lucas, 2006; Thelin, 2004).

The commonly listed purposes for early US higher education nowhere indicate that higher education was understood as a pathway for social mobility. In the first place, social mobility was, at the time, not framed as a promised social good. Although there were exceptions, possibilities for mobility at the time were largely achieved not through education but rather through securing land and other forms of private property. The promise of higher education as a pathway for social mobility was established only later, but within mainstream narratives this shift only gives further evidence of another promise: that higher education offers continual progress, both within society as a whole and in terms of its own development from an elite institution to a progressively more inclusive one.

The preparation of "lawyers, ministers, and statesmen" to serve the colonies and, later, the young US nation was accomplished largely through the transmission of "knowledge of rhetoric, classical scholarship, and the Bible" (Cohen & Kisker, 2010, p. 33). Many of the white men who orchestrated the US founding were educated in colonial colleges. As Cohen and Kisker (2010) explain, "The nation was founded by an educated minority whose writings evidenced their dedication to classical and contemporary political philosophy" (p. 53). Though situated within a particular social, cultural, and historical milieu, these philosophies were nonetheless framed as universally valuable, relevant, and revolutionary (Grosfoguel, 2013). Thelin (2004) suggests that "colonial college-building made a significant, positive contribution to the ideas and actions of the generation that shaped the American Revolution" (p. 36). He almost immediately qualifies this claim, arguing that the impact of the colonial college "was neither complete nor infallible, nor even indispensable. It was however, significant" (p. 37); yet it is evident that these early colleges indeed helped to nurture US "nation-builders."

For those who find in the US founding fathers inspirational and heroic protagonists of history and who believe the United States to be a benevolent domestic and global superpower, the foregoing history suggests that from its very beginning, US higher education was worthy of celebration. In contrast, decolonial perspectives understand the founding fathers as colonizers and enslavers who fought the Revolutionary War largely in order to resist British taxation, preserve the system of slavery that Britain was moving toward abolishing, and secure access to Indigenous lands beyond the Appalachian Mountains where Britain had forbidden settlement. This perspective views the United States as a nation-state premised on Black and Indigenous dispossession, imperial expansion, and gendered, racialized regimes of property. Rather than celebrate early US higher education, therefore, this perspective asks, as John Willinsky (1998) puts it, "What is the legacy of this possessive education, this right of ownership and property?" (p. 73).

The Colonial Epistemology of US Higher Education Histories

Numerous accounts trace the transit of tradition from European colleges to US higher education. But the story of how the Indigenous knowledges that emerged in and from the places where these institutions now sit came to be replaced with Western knowledge tends to remain unheard and unthought by most non-Indigenous people, even though it has not in fact gone untold (Simpson, 2014; Smith, 2012; Stanley, 2009; Stonechild, 2006; Wilder, 2013). It was through the settler colonial drive to "eliminate" Indigenous peoples and "replace" them with settlers that Indigenous communities, as well as Indigenous and other non-Western knowledges, were largely displaced, crowded out, and often violently suppressed in order to claim space for European people and thought (Arvin, Tuck, & Morrill, 2013; Battiste, 2017; Grosfoguel, 2013).

The white supremacist, colonial hierarchy of humanity produced what Santos (2007) describes as an "abyssal line," which rests on epistemological as well as ontological violence. The abyssal line serves as a divider between Western knowledge, understood as universal human truth, and all other ways of knowing and being, which are relegated to the other side of the divide, in the "abyss." These other knowledge systems are denied relevance and even existence—they are made to seem invisible and actually become illegible from within the frames of Western knowledge (Ahenakew, 2016). In abyssal thinking, non-Western knowledge systems are actively made to be *absent*, and those who hold them are deemed incapable of "universal knowledge" and thus denied recognition within the bounds of humanity.

The production and transmission of knowledge in early US higher education institutions helped to rationalize these racial hierarchies of knowing and being in society, and these institutions of higher education in turn materially depended on practices of colonization and slavery (Wilder, 2013). In this context, nonwhite communities were "placed in the role of providing information and culture, but not knowledge" (Mignolo, 2003, p. 109). Despite dismissing the value of knowledges held by nonwhite people, white settlers in fact extracted, appropriated, and commodified numerous technologies, techniques, and theories from both enslaved Black peoples and Indigenous peoples. White people took credit for these knowledges, often claiming them as their own novel discoveries, presuming that Black and Indigenous insights and practices needed to be translated through Western frames and modes of systematization in order to be considered valid and valuable. As Linda Tuhiwai Smith (2012) notes, colonialism entailed Western claims of authority and ownership not just over Indigenous lands and waters but also "over all aspects of Indigenous knowledges, languages, and cultures" (p. 126). Thus, European colonizers dismissed and demonized the knowledges of the Indigenous peoples they displaced, and of the Black peoples they enslaved, while simultaneously depending on those knowledges. This is a pattern that continues today whenever white researchers claim to have "discovered" insights, theories, and technologies that have been held by Black, Indigenous, and other racialized peoples for centuries. Furthermore, in many cases those "discoveries" are mobilized primarily for the benefit of white settler communities.

The White Male Protagonist of Early
Higher Education History

As the previous chapter notes, many mainstream texts implicitly narrate US higher education history from the perspective of a white, male, middle- or upper-class, Christian subject. Here, I offer a close reading of accounts of this era in three texts: Cohen and Kisker's *The Shaping of American Higher Education: Emergence and Growth of the Contemporary System* (2010), Thelin's *A History of American Higher Education* (2004), and Lucas's *American Higher Education: A History* (2006). I also refer to several others, including Geiger's *The History of American Higher Education* (2014). These texts implicitly presume a reader who identifies with this particular subject, or at least tolerates him being the center of the historical narrative.

For instance, Cohen and Kisker (2010) note that schools such as William and Mary, Harvard, and Dartmouth "had a mission of Christianizing and civilizing the indigenous [*sic*]. . . . But their efforts were largely unsuccessful" (p. 22). While, from the perspective of the white Christian male benefactors of these institutions, this "mission" might be deemed "unsuccessful," from the perspective of Indigenous peoples, it might be understood as a victory and an example of anticolonial resistance. As Bobby Wright (1991) notes, these missions "failed" in large part because Indigenous peoples resisted them, even many who initially agreed to attend the schools.

Yet Wright also leaves space for the complex personhood of Indigenous peoples (Gordon, 2008; Tuck, 2009), cautious not to romanticize, homogenize, or oversimplify their stories. He notes, "American Indians in the colonies—both individually and collectively—exhibited a full range of responses to missions and education" (Wright, 1991, p. 435), including "genuine conversation, accommodation, intense theological debate and criticism, and finally violent opposition" (p. 435).* A rare example of critical Indigenous responses to colonial higher education in the mainstream higher education history literature is found in Thelin's (2004) reference to an instance in which a group of Indigenous leaders "who initially agreed to send their sons to the colleges ... refused the colleges' offers to renew the scholarship program and politely suggested that college officials might want to send young Englishmen to the tribes for a truly beneficial education in leadership" (p. 30).

In general, however, in mainstream narratives of higher education history, the specific experience of the white male student collapses into a universal student-subject of history, and nonwhite people are either entirely invisible or framed as objects of that history. When white men become the center of historical narratives, they tend to be framed as protagonists, and consideration of other communities becomes at best an account of their exclusion from a presumably unmarked universal position. For instance, Cohen and Kisker (2010) write that in the colonial era "the frontier, new opportunities, a different environment always beckoned ... the frontier was ever expanding and a young man could work his way into a homestead of his own.... The geographic openness of the land was also reflected in the way that people could reinvent themselves" (p. 17). Here, the young man—implicitly white—is centered as the protagonist of the early colonies and, thus, early higher education. Certainly, it would be a very different story if a young Black or Indigenous person of any gender were centered.

---

* The term "Indian," or "American Indian," is considered to be an outdated and offensive term by many Indigenous peoples today, especially when it is used by non-Indigenous people. (Bobby Wright was Indigenous.) Throughout the text, I use these terms only when directly quoting an author.

Meanwhile, the racial, colonial, and ecological violence that enabled the opportunities for white men—including opportunities to access higher education—is generally elided. If addressed at all, that violence is framed as a footnote, an unfortunate result of ignorance and a lack of empathy, and thus as a side-effect of the inevitable march of progress and development. This is made especially evident in the framing of land in higher education history texts, which I examine more closely in the following section.

Denaturalizing the "Need for Land"

Cohen and Kisker (2010) write, "The more Europeans, the greater the need for land, hence the onerous displacement of the native peoples as the immigrants conquered the wilderness" (p. 15). Here, European peoples' colonization and settlement of Indigenous lands are named explicitly as conquest and yet are nonetheless naturalized as by-products of an uninterrogated imperative: "the need for land." The intention behind the use of the word "onerous" here is ambiguous, but both possible uses of the term are troubling. If it is meant to describe Indigenous peoples' violent dispossession and displacement as "onerous" for Indigenous peoples themselves, this is quite a euphemism for the experience of colonization and genocide. If it is meant to describe the labor of dispossessing and displacing Indigenous people as "onerous" for white settlers, it implicitly aligns and empathizes with their perspective. The lands that Indigenous peoples inhabited and stewarded for thousands of years are also framed here as "the wilderness," repeating the colonial fiction of terra nullius, in which "lands that ... were occupied and possessed by non-Europeans but not being used in a fashion that European legal systems approved were considered to be waste or vacant" (Miller, 2005, p. 15) and therefore available for European settlement.

European settlement was violent not only for Indigenous peoples but for other-than-human beings as well. Settlers did not merely make their homes atop expropriated, supposedly empty Indigenous lands; they also actively and destructively transformed those living lands and waters into property for their own purposes and profit. In the process, they disrupted and destroyed living ecosystems and attempted to break long-standing reciprocal relationships between those ecosystems and their Indigenous caretakers. Whyte (2018) writes that, in settler colonial contexts, "permanent settlement involves ter-raforming the landscape to reflect settler economies, cultures, and visions for the future so that there are few if any physical or ecological traces of Indigenous economies, cultures, and visions" (p. 285).

Davis and Todd (2017) similarly argue that slavery and co-lonialism were "always about changing the land, transforming the earth itself" (p. 770). They therefore suggest that the most appropriate starting point of our current geological era, the An-thropocene, is 1610—just before one of the first US universi-ties, Harvard, was founded in 1636. "To use a date that coincides with colonialism in the Americas," they argue, "allows us to un-derstand the current state of ecological crisis as inherently in-vested in a specific ideology defined by proto-capitalist logics based on extraction and accumulation through dispossession—logics that continue to shape the world we live in and that have produced our current era" (p. 764). Davis and Todd draw on the work of Simon L. Lewis and Mark A. Maslin (2015), who, they note, suggest 1610 as a possible starting point of the Anthro-pocene for two primary reasons:

> The first is that the amount of plants and animals that were ex-changed between Europe and the Americas during this time dras-tically re-shaped the ecosystems of both of these landmasses....

The second reason, which is a much more chilling indictment against the horrifying realities of colonialism, is the drop in carbon dioxide levels that can be found in the geologic layer that correspond to the genocide of the peoples of the Americas and the subsequent re-growth of forests and other plants. Lewis and Maslin note that in 1492 there were between 54 to 61 million peoples in the Americas and by 1650 there were 6 million. (Davis & Todd, 2017, p. 766)

Institutions of higher education were actively involved in the onset of this ecological transformation, the impacts of which we are facing today in the form of climate change and biodiversity loss.

In most narratives about the early history of US higher education, land is framed almost exclusively and uncritically as an object of accumulation and ownership that was key to the social, political, and economic structure of the emerging US nation-state. For instance, Cohen and Kisker (2010) describe the continent's "limitless land" (p. 17). While they rightly note that the promise of limitless land "influenced the way the colonies and eventually the nation developed," they do not consider the ecological violence of treating land as property and a resource, nor do they connect the dots to consider that this land was not simply available for the taking but was violently acquired through the dispossession of Indigenous peoples. In turn, this Indigenous land was often transformed into properties considered "useful" and "productive" by settlers through the forced labor of enslaved Black people. Making these connections might have led the authors to confront the ways that colonization and enslavement are at the very core of the US nation-state, as well as its higher education system.

In the same section, Cohen and Kisker (2010) write, "The colonists began importing slaves from Africa because they could not entice or coerce the natives to work in farms or industries" (p. 15). Here, enslavement is characterized as an inevitable outcome of white colonists' political and economic needs; the structures and systems of slavery that white politicians, plantation owners, traders, and merchants violently constructed and maintained are obscured. Furthermore, this outcome is framed as a result of the fact that Indigenous peoples could not be "enticed or coerced to work in farms of industries," which in turn suggests that Africans, by contrast, were more susceptible or open to being "enticed or coerced." Both groups are framed here as merely reacting to European intervention, while their own histories, educational traditions, and experiences are entirely outside the scope of interest.

Cohen and Kisker's discussion of Indigenous peoples drops off entirely in their review of the post–Revolutionary War antebellum era, in which, they claim, "only the African Americans remained apart as a completely separate group, sharing in neither the bounty nor optimism of the expanding nation" (p. 59). Despite referencing just a page earlier the notion of "manifest destiny" and the infamous imperial dictum "Go West, young man, and grow up with the country," they ignore the violent displacement, dispossession, and in many cases death of Indigenous peoples that enabled movement westward, thereby naturalizing US expansionism in this era. This naturalization is further cemented in their description of the young US government as "land rich" (p. 60), which they note in order to point to the fact that much of the nation's "building" was funded through the sale of this land. In turn, this enables Cohen and Kisker to frame the US government as the biggest benefactor of US nation-building. While this interpretation is useful for their intention to contest the claim of "contemporary capitalists that 'free enterprise built the nation'" (p. 60), it erases two underlying involuntary "benefactors": Indigenous peoples, whose stolen lands became "public lands" with a colonial sleight of hand, and enslaved Black peoples, whose stolen lives and labor fueled the creation of further wealth.

Cohen and Kisker (2010) draw attention to colonists' "compartmentalized notions of freedom—one for themselves, and another for their slaves and servants" (p. 19)—but do not offer a substantive consideration of its relationship to the formation of early US higher education. Lucas (2006) similarly notes that early-nineteenth-century "demands for the expansion and reform of higher education did not speak to aspirations of women, blacks, indigenous peoples, or other ethnic minorities" (p. 123), but quickly pivots back to a discussion of social hierarchy absent specific considerations of race, coloniality, and gender.

Finally, Thelin (2004) suggests that a "forthright statement of one Virginian sums up the worldview of the young men who typically went to the colonial colleges: 'I am an aristocrat. I love liberty; I hate equality'" (p. 26). While such a statement is indeed telling, Thelin does not engage explicitly with its racial and colonial implications, instead contrasting it with today's presumptively more inclusive vision of democracy. Yet, as Lisa Lowe (2015) notes, "the uses of universalizing concepts of reason, civilization, and freedom effect colonial divisions of humanity, affirming liberty for modern man while subordinating the variously colonized and dispossessed peoples whose material labor and resources were the conditions of possibility for that liberty" (p. 7). In other words, not only did these men seek to exclude others from access to liberty, but their subjugation of nonwhite communities is precisely what enabled liberty for them. Designating Indigenous, Black, and other racialized peoples as "unfit for liberty" or "incapable of civilization" (Lowe, 2015, p. 7) became justification for exploitation and expropriation. The colonial concept of liberty did not contradict colonial investments in inequality.

This is a distinct reading from that offered by Thelin (2004), who writes that those like the quoted man did not support "democracy in the modern sense of the world," which is "difficult for us today to accept" (p. 26). Those who continue to be framed as the "others" and interlopers of US society, and whose subjugation subsidizes the perpetuation of this society, might not see themselves in Thelin's "us." Further, they might find the Virginian man's perspective quite familiar and contemporary. Some might suggest that this statement from the past is not so different from certain sentiments expressed today on many US campuses—particularly in a context of white backlash against racial justice and decolonization efforts. In sum, even accounts that are somewhat critical of the elitism of higher education tend to erase the colonial conditions and implications of this elitism, emphasizing class hierarchies within whiteness at the expense of offering more multidimensional, intersectional, and decolonial analyses. These critiques also reproduce an implicit narrative in which elitism was eventually overcome or at least mitigated through the expanded inclusion of nonwhite communities into existing institutions, which are presumed to be otherwise benevolent and universal.

Having deconstructed some of the discourses that circulate within mainstream historical narratives about early US higher education, in the following sections I take a more direct look at examples of institutional complicity in colonization and slavery during this era.

Institutional Complicity in Colonization

According to Wilder (2013), "The fate of the American college had been intertwined from its beginning with the social project of dispossessing Indian people" (p. 150). From a deco-lonial perspective, this is not merely a shameful history that we have since moved away from. Instead, as Kaiwipunikauikawēkiu Lipe (2018) notes, "every university in the United States of America and Hawai'i is situated on Indigenous land" (p. 164). In turn, this means that every institution of US higher education is implicated in the dispossession of Indigenous peoples. The exact circumstances of how individual institutions obtained the legal title to those lands varies, but these histories can be dis-cerned and documented. The fact that most institutions do not do so points to their ongoing investments in *not knowing* their own colonial legacies (Vimalassery, Pegues, & Goldstein, 2017). If universities were to trace these legacies and take seri-ously the responsibilities for redress and reparations that follow from them, this would throw into question the literal and meta-phorical grounds on which the institutions stand. This fact may help explain why good-faith institutional engagements with complicity in colonization are so rare.

Universities' complicity is a matter not only of their direct role in the dispossession of land and lives but also of their in-direct role in reproducing the mundane political, economic, and epistemological infrastructures that naturalize ongoing settler colonial dispossession. As Wilder (2013) notes, "Col-leges were imperial instruments akin to armories and forts, a part of the colonial garrison with the specific responsibilities to train ministers and missionaries, convert indigenous peoples and soften cultural resistance, and extend European rule over foreign nations" (p. 33). Cohen and Kisker (2010) suggest that colonists "needed institutions to assist in acculturating the young, and the notion of civilizing the Indians was not far from the surface" (p. 24). To take the example of Harvard, many of the school's ministers sought to evangelize Indigenous communities, and the school's charter actually includes this as one of its missions—although only one Indigenous student graduated from the school during the colonial era. Many of Harvard's benefactors and leaders participated in the colonial war against the Pequot people, and the school eventually acquired much of the land that was expropriated from them following the British victory (Wilder, 2013).

The founding of the College of William and Mary in 1693 was first initiated in the early seventeenth century through a grant of land that had been expropriated from Indigenous peoples by the British crown. The institution's establishment was delayed by decades due to various events, including an uprising by the Powhatan tribes. Powhatan resistance was ultimately suppressed, and the school was built in a different location (Geiger, 2014), but the college's founding was nonetheless framed as a necessary response "to the lingering problems of defending the colony's expansive borders with Indian nations, regulating a large population of enslaved people, and governing a free population with a history of resisting political and religious authority" (Wilder, 2013, p. 42). William and Mary's inception was therefore justified in part as a means to maintain the power of colonial authority over Indigenous peoples and lands, enslaved Black people, and nonelite white people. Although the school's initial charter did not address the education of Indigenous peoples, later versions did, reflecting the perception that doing so would garner financial support (Carney, 1999). The final charter notes the school was created in part so "that the Christian faith may be propagated amongst the Western Indians" (as cited by Wright, 1991, p. 432). Among other things, the college received a grant to construct a building for Indigenous higher education students, though only a handful of Indigenous students actually attended the school in its early years (Carney, 1999).

As the case of William and Mary shows, while northeastern Ivy League schools are often centered in early histories of US higher education, a handful of southern institutions also emerged in this era, though some did not secure degree-granting powers until after the Revolutionary War. Further, many more institutions emerged around the time of the Revolutionary War or shortly thereafter. Although founded at or toward the end of the British colonial era and thus dubiously included in this chapter, I highlight them here in order to gesture toward the ways higher education was understood as part of emergent nation-building efforts for the young US nation-state. These institutions helped to secure the United States' settler colonial claims to recently expropriated Indigenous lands and to train young people (specifically, white men) to be good citizens and public servants. Thus, as Grande (2018) writes, colleges and universities operated as "arms of the settler state" (p. 47). I unravel this thread about the role of higher education in US nation-state-building to an extent in this chapter, and develop it further in subsequent chapters.

The founding charter of the University of Georgia (1785) declares the school's primary purpose to be the development of the citizenry: "It is the distinguishing happiness of free governments that civil Order should be the Result of choice and not necessity, and the common wishes of the People become the Laws of the Land, their public prosperity and even existence very much depends upon suitably forming the minds and morals of their Citizens." This formation of "minds and morals" can be achieved, the charter continues, "only by religion and education." As a result, the university's founding is said to be a response to "the strongest obligation to form the youth, the rising hope of our Land to render the like glorious & essential Services to our country."

If we understand early higher education institutions as nation-building institutions, decolonial critiques suggest the need to understand them also as efforts to sediment and legitimate the settler nation-state's colonial claims to possess Indigenous land in perpetuity. By using universities as a means of importing and imposing Western social relations and imaginaries of development onto Indigenous lands, colonial powers sought to erase the histories and political claims of Indigenous peoples who had occupied and cared for those lands for thousands of years. Such efforts generated an overall impression that the issue of colonization had been settled, but also that lands were "improved" by the presence of "Western civilization." Again, the charter of the University of Georgia notes that, without the "cultivation" provided by (higher) education and religion, "a free government will be attended with greater Confusions and with Evils more horrid than the wild, uncultivated State of Nature."

The "state of nature" evoked here is a colonial concept developed within classical liberal philosophy to describe the US continent before colonization: "the wild woods and uncultivated waste . . . left to nature, without any improvement, tillage, or husbandry" (John Locke as cited by Silva, 2007, p. 204). This description, which implies that the Indigenous peoples who inhabited the continent failed to adequately "develop" land and institute a "proper" political and economic system, has served as an enduring alibi to justify the colonial expropriation and occupation of that land by settlers (Lowe, 2015; Silva, 2007). In this context, the University of Georgia charter suggests that higher education was understood as a safeguard against the possible chaos and waste that were associated with non-European peoples.

Clearly, the central role of colonization in the founding of US universities did not cease with the Revolutionary War. The young nation-state removed Indigenous peoples from their lands, using the rationale that its "economic configuration ... increasingly required more and more [Indigenous] lands, natural resources, and exploitable labor" (Silva, 2007, p. 205).

Universities were often understood as part of the vanguard of colonial settlement. The University of Georgia was to be funded in part through the sale of land claimed by the state of Georgia after it declared its defeat of the Muscogee (Creek) peoples. But efforts to build the new school were interrupted by Muscogee efforts to take back their land, as the university's first president, Abraham Baldwin, reported in his diary in 1786:

> I went out to the intended seat of Government Louisville by name at your service, contracted for a tract of 300 acres adjoining the town chose the spot for the University, and such a delightful situation for a garden of 50 to 100 acres I never saw, there I have been and there I expected to have passed the summer, but I have been obliged to retreat. I had been there planning and pleasing myself with the prospect of what a few months and a few years would accomplish there till I had begun to consider it my home, where I should soon be located, when our first news was, that the Creek nation were preparing for war and that we might soon expect them down. (pp. 2–3)

Five decades later, the Muscogee people would be forcibly removed from their territories in the Southeast and relocated to what is now Oklahoma as part of the Trail of Tears. In 2004, the Muscogee Nation founded its own college in Okmulgee, Oklahoma, where the nation is headquartered.

The examples offered thus far illustrate how early US colleges were complicit in and dependent on colonization. Beyond the fact that no settler institutions of higher education would exist were it not for the original and ongoing occupation of Indigenous lands, specific histories also point to colonization as a direct material condition of possibility for colleges in the colonial era. I review some of these below.

Mobilizing Missionary Monies for White Education: The Case of Dartmouth

The coloniality of US higher education is not primarily defined by the exclusion of certain communities from otherwise universal institutions, but rather by the fact that those institutions exist at the expense of those communities (Rodríguez, 2012). The importance of going beyond the frame of exclusion is made evident in the case of institutions that positioned themselves as sites of Indigenous religious conversion. Not only did their promised inclusion of Indigenous peoples rest on the presumption of white Christian supremacy, but many of the funds raised in the name of Indigenous education ultimately went toward the education of white settler students (Wright 1988, 1991). Although many colonists were earnestly committed to Indigenous conversion, which could be understood as "inclusion by assimilation," the European presence in the colonies was more about seizing lands and securing profits than religious conviction.

Yet institutional leaders took advantage of others' missionary moral imperative to raise funds for "Indian education" at Harvard, William and Mary, and Dartmouth. As Michael Carney (1999) argues, "Virtually every instance of professed devotion to Indian higher education by the colleges during the colonial period was actually an exercise in fund raising or in access to funds requiring an Indian mission" (p. 3). To illustrate this dynamic, I focus on the case of Dartmouth.

Dartmouth's founder, Eleazar Wheelock, "amassed hundreds of acres of land through his educational ventures, he owned slaves, and his prescription for the education and salvation of Native Americans was predicated on the unquestioned superiority of his own culture and the eradication of theirs" (Calloway, 2010, p. 1). Through education, he sought to convert, civilize, and thus "save" Indigenous peoples. Specifically, he sought to remove Indigenous peoples from their communities to be educated in Puritan, English-style education. He encouraged Indigenous people to become missionaries and teachers in their own communities.

Before founding Dartmouth, Wheelock established Moor's Indian Charity School, whose stated purpose was "Educating Such of the Indian Natives, of any or all the Indian tribes in North America, or other poor Persons, in Reading, Writing, and all Liberal Arts, and Sciences . . . & More Especially for instructing them in the Knowledge & Practice of the Protestant Christian Religion." At Moor's, Wheelock "demanded unquestioning obedience, subordination, and even expressions of self-loathing" from the Indigenous students (Calloway, 2010, pp. 10–11). The school enrolled Indigenous as well as white people whom Wheelock deemed to be promising potential missionaries. He admitted not only Indigenous boys but also girls, whom he sought to prepare as domestic workers and supporters of missionary work. To finance his school, Wheelock sought funding from missionary societies in England and Scotland.

The origins of Dartmouth came when Wheelock, deciding to extend his work at Moor's, wrote "A Proposal for Introducing Religion Learning, Agriculture, and Manufacture Among the Pagans of America." After British authorities in the colony refused Wheelock's request for land on which to build this school, he turned to Europe in search of funding. He found that whereas white people in the colonies largely rebuffed his requests because Indigenous peoples were perceived as an immediate threat, Europeans perceived Indigenous peoples as "exotic" and distant, making it easier to raise funds from among them (Carney, 1999, p. 32). Wheelock's fund raising in England and Scotland for the new college was undertaken by a white colonial reverend, Nathaniel Whitaker, and Samson Occom, a Mohegan minister who had studied with Wheelock as a young man (Carney, 1999).

Occom was a scholar, preacher, and tribal leader who encountered resistance to his work from both white and Indigenous communities throughout his life; he often worked to mediate conflict between the two communities (Calloway, 2010; Carney, 1999). Occom was chosen to undertake a fund-raising trip in Europe because Wheelock perceived him as "a model of what [his] school could accomplish—given the right level of funding" (Calloway, 2010, p. 16). During his European travels, Occom helped to collect an endowment for Dartmouth of 12,000 pounds (Wright, 1991). Despite this fund-raising success, Occom himself achieved little financial security in his own life.

In 1769, the governor of New Hampshire signed the Dartmouth charter, claiming that the college would "civilize the Indians & spread Christianity among them [more] than any other public or private Measures hitherto granted for Indian Instruction" and in turn help prevent further Indigenous resistance (Calloway, 2010, p. 21). The school's charter declared that:

> We, considering the premises and being willing to encourage the laudable and charitable design of spreading Christian knowledge among the savages of our American wilderness, and also that the best means of education be established in our province of New Hampshire, for the benefit of said province, do, of our special grace, certain knowledge and mere motion, by and with the advice of our counsel for said province, by these presents, will, ordain, grant and constitute that there be a college erected in our said province of New Hampshire by the name of Dartmouth College, for the education and instruction of youth of the Indian

tribes in this land in reading, writing, and all parts of learning which shall appear necessary and expedient for civilizing and christianizing children of pagans, as well as in all liberal arts and sciences, and also of English youth and any others. (as quoted in Calloway, 2010, p. 22)

The choice to emphasize the education of Indigenous youth (characterized in the charter as "savages" and "pagans") and consider the education of English youth as an afterthought was a reversal of Wheelock's original draft phrasing, done to align with the characterization of fund-raising efforts as soliciting support for Indigenous education. Nonetheless, the original phrasing reflected the new institution's already-shifting focus (Wilder, 2013). Ultimately, Wheelock kept Moor's primarily as a school for Indigenous youth, and Dartmouth primarily as a school for white youth, while drawing heavily on monies raised in the name of Indigenous education to fund Dartmouth (Calloway, 2010). This created a rift between Wheelock and Occom as Occom became frustrated by the lack of Indigenous students at Dartmouth; he wrote that Wheelock had used him to fund-raise for white students (Carney, 1999).

Dartmouth offers just one of many examples of how early institutions both depended on colonization to secure the lands on which they built their campuses and instrumentalized Indigenous peoples to raise funds for white education. Indigenous peoples were leveraged for colleges' financial viability. Wright (1988) concludes that colonists sought to "further their own political, economic and educational agendas, which included Indian education as an ancillary aim at best, while all the time professing their own piety as if this were their singular motivation" (p. 78).

Yet, even if fund raisers' motivations had been purely religious or missionary, those would not have made them more benevolent nor less colonial. In one of the few references to Indigenous peoples in his account of early US higher educa- tion, Geiger (2014) writes, "Wheelock's intentions would today be labeled cultural imperialism, predicated on a typically dep- recating view of Native American peoples and cultures; but few contemporaries possessed as genuine a concern for their wel- fare" (p. 69). Yet one need not erase Wheelock's intentions— which some might label as good or at least better than some others in his time—in order to critique their underlying colo- nial assumptions and implications. To minimize or dismiss cri- tiques of Wheelock as rooted in presentism also dismisses the diverse and often resistant responses of Indigenous peoples to colonial overtures delivered via education in Wheelock's time (Wright, 1988). To critique the underlying colonial rationales and behaviors of white college and university founders, one also need not erase the fact that while many Indigenous people resisted white Western (higher) education, others (like Oc- com) ambivalently sought access to it (Carney, 1999).

These colonial histories challenge the notion that US higher education is intrinsically benevolent. They also compel us to consider how the most significant colonial violence of early US higher education was *not* that most Indigenous peoples were excluded from access. The liberal inclusion-exclusion para- digm fails to recognize that the underlying goal of settler colo- nialism is "the obliteration rather than the incorporation of Indigenous peoples" (Trask, as cited by Arvin, 2019, p. 336). In- clusion cannot be viewed as an unmitigated good if the price of that inclusion is assimilation of Indigenous peoples into Western Christian knowledge systems and societies and the continued colonial occupation of their lands. Further, the inclusion-exclusion frame reduces a heterogenous range of modes and expressions of Indigenous responses to coloniza- tion into a single struggle for inclusion in settler institutions.

Particularly in early US higher education history, most Indigenous peoples were not seeking "inclusion" in settler colleges.
This is evident if we consider the difficulty of recruiting and
retaining Indigenous youth in early institutions such as Dartmouth (Calloway, 2010; Wright, 1991).

The Coloniality of Contemporary
Organizational Sagas

Before moving on, it is worth briefly examining the sanctioned narratives or organizational sagas that are told about
colonial institutions like Dartmouth today. The Dartmouth undergraduate admissions website includes a "History and Traditions" section in which it is noted that "Dartmouth's founder,
Eleazar Wheelock, a Congregational minister from Connecti-
cut, established the College 'for the education and instruction
of youth of the Indian tribes in this land, . . . English Youth,
and any others.' Samson Occom, a Mohegan Indian and one
of Wheelock's first students, was instrumental in raising the
funds necessary to found the College" (Dartmouth University, n.d.). This account portrays Wheelock as a benevolent
founding figure, and its uncritical use of the term "Indian" is out
of sync with contemporary terminology about Indigenous
peoples.

The "History and Traditions" page of the Dartmouth admissions website does acknowledge that, "during its first
200 years, Dartmouth did little to actualize its founding commitment to Native students." The establishment of the college's Native American studies program in 1972 is portrayed as
a moment in which Dartmouth "reaffirmed its founding mission," and the annual Dartmouth Powwow is framed as "honoring Dartmouth's long-standing mission of educating Native
students." Thus, a small effort to honestly acknowledge Dartmouth's history is situated as part of a redemptive narrative

arc, one that glosses over the early college's assimilative mission and elides the fact that Dartmouth's contemporary Native American and Indigenous studies program and support for Indigenous students were made possible largely because of the activism of Indigenous students in the 1970s.

For most of Dartmouth's history there were few Indigenous students, and "the college's main commitment to things native was through an increasing institutional use of racial symbols" (Daniell as cited by Calloway, 2010, p. 131). In particular, "stereotypical Indians, wild and free, served as oppositional figures against which Dartmouth men could imagine their own civilized and educated selves" (Calloway, 2010, p. 132). These racist caricatures manifested in various institutional traditions, including poems, songs, imagery, and especially sports-related traditions. When more Indigenous students started to enroll at Dartmouth in the 1970s, they were often victimized by white students. In 1971, Indigenous students issued a statement critiquing Indigenous caricatures and recommending strategies for recruiting and supporting Indigenous students, including successfully advocating for the founding of what is now the Department of Native American and Indigenous Studies.

While there is growing interest among higher education institutions like Dartmouth to address the shadow sides of their histories, thus far, most of these efforts have been centered on histories of institutional complicity in slavery. I consider these next.

Institutional Complicity in Slavery

My engagement with institutional complicity in slavery is somewhat abridged compared to the discussion of complicity in settler colonialism, in part because other scholars have already examined the former and have done so more thoroughly, though certainly not exhaustively, than they have the latter. In his introduction to a special forum focused on slavery and universities in the journal *Slavery and Abolition*, Alfred Brophy (2018) offers a useful review of existing strains of research on this topic. He notes that most studies emphasize one of three dimensions: the intellectual dimension of universities' role in slavery; universities' financial connections to slavery; and the experiences of enslaved people who lived and labored on campuses or elsewhere in the service of higher education institutions.

Texts on the subject of slavery and the university include *Ebony and Ivy: Race, Slavery, and the Troubled History of America's Universities* (Wilder, 2013); *Scarlet and Black: Slavery and Dispossession in Rutgers History* (Fuentes & White, 2016); *Slavery and the University: Histories and Legacies* (Harris, Campbell, & Brophy, 2019); *University, Court, and Slave: Pro-slavery Thought in Southern Colleges and Courts and the Coming of Civil War* (Brophy, 2016); and numerous scholarly articles. Accounts of slavery at particular institutions can be found in the reports that universities have thus far produced out of a publicly stated commitment to examine their own histories of slavery, or that those who are otherwise connected to the institutions (such as students, faculty, local community members) have written in the absence of official institutional efforts. Some of these reports are referenced here.

It is no simple task to trace the myriad entanglements of higher education institutions with slavery. As the report about Yale University authored by three Yale doctoral students notes, "There was no escaping the influence of slavery in colonial times. Not only did most prominent leaders have slaves, but most financial transactions depended at some point on slavery. Three of the financial endowments that allowed Yale to thrive in its early days depended upon slavery: Yale's first endowed professorship, Yale's first scholarship fund, and

Yale's first endowed library fund" (Dugdale, Fueser, & de Castro Alves, 2001, p. 3).

These often-opaque entanglements are also addressed in *Slavery and Justice: Report of the Brown University Steering Committee on Slavery and Justice* (2006): "Determining what percentage of the money that founded Brown is traceable to slavery is impossible ... slavery was not a distinct enterprise but rather an institution that permeated every aspect of social and economic life in Rhode Island, the Americas, and indeed the Atlantic World. But there is no question that many of the assets that underwrote the University's creation and growth derived, directly and indirectly, from slavery and the slave trade. Links with slavery are particularly apparent in the University's first endowment campaign ... launched in the late 1760s" (p. 13).

Many other higher education institutions were implicated in slavery—likely all those founded before the Civil War. As Clarke and Fine (2010) note, "We can assume that most institutions of higher education founded prior to emancipation will have some connections to answer to, whether they have currently begun the process of exploration or not" (p. 84). These "connections" include, among others, institutional ownership of enslaved people; forcing enslaved people to build and serve institutions; students, faculty, administrators, and trustees who were (or whose family members were) enslavers and slave traders; soliciting and accepting donations from those who were involved in the slave economy, such as merchants, insurers, shippers, investors, and plantation owners; and producing and spreading knowledge that rationalized racism and white supremacy, thereby "providing intellectual cover for the social and political subjugation of non-white peoples" (Wilder, 2013, p. 3).

Colleges thus not only forced enslaved people to labor on their campuses; they also served as sites for the reproduction of wealthy and elite social networks embedded in the slave trade and plantation economy. In this context, the "politics of the campus conformed to the presence and demands of slave-holding students as colleges aggressively cultivated a social environment attractive to the sons of wealthy families" (Wilder, 2013, p. 77). Historical complicity with slavery can also be tied to the contemporary wealth of these institutions. For instance, in 2021, Brown's endowment was $6.9 billion. In the Brown University report, one of the recommendations is to "maintain high ethical standards in regard to investments and gifts." Yet this is an entirely forward-looking recommendation. If, as the report suggests, "Brown's early endowment benefited from contributions made by slaveowners and slave traders" (p. 85), what are the implications for the existing endowment monies? A glance at other universities' endowments invites questions about the origins of these vast sums of money, as well as institutions' contemporary responsibilities in relation to these funds.

Harvard is perhaps the most extreme example, with an endowment nearly eight times that of Brown, reaching $53.2 billion in 2021. It can be argued that Harvard receives too much emphasis and attention for an institution that educates a very small portion of US university students and that looks exceedingly different from the public institutions where most US students are enrolled. Yet, if we think about its cultural and political influence, this excess of attention starts to make more sense. Eight US presidents have been Harvard graduates; the university regularly has the highest number of graduates in Congress; and it shares top billing with Yale as the alma mater of the most (currently appointed) Supreme Court justices.

For some people, Harvard's age and power are enough to explain its outsized influence and wealth. As a 1963 Harvard admissions brochure noted, "Wealth, like age, does not make a university great. But it helps" (as cited by Thelin, 2004, p. xiii). However, we still have to ask, Where did all this wealth come from? We can trace Harvard's wealth in large part to its origins. Wilder (2013) documents that "Harvard's history was inseparable from the history of slavery and the slave trade. . . . Harvard . . . was a pillar of the antebellum racial order. Not only were the students, the faculties, the officers, and the trustees white, but people of color came to campus only as servants and objects." (p. 3).

As Wilder (2013) shows, many of Harvard's benefactors and donors accumulated their wealth through the trade of enslaved peoples or through plantation ownership, or both. For instance, colonial merchant Nicholas Bolyston, who acquired his wealth largely through a family inheritance derived from the trade of enslaved peoples, funded one of Harvard's first endowed chairs. Owner and trader of enslaved peoples Isaac Royall donated lands that were later used to fund Harvard Medical College and Harvard Law School, and Dorothy Saltonstall and her husband gifted Harvard part of their fortune acquired through the trade of enslaved peoples in Barbados. Like many schools at the time, Harvard enrolled the sons of wealthy plantation owners from the US South and the West Indies; many Harvard graduates fought in genocidal wars against Indigenous peoples in what is now New England; Harvard alumni and officers often purchased enslaved people from other Harvard graduates; and "many Harvard men built their careers on the Caribbean and Africa trades" (Wilder, 2013, p. 89).

The enduring impact of Harvard's origins in enslavement, colonization, and other forms of expropriation is evident not only in the university's massive endowment but also in the specific investments constituting that endowment today. For instance, in the past decade, the university has acquired farmland, forests, and "natural resources" around the world, including in Latin America, Africa, Europe, and the United States, especially California. Critics suggest that many of these acquisitions—

some of which have been deemed land grabs—were undertaken without consideration of their social and ecological implications and accountabilities, and argue that Harvard is capitalizing on environmental uncertainty as well as lax human rights protections (Fairbairn et al., 2021; GRAIN & Rede Social de Justiça e Direitos Humanos, 2018; Civil Society Leaders, 2014). Several other US universities have made similar investments. Indeed, as the following section makes clear, while Harvard may be exceptional in its wealth and contemporary standing, it is not unique—certainly not in its early ties to slavery.

Pre–Civil War Complicity in Slavery

As with considerations of settler colonization, it is important to look beyond the first few New England colleges to consider how *all* schools built prior to the Civil War are implicated in slavery. This is especially true for schools with campuses in the southern United States. But it is also important to remember that although the forced labor of enslaved people in building or maintaining higher education institutions may have ceased in northern states as slavery was gradually abolished there during or in the decades following the Revolutionary War, northern states and the individuals and institutions within them nonetheless remained deeply entangled with the practice of slavery in the South and the West Indies through their domestic and international political and economic relations.

Here, I consider the case of University of Virginia (UVA), my undergraduate alma mater. Given the ways students and alumni jealously guard its institutional traditions (see Office of the Dean of Students, 2015), UVA offers a compelling example of the abiding strength of romantic organizational sagas in higher education. Proud narratives about UVA's idealistic provenance and idyllic early days are central to its institutional identity (Longstreth, 2014), as is the outsized figure of UVA founder, Thomas Jefferson. Apart from founding UVA, Jefferson was a US and Virginia statesman, US president, and owner of enslaved people. Jefferson remains a ubiquitous presence at the university. He is regularly evoked at such formal events as convocation and graduation, memorialized in statues and scholarships, and frequently recalled in the colloquial designation of the institution as "Mr. Jefferson's University." The university celebrates his ambitious vision and detailed plans to create an "Academical Village" in which to educate future "statesmen, legislators, and judges, on whom public prosperity and individual happiness are so much to depend" (Jefferson, 1818). Given that Jefferson understood education as a "civilizing" cure for what he called "barbarism and wretchedness," it is telling that he is often uncritically celebrated for his democratic visions of schooling (Carpenter, 2013).

According to the UVA President's Commission on Slavery and the University (2018), "Slavery, in every way imaginable, was central to the project of designing, funding, building, and maintaining the school" (p. 15). When construction of UVA began in 1817, there were more enslaved people in Virginia than in any other state (President's Commission on Slavery and the University, 2018). "The work done to supply and create the University's built landscape," the President's Commission found, "was overwhelmingly done by enslaved people, who terraced land, hauled dirt, dug foundations, shaped and fired bricks, and did tinwork, carpentry, roofing, and stone masonry" (p. 17). Many of these people were not owned by the university but "hired from local owners, who were paid a set amount per slave" (Wolfe, 2013). Some free Black laborers also participated in construction, along with white laborers. When the institution was completed and opened in 1825, enslaved people, including children, "became a permanent fixture at the university" (Oast, 2009, p. 220).

The President's Commission on Slavery and the University (2018) reports that "between 1825 and 1865 . . . the population of enslaved African Americans at UVA grew, averaging well over one hundred people annually. . . . In most years, it is reasonable to imagine a fluctuating population of between 125 and 200 enslaved people at the University" (p. 17). A handful of these people were directly owned by the university (Oast, 2009; President's Commission on Slavery and the University, 2018; Wolfe, 2020). University professors and administrators owned the majority of enslaved persons on campus, some of whom were purchased from Jefferson himself (Faulkner, 2013; Longstreth, 2014). While students were prohibited from bringing persons enslaved by their families to the university, those people enslaved by hotels and inns where the students lived did labor on the university's grounds (Wolfe, 2013). It was also slavery that produced the wealth that enabled most of the students to attend UVA, as the majority of them came from families in the planter class that enslaved people (President's Commission on Slavery and the University, 2018). Further, many of the university's alumni later "became important southern politicians and intellectual leaders; they were congressmen and governors, leading voices in the pro-slavery movement, Confederate cabinet officers, and soldiers in the Confederate Army" (President's Commission on Slavery and the University, 2018, p. 16).

According to the President's Commission on Slavery and the University (2018), "The countless daily interactions between enslaved people and whites who were not their owners meant the enslaved were constantly in jeopardy" (p. 18) and "had not one master but hundreds, all of whom were steeped in the pervasive pro-slavery thought that was promulgated at the school" (p. 20). Enslaved women especially were extremely vulnerable to abuse, particularly sexual abuse. Upon their deaths, both free and enslaved Black persons were also used in numerous medical dissections at the university, often stolen by way of grave robbing (Bruce, 1920b; President's Commission on Slavery and the University, 2018). This was done "in the pursuit of a 'science' of medicine that re-confirmed false ideas about white superiority" (President's Commission on Slavery and the University, 2018, p. 37).

Minutes from the UVA Board of Visitors meetings document the board's involvement in the management of enslaved persons on university grounds, and university faculty adjudicated disputes between students and enslaved persons (Oast, 2009). In 1829, the university instituted a slave patrol to capture those who escaped (Wolfe, 2013). At the end of the Civil War, the UVA faculty overwhelmingly agreed that freedpeople were not deserving of any assistance or support, and the Board of Visitors put forth no provisions for them (Wolfe, 2013).

Jefferson founded UVA in part to meet the need he perceived for a southern institution that could shield young men from "abolitionist teachings in the North" (President's Commission on Slavery and the University, 2018, p. 15). Particularly in the decades leading up to the Civil War, several universities became sites of intense debate over abolition. The Brown University report (Brown University Steering Committee on Slavery and Justice, 2006) notes that in the wake of "the gradual abolition of slavery in the northern states and the rapid expansion of the institution in the South," Brown "was shaped by all of these developments, and members of the campus community, including students, vigorously debated their meaning and significance" (p. 5). As the organizers of a recent conference focusing on abolitionist university studies note, "In some instances, universities served as multiracial hubs for genuinely abolitionist organizing and imagining" (Boggs et al., 2019, p. 11). This activity included, for instance, faculty and students organizing for abolition at Oberlin College, many of whom "supported formerly enslaved African-American people on their journeys to freedom, took leadership from formerly enslaved people and their children, developed abolitionist tactics and strategies, built abolitionist networks with the surrounding community, and trained students to become abolitionist organizers, lecturers, journalists, and founders of new antislavery societies, towns, and colleges" (p. 11). However, as Boggs and colleagues (2019) also note, criticisms of slavery like those articulated at Oberlin did not necessarily extend to critiques of settler colonialism and the perceived role of the university as a "civilizing" force. And as the Brown University report notes, "most colleges took a more conservative approach" to slavery (p. 29). For instance, Harvard sought to prevent even discussion of the topic among students and faculty.

Comprehensive considerations of institutional entanglements with slavery cannot be limited to the pre-Emancipation era. For instance, at UVA, the legacies of slavery on campus "would live on at the University far past the general emancipation in 1865. Freedpeople often continued to work at the school for very low wages in the immediate aftermath of the conflict. That remained unchanged with the rise of de jure Jim Crow segregation and the white supremacist state in the early twentieth century. Echoes of that racially structured inequality, born in slavery and sustained long afterward, remain with us today at the twenty-first-century University" (President's Commission on Slavery and the University, 2018, p. 15). Meanwhile, the Yale report divides the impacts of slavery on campus into two eras: the university's early years; and the 1930s and 1960s, during which time "Yale chose to name most of its colleges

after slave owners and pro-slavery leaders" (Dugdale, Fueser, &
de Castro Alves 2001, p. 1). In fact, many commemorations
of enslavers, advocates of slavery, and those who otherwise
benefited from slavery are relatively recent phenomena at several institutions besides Yale. On campuses in the US South,
several statues of Confederate heroes were erected in the early
twentieth century (Harris, Campbell, & Brophy, 2019). Efforts to remove them or rename buildings or schools named
after enslavers, colonizers, and Confederates are ongoing, but
addressing the enduring legacies of slavery on campuses will
require much more than a change of name.

Contemporary Implications of the Colonial and Antebellum Eras

In this chapter I offer a decolonial historiographic reading
of mainstream narratives of early US higher education. I seek
to make visible the colonial entanglements, interdependen-
cies, and extractive relationships initiated in this era so that
their contemporary implications can ultimately be better understood. After all, as Hartman (2008) asks, "To what end does
one conjure the ghosts of slavery, if not to incite the hopes of
transforming the present?" (p. 170). The study of history
matters for its own sake, yes, but it is also important to ask how
the stories we tell about the past shape how we conceptualize
its connection to the (neoliberal and neocolonial) present.

By inviting attention to continuities between the past and
present of US higher education, I do not suggest that nothing
has changed. Higher education has not only adapted to but
also helped usher in new social, political, and economic relations, including the new forms of industrial capitalism in the
mid-eighteenth century, mid-twentieth-century Keynesian
liberal capitalism, and neoliberal financial capitalism, which
first emerged in the 1970s. Nonetheless, the colonial modes of

governance, property, knowledge, subjectivity, and social relations that shaped early higher education are the foundations
upon which new modes of racialized accumulation are consistently created and institutionalized.

Capital that was initially accumulated through processes of
slavery and colonization continues to circulate within and accumulate more wealth for many higher education institutions.
Furthermore, as Paula Chakravartty and Denise Ferreira da
Silva (2012) point out, new modes of accumulation are driven
by the search for "'new territories' of consumption and investment [that] have been mapped onto previous racial and colonial (imperial) discourses and practice" (p. 368). As a result,
Indigenous, Black, and other racialized and marginalized communities (both "at home" and "abroad") are thus perpetually
targeted for—and perpetually resist—the most brutal, un-
bridled strategies of accumulation (Kish & Leroy, 2015). Racial hierarchies and logics established during the "inaugural
moments of conquest" (King, 2016) still order the US political economy and social institutions, including higher education; and the US state facilitates the continuous racialized accumulation of capital and secures the capital that has already
been accumulated. As King (2016) suggests, "Realizing that
the relations of conquest have far from abated encourages a
reframing and rethinking of some of the urgent questions and
interdisciplinary concerns that critical theories continue to
grapple with in the neoliberal university" (n.p.).

Yet mainstream historical narratives often lack deep consideration of the role of colonial relations and rationalities in shaping the foundations of US higher education, let alone shaping
contemporary campuses. To rethink the present and imagine
different futures, we need not only to address these absences
with alternative historical accounts but also to consider how
and why these absences have been maintained for so long, and

how and why whitestream narratives of higher education history—as well as the material structures naturalized in these narratives—have been kept so firmly in place. This, in turn, may help clarify some of the challenges involved in interrupting these narratives and denaturalizing the higher education promises that have been cultivated along with them.

To simply frame the absence of histories of colonization and slavery as a product of ignorance due to a lack of information is to depoliticize the active, ongoing, and systemic practice of disavowal that sustains and sanctions that absence in white settler memory. As Bruyneel (2013) notes, what we face is not "a lack of knowledge about the treatment of Indigenous peoples but a lack of acknowledgement that . . . the American liberal colonial tradition is created through a combination of settler colonial logic and the constitutive disavowal of said logic so as to reproduce the American exceptionalist mythos" (p. 315). This disavowal is foundational to the structure of US society itself, because acknowledging the central role of colonization and slavery in enabling that structure would challenge national narratives of freedom, sovereignty, independence, exceptionalism, and innocence. To acknowledge the foundational role of colonization and slavery also challenges the tropes of higher education exceptionalism manifest in many organizational sagas.

This chapter offers an initial glimpse at how the socially sanctioned disavowal of the constitutive role of violence in the creation of early US society extends to disavowal of that violence in US higher education. This disavowal is sustained even in many contemporary efforts to address these violent histories. While these efforts engage with disavowed histories *to a certain degree*, they rarely acknowledge slavery and colonization as a primary condition of possibility for US higher education's emergence and survival, and a deeply influential force in the shaping of its orienting logic, practices, and structures. As a result, these efforts also often fail to challenge widespread beliefs in the underlying benevolence of the US university, or to question the possibility or the desirability that higher education can fulfill a promise of continuous progress and social mobility for all. Racial and colonial violence remain widely understood as exceptional and incidental to the origins of US higher education. As a result, institutional complicity in slavery and colonization is understood as the unfortunate past price of an imagined egalitarian present and future. What would happen if instead we understood these foundational violences as only the initial instances of an ongoing colonial grammar that continues to govern contemporary life, including higher education?

In response to this question, I turn next to the land-grant era of US higher education to examine how efforts to mobilize the "public good" rely on myths about the past that further elide colonialism as a structural precondition of higher education's existence.

Dispossession at the Roots of "Democracy's Colleges": The Colonial Legacy of Land-Grant Institutions

The land grant idea was one of the great ideas in the history of the United States and of higher education around the world.

—Clark Kerr, 1991, p. 310

The United States has believed that it had an original contribution to make to the history of society by the production of a self-determining, self-restrained, intelligent democracy.

—Frederick Jackson Turner, 1910

The deed to almost all real estate in the United States originates from a federal title that itself came from an Indian title.

—Robert Miller, 2005, p. 3

Land-grant colleges and universities have been designated by US states and territories to receive federal financial and other benefits through the Land-Grant College Act, or Morrill Act, of 1862 and subsequent related legislation (APLU, 2012). Land-grant schools make up only a small segment of US public higher education institutions, but they loom large within the national imaginary, particularly in relation to their perceived democratizing intent and impact (Eddy, 1957; Nevins, 1962; Ross, 1942). According to Allen Nevins (1962) in his classic book *State Universities and Democracy*, "The most important idea in the genesis of the land-grant colleges and state universities was that of democracy" (p. 16).

The "romantic school" of historical accounts from the mid-twentieth century such as Nevins's, which celebrated land grants for their role in the democratization of US higher education, has been significantly complicated by revisionist historians who point to the central economic role of industrialization and global competition in motivating the land-grant movement (Geiger, 2014; Sorber, 2011; Sorber & Geiger, 2014). Yet, in mainstream higher education scholarship and in popular discourses, land-grant colleges and universities still serve as a powerful metonym for the democratic promise and potential of public higher education, particularly in the current context of neoliberal privatization. In this regard, the land-grant legacy is periodically evoked in an effort to reclaim and reinvigorate higher education's role in serving the public good and to solicit further public financial and political support.

For instance, Nathan Sorber and Roger Geiger (2014) find that documents from land-grant institutions and associations "harken to the Morrill Act's egalitarian past to support contemporary calls for access [and] increased state funding" (p. 387). Danika M. Brown (2003) observes, "Scholars tend to construct the land grant mission within the rhetoric of democracy and access ... in this discourse, the land grant mission serves as a foil to critique the relationship between education and corporate interests" (p. 328). Many of these discourses about land grants draw on nostalgic historical narratives that challenge certain neoliberal rationalities and rhetorically advocate for equality. When read from a decolonial perspective, however, these narratives ultimately reaffirm the underlying imperatives of capitalist growth and racialized socioeconomic hierarchy that were built into the colonial foundations of US public higher education. In this chapter, I trace and denaturalize these imperatives.

As Scott Peters (2013) points out, "There is not and can never be just one objectively correct way for historians (or anyone else) to story the land-grant system" (p. 336). It is in this spirit that I seek to supplement rather than replace existing efforts to "story" the land-grant system by analyzing how colonial assumptions and investments are reproduced within common modes of narrating the foundations of these institutions. The stories we tell about the past have significant effects on how we conceptualize the problems of the neoliberal present and on what we imagine as viable and desirable possibilities for the future. In this chapter, I focus on a dimension of land-grant legislation that has gone "unthought" or "unstoried" within both romantic and revisionist historical narratives: its colonial origins.

Roxanne Dunbar-Ortiz (2014) notes that after the Revolutionary War, for the young US nation-state, "land became the most important exchange commodity for the accumulation of capital and building of the national treasury. To understand the genocidal policy of the US government, the centrality of land sales in building the economic base of the US wealth and power must be seen" (p. 124). From a decolonial perspective, the US government's vigorous and violent efforts to accumulate and settle Indigenous lands in the eighteenth and nineteenth centuries provided the conditions of possibility for the distribution of those lands through the Morrill Act of 1862. Further, the act itself helped to solidify and extend claims of US sovereignty over the continent, especially in areas that had only been recently claimed.

Rather than view colonization as an isolated historical event, in this chapter I argue that the US nation-state's genocidal and ecocidal efforts to extend its land base westward helped to solidify a settler colonial template of state-facilitated capital accumulation premised on the conquest of a perpetual "frontier." As Sarah Launius and Geoffrey Alan Boyce (2021) note, "The frontier and its colonial logic are structural features of racial governance and capital accumulation that remain continuously operative over time" and that devalue "nonwhite territorial and economic relations to accomplish and stabilize white settler control over property and land" (p. 157). Within this settler colonial logic, "the frontier comes to designate a threshold between higher and lower stages of productivity and development, its advancement interpreted as simultaneously a spatial and a temporal phenomenon" (p. 159).

Thus, rather than serve as a foil for the present, early land-grant legislation and its dependence on and extension of US efforts to "conquer the frontier" illustrate how, from their beginnings, US public goods like higher education have been shaped by the imperative of continuous racialized capital accumulation. The harmful impacts of that accumulation, while increasingly generalized, are nonetheless unevenly distributed in ways that maintain the taken-for-granted colonial nature of the United States, and thereby presume its perpetuation.

The Origins of This Chapter

This chapter first took form as a conference paper proposal in 2014. As a new doctoral student, I was eager to make critiques of settler colonialism relevant to the higher education field, but uncertain how to do so. The ongoing displacement and dispossession of Indigenous peoples underpin the existence of *all* US higher education institutions, both public and private. I decided to focus on land-grant institutions specifically, because they have significant symbolic weight in discourses about public higher education, and because their explicit relationship to *land* offers a fruitful opening through which to identify more expansive, insidious patterns of colonization. As La Paperson (2017) notes, "Land-grant universities are built not only *on* land but also *from* land." Because of the way the Morrill Act was set up (as I detail later in this chapter), these institutions are linked to Indigenous lands that are often thousands of miles away from their campuses. I was also inspired by decolonial scholars who referred to but never fully elaborated the place of land-grant higher education institutions in our colonial present (e.g., Barker, 2016; Rodríguez, 2012).

In their feedback, the reviewers of the proposal said that while it sounded interesting, they could not understand how the admittedly unfortunate role of colonialism in the founding of land-grant institutions was relevant to the present. No doubt part of the issue was my adequate articulation of these connections and their contemporary implications. However, the inability or unwillingness to link the past to the present in this way also indicates a broader tendency to see these histories of violence as exceptional moments that have been or at least can be healed through the inevitable march of progress. Decolonial critiques invite us instead to consider that the very ideals many people value most about higher education—public goods, universal truths, social mobility, broadly distributed affluence, liberal democracy—are not the opposite of colonial violence, but instead in many ways require for their realization the symbolic and material value that this violence produces. And the violence is not just historical, it is ongoing.

Eventually this rejected conference paper became an article, first published in 2017, which forms the basis of this chapter. That same year, La Paperson, in *A Third University Is Possible* (2017), offered an extended engagement with land grants as part of a wider discussion about (de)colonization and the university. Since then, Margaret Nash (2019) has traced the Indigenous nations whose lands were sold to fund the founding of several land-grant institutions, as well as the treaty, cession, or executive orders through which those nations were initially separated from their lands. In 2020, *High Country News* published an award-winning, widely read investigatory article, "Land Grab Universities," along with an open database that traces all lands granted to institutions through the Morrill Act to the original Indigenous inhabitants and caretakers of those lands (Lee & Ahtone, 2020). The project has inspired several subsequent scholarly engagements and institutional conversations about the colonial legacy of land-grant universities, including a special issue of the journal *Native American and Indigenous Studies.*

This chapter extends my earlier article and puts a decolonial reading of land grants in conversation with various other narratives about US higher education in this era.

Before I proceed, I note an ambivalence that accompanies many efforts to write critically about settler colonization. Such writing is not necessarily "about" Indigenous peoples, because Indigenous peoples are not defined by their experiences of colonization. In fact, to make settler colonization primarily about Indigenous peoples is to ignore how the occupation of their lands is central to the production of the settler nation-state, settler citizens, and imagined settler futures. At the same time, failing to emphasize Indigenous perspectives in this conversation—including ongoing critiques, refusals, and resistances to colonization—would reproduce tropes of Indigenous vanishing and recenter settlers (Snelgrove, Dhamoon, & Corntassel, 2014; Macoun & Strakosch, 2013). In this chapter, I address these considerations by emphasizing the colonial processes enacted by settlers that underlie the Morrill Act, while drawing primarily on the critical and decolonizing insights of Indigenous scholars who insist upon the imperative to make colonial violence visible and who assert the continued presence and inherent rights of Indigenous peoples in what is currently but need not always be known as the United States.

Critiques of (Settler) Colonization

Decolonial critiques identify the United States as a settler colonial state. Scholars argue that while exploitation or metropole colonialism is characterized by the extraction of wealth and resources that are then transferred back to the metropole and its people, settler colonialism is premised on the removal and perpetual displacement of Indigenous peoples from their lands to enable permanent settlement by non-Indigenous people (Tuck & McKenzie, 2014; Wolfe, 2006). In this analysis, the settler nation-state, in both its conservative and progressive iterations, is premised on the ongoing violence of Indigenous dispossession (Trask, 2004).

These critiques also argue that while Indigenous people are racialized under settler colonialism, settler colonialism is irreducible to racism alone; it also entails attempted territorial conquest, denial of Indigenous peoples' existence and rights as sovereign political entities, and the assertion of settler ownership of Indigenous lands (Byrd, 2011). In turn, this means that "Indigenous political economies and relations to and with land" (Coulthard, 2014, p. 4) are treated as obstacles or even threats to be eliminated through physical violence, policies of hyperdescent, and assimilation—including assimilation through the imposition of colonial forms of education (Arvin, Tuck, & Morrill, 2013; Battiste, 2017).

Tuck and McKenzie (2014) describe how, "through the process and structuring of settler colonialism, land is remade into property, and human relationships to land are redefined/reduced to the relationship of owner to his property" (p. 64). This restructuring ignores Indigenous sovereignty and Indigenous understandings of land as a reciprocal, living relation, rather than an object or resource to be possessed (Ahenakew et al., 2014). In settler colonial contexts, the nation-state and capitalism are interdependent as the state facilitates the initial accumulation of Indigenous lands, as well as the subsequent commodification and private sale of those lands (Nichols, 2017); the extraction of "natural resources" from those lands; and all subsequent economic activity that depends on the "real estate" (land) on which it operates (Dunbar-Ortiz, 2014, p. 141). At the same time that the US nation-state facilitated the creation of a capitalist economic system through processes of enslavement and colonization, the nation-state also became entangled with and dependent on that system (Nichols, 2017).

The forced separation of Indigenous peoples from their territories for the purposes of settlement and resource extraction resulted in the disruption of established reciprocal and consensual relationships and led to widespread ecological destruction. Whyte (2018) describes settler colonialism as a form of ecological violence premised on the denial of human interdependence with the environment. In the United States, this ecological violence has entailed the clear-cutting of forests, the mining of coal and various minerals, oil and gas extraction, industrial agriculture, and destructive irrigation projects (Whyte, 2018). Many of the most polluted and otherwise negatively affected areas are concentrated in or near Indigenous and other racialized communities, and all of this ecological destruction happens on Indigenous lands.

Higher education has been central to efforts to make land in the United States more profitable and productive under capitalist logics. For instance, universities have trained scientists and managers to work in resource extraction industries and have developed Western scientific and industrial technologies and techniques for maximizing products and profits in various sectors at the expense of many communities' social and ecological health and well-being. They have also trained lawyers, judges, legislators, and administrators who argue for, implement, and manage different state and state-sanctioned modes of Indigenous dispossession. As La Paperson (2017) notes, "The public university, with its charge to underwrite industry and agribusiness, literally changed the landscape of the Americas"; this was especially the case for land-grant institutions, which were charged with supporting the development of the academic fields and professions of agriculture, science, and engineering.

Across time, settler colonial processes have been continually revised to maintain the literal and figurative grounds for capital accumulation and settler sovereignty (King, 2016). I argue that the colonial aspects of public higher education that emerged with land-grant institutions continue to shape US higher education today and circumscribe imaginable higher education futures in ways that presume the inevitable persistence of colonization. Although specific modes of settler colonization are continuously rearticulated in ways that seek to supress or co-opt Indigenous resistance, enable new modes of capital expansion, and ensure settler futurities, one constant is the justification and banalization of colonial violence in the name of progress, democracy, social mobility, economic development, and even equality.

In this chapter, I identify the central role of Indigenous dispossession and settler colonial logic in the founding and expansion of US public colleges and universities. I begin by reviewing the basic elements of the Morrill Act and then survey different historical narratives about the act before offering a decolonial reading of land-grant history. To engage this reading, I review the history of colonization in the nineteenth century, which enabled the US state to accumulate Indigenous land that was then dispersed, in part, through the Morrill Act. I therefore argue that there is an indirect but dependent relationship between the dispossession of Indigenous lands and the founding of the land-grant colleges and universities. I further suggest that it is important to trace the "structural and material continuities in the settler colonial logic" (Launius & Boyce, 2021, p. 162) that underpin the possibility for US public higher education today.

The Morrill Act

By the time of the first Morrill Act in 1862, there was already a history of public federal land grants for educational institutions. Between 1796 and 1861, seventeen states received federal land grants for higher education; several states offered their own land grants, as well (Thelin, 2004). In 1850, minister and professor Jonathan Baldwin Turner unsuccessfully proposed a "University for industrial classes" and encouraged farmers to demand appropriations of public land with which to expand industrial education (Cross, 2012). When Senator Justin Morrill first introduced his land-grant bill in 1857, Congress passed it, but President Buchanan vetoed it. In 1862, with seceded Southern states having no representatives in Congress to object to the legislation during the Civil War, both chambers passed a revised version of the legislation, and President Lincoln signed it into law.

The Morrill Act granted to each state 30,000 acres of federal public lands per senator and representative, sale of which land would fund "the endowment, support, and maintenance of at least one college where the leading object shall be, without excluding other scientific and classical studies, and including military tactics, to teach such branches of learning as are related to agriculture and the mechanic arts, in such manner as the legislatures of the States may respectively prescribe, in order to promote the liberal and practical education of the industrial classes on the several pursuits and professions in life."

According to Geiger (2014), "The act immediately affected the expansion and structure of higher education and, eventually, the productivity of the American economy" (p. 281). Some states implemented more comprehensive approaches to education, and others emphasized agricultural training; some created entirely new institutions, while others conferred land-grant status on existing schools (Sorber & Geiger, 2014; Williams, 1991). Western states would select land parcels from their own (federally held) lands, and they could build on part of that land and sell the rest of it, or they could sell the whole of the granted land, use the funds to build their institution elsewhere, and apply the remaining funds to supporting the institution. Eastern states that no longer held much public land received scrip to be used in selecting public land farther west (Cross, 2012; Nash, 2019). In both cases, the states were supposed to sell any land they acquired and did not build on in order to buy stocks so as to create profits to continuously fund the activities outlined in the act. According to the act, "The moneys so invested shall constitute a perpetual fund, the capital of which shall remain forever undiminished (except so far as may be provided in section fifth of this act), and the interest of which shall be inviolably appropriated, by each State which may take and claim the benefit of this act." In other words, states had to invest the profits from the sales of the granted land. The "public good" of land-grant institutions depended from the outset on profits from capitalist markets and, thus, on continuous capital accumulation. However, none of this subsequent accumulation would have been possible without the federal government's *initial* accumulation of Indigenous lands through dispossession.

Although Morrill Act funding is marginal in the context of today's massive land-grant institution budgets, as Robert Lee and Tristan Ahtone (2020) note, "Morrill Act funds were the entire endowment of more than a third of land-grant colleges a century after the law's passage" (p. 41). Further, the moneys acquired from those land sales "still remain on university ledgers to this day" (p. 35), with the total grants of 10.7 million acres—land taken from close to 250 tribes and communities— being valued at around $500 million adjusted for inflation. Today, several states also yield income from as-yet-unsold lands still held in trust, for example, in the form of mineral rights or resource harvesting (Lee & Ahtone, 2020).

When the 1862 provisions proved insufficient for supporting the various land-grant responsibilities, Congress passed the Hatch Act in 1887 to fund "agricultural experiment stations" for scientific research at land-grant institutions, and the Smith-Lever Act in 1914 to support cooperative extension programs across each state.

Roderick Ferguson (2012) describes the Morrill Act of 1862 as, in part, an effort to distinguish white people from recently freed or soon-to-be-freed Black people after the Civil War: "The professional (i.e., white subject) who would become the academic ideal of that act would thus be the fully industrialized alternative to the unlettered slave who hailed from a plantation-based economy" (p. 85). Meanwhile, Black students who enrolled in northern land-grant institutions were subject to discrimination, and in the South they were excluded from enrollment altogether (Sorber & Geiger, 2014). In 1890, the Second Morrill Act made further appropriations for the 1862 land-grant schools, but withheld funds from states with institutions that had anti-Black legislation and discriminatory admissions policies, unless they created separate institutions for

Black students. This led to the founding of nearly twenty Black land-grant schools in the southern states. The land-grant legislation that passed after 1862, including the Second Morrill Act, was not directly funded through grants of land or scrip.

While it expanded access to higher education for Black students, the Second Morrill Act also further entrenched and naturalized racial segregation, foreshadowing the "separate but equal" legal doctrine set forth in 1896 in the Supreme Court's *Plessy v. Ferguson* ruling (Ferguson, 2012; Wheatle, 2019). The 1890 Morrill Act was deeply shaped by racist attitudes within the US Congress and, according to Katherine Wheatle (2019), was motivated primarily by the intention to enhance general funding for agricultural research and instruction at the 1862 institutions, not to ensure racially democratized access to higher education. As a result, "equitable resources for educational opportunities were still rarely afforded to the 1890 institutions or African American students" (Wheatle, 2019, p. 4), and the 1890 law "ultimately protected and maintained white property interests of white policymakers, educational administrators, institutions, and students" (p. 2). This highly conditional inclusion of Black people in ways that did not threaten white dominance foreshadowed the more expansive forms of conditional inclusion that emerged in the post–World War II era of US higher education (Ferguson, 2012).

Several subsequent pieces of legislation supplemented and transformed existing land-grant institutions and their research and education efforts. In 1972, universities in the US territories of Guam, the Mariana Islands, American Samoa, and the US Virgin Islands were granted land-grant status. In 1994, after a successful campaign from tribal colleges and universities, Congress passed the Equity in Educational Land-Grant Status Act, which granted tribal institutions land-grant status with an accompanying endowment (AIHEC, 2014; APLU, 2012).

In 2012, the Morrill Act turned 150, which led to several commemorations of the legislation at individual land-grant schools and by the Association for Public and Land Grant Universities. The exact benefits derived from land-grant status have shifted over time, and institutions now receive funding from several different sources (APLU, 2012). However, historically Black land-grant colleges and universities and tribal land-grant institutions remain grossly underfunded in comparison to their historically white 1862 counterparts (AIHEC, 2014; Lee & Keys, 2013).

The Romantic School of Land-Grant History and Its Revisionist Counterparts

Writing thirty years ago, Roger L. Williams (1991) noted that the literature on land grants was dominated by "romantic" texts that suggested "the land-grant movement was inevitable, the colleges [having been] called into being by the educational demands of a rapidly expanding and democratizing nation" (p. 2). Recently, in their review of land-grant historiography, Sorber and Geiger (2014) observe that despite several decades of revisionist historians' work, these more romantic accounts continue to orient the scholarly literature and popular discourse. Romantic historical narratives, they note, tend to paper over significant tensions and conflicts within the land-grant movement and its subsequent implementation, and give inadequate attention to the layered rationales for the Morrill Act, which include "interrelated movements of industrialization, the rise of science, international competition, nation-building and bureaucratization, academic professionalization, agricultural modernization, the rise of professionalization in fields like engineering, and an emerging middle class" (p. 388).

Several revisionist historians offer analyses of these and other rationales for the legislation. Many note the role of education and business reformers in pushing the act forward, challenging the assertion that it was a democratic demand that came from "the people" (Brown, 2003; Key, 1996; Williams, 1991; Sorber & Geiger, 2014). Others emphasize that support for the bill was largely motivated by concern about low national productivity levels and their effect on US economic competitiveness. Some feared the United States would fall behind Europe if it did not embrace a more scientific approach to industry and agriculture and train workers to use this approach (Cross, 2012; Sorber, 2011; Williams, 1991). Mark Paschall (2016) argues that while earlier modes of higher education were more suited to reproducing the aristocratic class of merchant capitalism, the transformation of US higher education in the late nineteenth century signaled a shift in power toward the middle classes and the utilitarian knowledge of an ascendant industrial capitalism. Scott Key (1996) also concludes that the land-grant legislation was not so much an educational policy as a political and economic one intended to promote settlement and thereby indirectly promote "national development" and prosperity, including through productivity gains from improved agricultural production techniques.

In sum, these revisionist critiques of romantic histories of land-grant institutions emphasize that national political and economic rationales for the legislation were as important as "purely" educational or populist motives, and likely more important. Yet even if land grants did not represent a popular desire for practical higher education at their founding, they nonetheless played a role in eventually generating that demand. Their growth also contributed to the strengthening of conceptual and material relationships between US democracy, the nation-state, and capitalist growth, and affirmed the role of higher education in mediating between them.

Linking Democracy and Social Mobility to Higher Education

In his famous writings on the United States in the nineteenth century, Alexis de Tocqueville asserted that the strength of a society's democratic system was tightly linked to the possibilities that it offered for social mobility, that is, opportunities to compete for a spot within the middle or even upper socioeconomic classes (Acemoglu, Egorov, & Sonin, 2016). Such perceived links between democracy and economic opportunity became deeply embedded in the national ethos.

Today, opportunity for social mobility has come to be understood as tightly woven into access to higher education, and many believe that "a college degree can be a ticket out of poverty" (Greenstone et al., 2013, p. 13). As Steven Brint and Jerome Karabel (1990) noted, "The idea that the higher education system in general, and higher education in particular, should provide ladders of upward mobility is so familiar as to be taken for granted" (p. 5). Social mobility via higher education is also closely associated with ideals of meritocracy, the presumption that "those who are the most talented, the hardest working, and the most virtuous get and should get the most rewards" (McNamee & Miller, 2009, p. 4). It is for this reason that Gordon Gee (2012) celebrates the fact that "the Morrill Act set the country on an accelerated path to realizing its founding promise to create a meritocracy based not on wealth or family connections but on ability, determination, and effort" (p. 53). Were land grants really founded on this promise? If so, to whom was this promise extended, and who paid the costs of its fulfillment? I address the first question in this section, and the question of costs in the following section, emphasizing colonization of Indigenous lands as a primary but generally disavowed cost.

The notion that land grants expanded access and opportunity, thus increasing social mobility, remains a prominent trope. Yet revisionist historians argue that the schools did not, in any immediate sense, affect the substantive expansion of access beyond the middle and upper-middle classes (Behle, 2013; Sorber & Geiger, 2014). As David Levine (1988) notes, while today it is taken for granted that education is associated with US economic growth and individual advancement, "higher education has not always been a critical criterion of economic and social mobility in American society" (p. 13). Levine dates the codification of the link between higher education and mobility to the years between 1915 and 1940.

Sorber (2011) dates this link earlier, arguing that by the end of the nineteenth century, "the state college was the place where children of farmers and workers, properly fitted in a public high school, could go at a reasonable price to pursue middle class aspirations" (p. 312). According to Labaree (2016), it was around this time that "going to college finally came to be seen as a good investment for a growing number of middle-class student-consumers" (p. 24). In this sense, land grants were part of the vanguard framing higher education as a central means of social mobility (or, for those who already held a middle-class position, retaining it) within the context of an emerging industrial US economy. As power and resources shifted from a class of agricultural gentlemen to a middle class of "businessmen, bureaucrats, and skilled technocrats" (Sorber, 2011, pp. 10–11), this new middle class, which made up 25 percent of the US workforce by the early 1900s, required preparation in engineering, agriculture, industrial science, and bureaucratic organization (Sorber, 2011). Beyond knowledge and skills, a college degree also signaled to employers that potential employees adhered to "proper" (i.e., white middle-class) values and behaviors (Bledstein, 1976).

By the mid-twentieth century, land-grant institutions served as a powerful symbol of higher education's "democratic promise," which specifically meant a means of social mobility, which was in turn tied to national economic growth. This promise is frequently reinvigorated today in response to declining public higher education funding. The perceived relationship between democracy, national economic growth, and social mobility is often reproduced in contemporary evocations of the land-grant ideal (Sorber & Geiger, 2014). For instance, in celebrating the democratic and egalitarian promises of land grants, Nancy Folbre (2010) asserts that these promises are tightly related to national economic growth and the associated opportunities for social mobility that enable people to benefit from that growth. Folbre emphasizes that US ideals of egalitarianism and opportunity have never been antithetical to capitalist growth; rather, the two have been tightly linked and codependent. Thus, at the same time that she is critical of the current configuration of capital-state relations, she holds out hope for an equitable arrangement with "more cooperative, sustainable, and egalitarian economic policies" (p. 60).

While critiques like Folbre's lament austerity measures that lessen public funding for higher education, they rarely question the overall effect of defining "progress and efficiency in terms of economic development" (Brown, 2003, p. 332). As a result, there is little concern about the fact that economic development always comes at a cost—one that is usually distributed in highly uneven, racialized ways. Effectively, critiques like Folbre's are oriented by a frustration that the people that previously benefited from the United States' economic expansion—in particular, those who were able to achieve social mobility through higher education—have fewer opportunities to do so today and lower returns when they do. The question of who pays and has paid the true price of these opportunities is generally invisibilized. One can ask about the rhetorical and political effects of choosing these narratives to catalyze resistance to neoliberalism over other possible narratives. In the remainder of this chapter, I offer a decolonial reading of the land-grant era as an alternative to both romantic and revisionist histories. This reading suggests that not only exploitation and expropriation of labor but also expropriation and dispossession of land have always been and continue to be central to US public higher education.

A Decolonial Reading of Land-Grant History

In the opening pages of his romantic account of land-grant history, *Democracy's College*, Earle Ross (1942) unwittingly captured the colonial grammar that underpins the democratic promises of US higher education and, more generally, the underlying colonial basis of "public goods": "American educational evolution has shown a degree of continuity that reflects a dominant and unifying motive. The determining influence has been that of . . . a democratic system according to the expanding conceptions of that term. . . . The material basis for the establishment of such a democratic system lay in the peculiar national resource. . . . *It was land, the main incentive in colonization, transoceanic and transcontinental, which provided down to the Civil War the financial resources necessary for public enterprises, 'internal improvements' and education*" (pp. 2–3; emphasis added).

Despite Ross's use of the term "colonization," Indigenous dispossession is absent from his narrative. Nor does it appear as a concern in revisionist accounts. For example, in his critical reassessment of land-grant histories, Key (1996) observes: "Like most nations, one of the main pillars of prosperity and power was agriculture; however few nations had been so richly blessed with such an abundance of land. This abundance became the principle resource of the new government when the colonies joined together and unoccupied land was ceded to the new Union" (p. 199). Here, Key employs "discourses of conquest" (Williams, as cited by Wolfe, 2012, p. 6) by suggesting a divine providence of land ("so richly blessed") that erases the human processes of dispossession by which that land was acquired. This discourse also reproduces the colonial fiction of terra nullius, according to which that the lands occupied by Indigenous peoples for millennia were empty and open for settlement ("unoccupied land").

In her effort to link land-grant institutions to the promise of equal opportunity in the early United States, Folbre (2010) writes, "Expanded opportunities reinforced the bootstrap vision of upward mobility that held the country together. The advice 'Go west, young man,' combined with the practical opportunity of virtually free land offered by the Homestead Act, held men accountable for their own economic welfare" (p. 30). Again, the origins of this "free land" and the colonial impetus of westward settlement are erased here in the effort to emphasize opportunity for socioeconomic mobility and the image of the self-made settler student. In the following section, I consider how Indigenous removals in the nineteenth century resulted in the US government's accumulation of land that was then distributed through the Morrill Act.

Conquering the Frontier

The United States' territorial claims are largely rooted in the so-called Doctrine of Discovery. Starting in the fifteenth century, this doctrine authorized European Christian colonization of non-European, non-Christian lands and peoples (Miller, 2005). Through the doctrine, in the colonies that would later become the United States, Britain claimed that its "discovery" diminished the sovereignty of Indigenous peoples, secured preemptive rights to purchase their lands, and barred any other colonial power (or individual colonists) from claiming those lands. The doctrine was later secularized and enshrined in US law. Robert J. Miller (2011) notes that when the term "manifest destiny" was first coined to describe the "predestined and divinely inspired expansion" of US empire in the mid-nineteenth century, it drew on "the same rationales and justifications that created the Doctrine" (p. 332).*

After achieving independence from Britain in the late eighteenth century, the young United States sought unfettered access to lands and resources for its developing capitalist economy (Silva, 2007). The Declaration of Independence already deems the frontier to have fallen under the purview of the emergent US nation-state, while it describes the Indigenous peoples beyond it as "merciless Indian Savages." Byrd (2011) points out that this foundational articulation frames Indigenous people "as abjected horror through whom civilization is articulated oppositionally" (p. xxi), and this perspective served as further justification for their attempted obliteration and violent replacement by "civilized" settlers and their government.

The young nation established processes for the settlement and sale of western lands as a means of both asserting US sovereignty and raising revenues (to fund public education, for example). All "unsettled" lands were claimed for the US federal government, and processes were established to enable individual land ownership and the founding of new states. In 1801 Thomas Jefferson wrote about the current boundaries of the US nation-

---

*According to Miller (2011): "Manifest Destiny is generally defined by three aspects.... First, the belief the United States has some unique moral virtues other countries do not possess. Second, the idea the United States has a mission to redeem the world by spreading republican government and the American way of life around the globe. And, third, that the United States has a divinely ordained destiny to accomplish these tasks" (p. 332).

state, "It is impossible not to look forward to distant times when our rapid multiplication will expand itself beyond those limits, and cover the whole northern, if not the southern continent" (as cited by Miller, 2006, p. 79). Shortly thereafter, Jefferson sought to actualize this future vision by commissioning the Lewis and Clark "expedition" and facilitating the Louisiana Purchase in 1803. He also declared that the European Doctrine of Discovery should extend to the United States, though it was not solidified as law until the early-nineteenth-century Marshall trilogy rulings (Pommersheim, 2009).

While never inevitable, continental expansion was taken for granted by US founders and early leaders such as Jefferson. Indigenous peoples maintained their assertions of sovereignty and self-determination, but the young US government considered them nuisances to be overcome rather than equal nations that would continue to exist and inhabit their traditional territories. Jefferson advocated for Indigenous assimilation so as to "extend to them the full blessings of civilized life & prepare their minds for becoming useful members of the American family" (as cited by Miller, 2006, p. 86), and of course to ensure that the United States would have full access to their lands. This understanding of the inevitably conquered frontier, and Indigenous peoples as an "uncivilized," expendable barrier to progress, is firmly implanted in white settler memory, including within discourses of higher education.

The Colonial Conditions of Possibility for the Morrill Act

Since the beginning of the United States, according to Gates (1976), "the power to own, manage, grant, and otherwise dispose of the public lands was to be one of the most nationalizing factors in the life of the federal republic" (p. 213). And these "public lands" were all wrested, by various, generally violent means, from the original Indigenous inhabitants. Yet, even as Indigenous removal and replacement by settlers was presumed to be inevitable, the US government nonetheless had to address the fact that the supposedly "empty" lands beyond its initial "frontier" were inhabited by hundreds of Indigenous nations that were designated in the Constitution as foreign entities and should therefore be engaged "in the way sovereign collectivities relate to others, namely, trade, treaties, and war" (Silva, 2007, p. 205). Beyond this, the United States had to address the fact that most Indigenous peoples strongly maintained and defended their claims to be the rightful inhabitants of their traditional territories.

By the nineteenth century, many questions still remained about how settlement would be realized, particularly without appearing to contradict the country's "self-image as [a] distinctly free societ[y] governed by law" (Nichols, 2017, p. 14). These questions were partially answered by three landmark Supreme Court cases between 1823 and 1832, presided over by Chief Justice John Marshall, now known as the "Marshall Trilogy." These were the first major cases about Indigenous peoples to be reviewed by the Supreme Court, and their rulings still form much of the backbone of federal law relating to the US government's relationship to Indigenous peoples (Barker, 2015; Goldstein, 2008; Miller, 2005).

In the first case in the trilogy, *Johnson v. M'Intosh* (1823), Marshall wrote for the Court: "Conquest gives a title which the Courts of the conqueror cannot deny," thereby formally enshrining into US law the Doctrine of Discovery. This approach contrasted with what international law would have enjoined the US government to do in its dealings with European nations. The ruling famously stated: "Even if it should be admitted that the Indians were originally an independent people, they have ceased to be so. A nation that has passed under the dominion of another, is no longer a sovereign state. The same treaties and negotiations, before referred to, show their dependent condition" (as cited in Barker, 2015, p. 250). The Supreme Court ruled that following "discovery" by a European power, Indigenous land title consisted not of full ownership or sovereignty but of mere occupancy (Barker, 2015). Joanne Barker argues that Marshall's "self-fulfilling narrative of legal, moral and social superiority . . . reinvented a sovereignty for indigenous peoples that was void of any of the associated rights to self-government, territorial integrity, and cultural autonomy that would have been affiliated with it in international law at the time" (as cited by Byrd, 2011, p. xxii). Effectively, the Marshall rulings affirmed that the US claims to mutually exclusive territorial sovereignty could go unchallenged only if the sovereignty of Indigenous peoples was significantly diminished, if not eradicated. Another way of describing this result is that the colonial structure of US sovereignty required, and continues to require, the presumption of inevitable Indigenous dispossession.

In its ruling in *Johnson v. M'Intosh* (1823), the Court asserted that Indigenous peoples were "fierce savages, whose occupation was war, and whose subsistence was drawn chiefly from the forest." Thus, the Court's ruling states, "to leave them in possession of their country was to leave the country a wilderness." Underlying this assertion, among other things, was the Lockean logic by which Indigenous nations were deemed not to have cultivated the land according to European standards of productivity and property and therefore could make no rightful claim to it (Barker, 2015; Byrd, 2011). The Court also ruled that Indigenous nations "remain in a state of nature, and have never been admitted into the general society of nations." Within European political theory, the notion of a "state of nature" relegates Indigenous peoples to an earlier stage of human social and political development, while European-descended peoples

are understood to be more advanced, having chosen of free
will to enter into a social contract, thereby "exiting the state of
nature" in order to create a political system that would protect
and secure their lives and private property and thus maximize
their freedom, and profits (Silva, 2007). Within this white-
supremacist story of human progress and development, European people are understood to be the leaders of humanity and
Indigenous people are presumed to be following behind—less
evolved and thus, justifiably, subject to colonization. Meanwhile, Indigenous claims of reciprocal relationships and responsibilities to land were illegible and invalid according to
Western political, economic, and legal systems.

The Marshall decisions and their representations of both
Indigenous peoples and white US settlers were rooted in a
framework of liberal property rights and personhood that per-
sists today. Patrick Wolfe (2012) argues that the Marshall Trilogy
"yielded more than land for settlers. It also yielded sovereign
subjecthood: they became the sort of people who could own,
rather than merely occupy" (p. 10). The rulings not only justified further Indigenous dispossession but also reified categori-
cally different subjectivities and rights for white citizens and
Indigenous peoples and sought to invalidate and erase the latter's relationships to their ancestral lands.

In sum, the Marshall Trilogy helped solidify the presumption
of inevitable Indigenous dispossession and disappearance. As
Wolfe (2012) notes, "Most of the forced removals perpetrated
against Indian peoples took place during the half century following *Cherokee v. Georgia* [1831]," the second case in the trilogy (p. 7). According to Paul Frymer (2014), "During the first
half of the nineteenth century, the territory of the United
States nearly tripled in size as the nation expanded across the
continent from thirteen Atlantic-side states south to the Rio
Grande and west to the Pacific Ocean" (p. 119). By 1850, US

federal landholdings had grown to approximately 1.2 billion acres (Rifkin, 2013). This expansion was made possible through treaties with other countries (Britain, France, Mexico, Spain) in which Indigenous lands were transferred from other colonial powers to the United States; treaties and wars with Indigenous nations; and policies that promoted western settlement (Frymer, 2014; Wolfe, 2012).

Even when the United States acquired Indigenous lands through purchase or treaty, there were and remain serious questions about the extent to which these land cessions were consensual and not made under duress, coercion, or threat of (further) violence. Historians and legal scholars also disagree as to their interpretation, especially given conflicting interpretations by settler courts and Indigenous communities. As Vine Deloria (1996) observes, most treaties "occur at the end of political and military crises in which the respective Indian nations have been forced to surrender tracts of land. But even here there are many anomalies, . . . for example, some very large areas of land are classified as being ceded in unratified treaties" (p. 978). Today the United States is in violation of even many ratified treaties (Dunbar-Ortiz, 2014).

During the second half of the nineteenth century the US Army continued its war on Indigenous communities, particularly in areas where settlement was relatively recent and precarious. Some of the land ultimately granted through the Morrill Act was acquired by the US government through cessions, seizures, and treaties that occurred after the act was passed (Lee & Ahtone, 2020). For instance, nearly half of Colorado State University's grant consisted of land stolen from the Arapaho and Cheyenne nations less than a year after two hundred of their people were murdered in the 1864 Sand Creek Massacre (Lee & Ahtone, 2020). As the US government colonized more Indigenous land, settlers were moving into the West in large numbers thanks in no small part to the Morrill Act, as well as two other pieces of legislation passed in the same year: the Homestead Act, which offered 160 acres of land to settlers who agreed to occupy and improve ("cultivate") it for five years (Sauder & Sauder, 1987), and the Pacific Railroad Act, which provided nearly 200 million acres to private companies to build the transcontinental railroad (Dunbar-Ortiz, 2014). Settlers were also drawn west by the allure of gold mining.

At the end of the Civil War, three years after the Morrill Act became law, many demobilized troops went west to fight on a new front. As Dunbar-Ortiz (2014) notes, "In much of the western lands, the army was the primary U.S. government institution" (p. 133). Infamous actions by the US military against Indigenous communities during this era include the Sand Creek Massacre (1864), Battle of Little Bighorn (1876), and Wounded Knee Massacre (1890). The army also supported decimation of the buffalo population, which was central to Plains Indigenous nations' social, political, and economic life. Many politicians and state governments also sponsored the destruction of Indigenous life. For instance, in California the first state governor promised "a war of extermination will continue to be waged between the races until the Indian race become extinct," and the state legislature sanctioned this call and paid bounties to individual settlers and militias for each Indigenous life taken. As a result, "whole tribes, bands, and families were massacred" (Barker, 2015, p. 263). California state legislation also legalized the forced labor (enslavement) of Indigenous peoples, including children.

The US unilaterally suspended treaty making in 1871 (Dunbar-Ortiz, 2014; Goldstein, 2014). In 1887, Congress passed the General Allotment Act, commonly known as the Dawes Act, in an effort to eradicate remaining Indigenous collective land-holdings and, in the process, Indigenous collective life. The act

sought to divide collectively held tribal lands among Indigenous individuals in an effort to encourage them to develop a
strong sense of individualism and value private property; the
land left over after allotment was declared surplus and sold to
white settlers and corporations (Chang, 2011; Goldstein, 2008).
Barker (2015) describes the Dawes Act as having effected the
"virtual obliteration of tribal rights" (p. 256); it reduced Indigenous tribal and individual landholdings by about two-thirds
and made the collective use of land nearly impossible.

David Wallace Adams (1988) argues that it is not a coinci-
dence that the Dawes Act was passed around the same time
that the US government began to fund boarding schools for
Indigenous children. These schools were founded in the late
nineteenth century with the genocidal intention to "kill the
Indian and save the man," in the words of US Army captain
Richard Henry Pratt, the founder of the first off-reservation
boarding school, Carlisle Indian Industrial School. These
schools were established as explicit efforts to "Americanize"
Indigenous children, that is, assimilate them into middle-class
Euro-American social mores and Christianity, which were
presumed to be the height of human progress and development (Adams, 1988; Brayboy, 2005). While various rationales
undergirded the schools' design and implementation, always
present was assimilation as a means to the end of accumulation: if Indigenous peoples fully assimilated into US society,
they would cease to be Indigenous peoples as such, and therefore white settlers could claim ownership of their lands without
impediment. The schooling of Indigenous children was seen as
a primary means through which to achieve this assimilation.

By 1900, nearly 85 percent of Indigenous children who
were enrolled in school attended boarding schools, some of
which were located off reservations and others on reservations (Adams, 1988). Over half of all school-aged Indigenous

children were enrolled in some form of school. Adams (1988) describes boarding schools as undertaking "an all-out assault on the child's 'otherness' . . . waged uncompromisingly on every aspect of the child's being" (p. 14). The schools separated Indigenous children not only from their families and communities but also from their cultural, political, spiritual, and educational practices. They were forced to speak English and not allowed to speak in their Indigenous languages, their hair was cut, and they were given Western-style names and clothes. The schools sought to cultivate among Indigenous children individualistic subjectivities that would make them fit for capitalist society. Administrators and teachers managed the schools in extremely militaristic ways, with harsh disciplinary practices and forced labor, to ensure Indigenous children's obedience to white authority and to teach boys industrial skills and girls domestic skills. Many of the boarding schools were overcrowded and unsanitary—conditions in which disease spread unchecked. In the midst of this violence, Indigenous children and their families resisted the schools in various ways; for instance, students practiced their spiritual traditions in secret or ran away from the schools (Davis, 2001).

While the US has only just started to have a national collective reckoning with the history of Indigenous boarding schools—a process that has begun, but hardly been completed, in Canada—they are relevant to higher education in at least two ways. First, many of the legislators, teachers, and various other professionals involved in designing and running the schools were trained in institutions of higher education. There is significant research yet to be done to unravel the multiple roles that US colleges and universities played particularly in training professionals in the practice of institutionalizing colonization through the boarding schools, but also in general. The second is that there is resonance and sometimes even direct relationships between the ways that the boarding schools and institutions of higher education treated Indigenous students (for a discussion of the relationship between Carlisle and Hampton University, see, e.g., Boggs et al., 2019).

An Indirect but Dependent Relationship

While Indigenous dispossession and removals were not enacted for the express purpose of funding or making space for land-grant higher education institutions, these removals were nonetheless prerequisites for their founding and existence. That is, the US government's violent efforts to accumulate Indigenous land throughout the eighteenth and nineteenth centuries helped to create the conditions of possibility for land-grant colleges and universities to exist. I describe this as an *indirect but dependent* relationship: without violently accumulating Indigenous lands through various means, the US government would not have been able to then grant it to the states to found and fund their institutions.

Further, these institutions helped to extend and solidify the US settler colonial project, particularly in the West, as did other higher education institutions. According to Michael Sedlak, "Colleges were often founded right on the frontier line—not a generation after the founding of a town or of a state, but at the same moment as the founding of the town or state" (as cited by Goodchild and Wrobel, 2014, p. 5). Meanwhile, Eldon Johnson (1981) has contended, land-grant institutions "were a boon to frontier settlement and an important ingredient in the frenzy of 'internal improvements' in many states" (p. 226). Finally, through settlement itself and through the forms of research and education—agricultural and industrial— that were encouraged by the Morrill Act, land-grant institutions also contributed to the further objectification and transformation of land and other-than-human beings into so-called natural resources and sites of extraction for the ends of capitalist profit (La Paperson, 2017).

The Morrill Act, along with the other legislation passed in 1862, which distributed grants of land to settlers and settler corporations, was significant in enabling and encouraging further white-majority expansion and settlement and the capitalist economic development of the US nation-state. All of these acts also helped to shore up US federal authority over recently acquired lands. Beyond the material dimensions of this authority, land-grant universities further naturalized dispossession and settlement through their approach to both curriculum and research, which treated the land as property to be "developed" by settlers according to Western notions of extractivism, profit, and efficiency. It is therefore telling that this set of laws has been termed "the blueprint for modern America" (McPherson as cited by Geiger, 2014, p. 281). Thus, it can be argued that the blueprint for modern America was settler colonialism.

As the United States secured its sovereignty, expanded higher education also represented a means by which the nation-state could develop and promote a more cohesive national identity. Adam Dahl (2014) notes that US popular sovereignty "was forged through processes of settler expansion" as people not only physically migrated West but also projected the nation's futurity across the continent, intensifying their investment in colonization (p. 17). Some advocates of westward expansion viewed land appropriations as a means to guarantee democratic egalitarianism, by spreading wealth rather than concentrating it in a few hands. Yet this democracy was underwritten by colonial violence. Further, even this already-distorted democratic vision was shaped by imperatives of economic growth and capital accumulation, not only in the structure of funding but also in the drivers and effects of the land-grant legislation.

Metaphorizing the Frontier

While colonial violence is largely missing from US national narratives, it is an absent presence in one of the country's most famous origin stories: Frederick Jackson Turner's late-nineteenth-century "frontier thesis." Turner (1920) argued, "The existence of an area of free land, its continuous recession, and the advance of American settlement westward, explains American development" (p. 1).

For Turner, US national identity, economic growth, democratic institutions, and individualism all derived from lessons and values learned by "pioneers" as they pushed west. He argued that the promotion of democracy was "the most important effect of the frontier" (Turner, 1920, p. 30) and, specifically, that "the effective force behind American democracy was the presence of the practically free land into which men might escape from oppression or inequalities" (p. 274). In this sense, Turner uncritically acknowledged that as colonization produced capital and secured state sovereignty, it also enabled the self-actualization of white, property-owning citizens (Silva, 2007). The US citizen-subject emerged through the very processes that subjugated and dispossessed Black and Indigenous peoples (King, 2016).

Turner's writings about the frontier also coincided with the United States' decision to turn its gaze to a new, extracontinental colonial frontier in the late nineteenth and early twentieth century, which led to US colonial incursions and territorial acquisitions in the Pacific and the Caribbean, including Hawai'i, Puerto Rico, Guam, the Philippines, American Samoa, the Marshall Islands, Alaska, the Virgin Islands, and Northern Mariana (Dunbar-Ortiz, 2014).

Despite the critiques that can and have been focused on Turner's frontier thesis about both the factuality of its claims and its deeply colonial grammar, this frontier logic remains powerful within narratives of higher education. With the so-called closing of the frontier in the continental United States in the late nineteenth and early twentieth century, along with the transition from agricultural to industrial labor, farm or other land ownership no longer guaranteed social mobility; now one needed to obtain a higher education credential (Chaput, 2004; Folbre, 2010). This shift in middle-class aspirations was premised on the shift from the literal frontier to a metaphorical frontier (Barrow, 1990). As Samuel Bowles and Herbert Gintis (1976) asserted, "A new ideology of opportunity became the order of the day. The folklore of capitalism was revitalized: Education was the new frontier" (p. 3).

This shift from the literal to the metaphorical educational frontier helped ensure white peoples' continued buy-in to a capitalist political economic system that exploited them but nonetheless offered many rewards, particularly in comparison to those offered to Indigenous, Black, and other racialized people. This was the vision outlined by Turner in a 1910 commencement speech in which he expressed concern that the democratic spirit and egalitarianism fostered by the frontier and the perceived imperative to "conquer" it was being threatened by expanding inequality and class conflict, particularly given "the practical exhaustion of the supply of cheap arable public lands open to the poor man" (p. 11). In light of these changes, he argued, public universities had a "duty in adjusting pioneer ideals to the new requirements of American democracy" (p. 27). Turner called upon state universities to train experts for new fields such as public health and manufacturing, "as the test tube and the microscope are needed rather than axe and rifle in this new ideal of conquest" (p. 24).

Catherine Chaput (2004) suggests that this kind of rhetorical metaphorization of the frontier helped suture the potentially contradictory logics of democracy and industrial capitalism. In this way, the promise of opportunity through education mitigated the fact of inequality and exploitation. But, although land-grant institutions supported capitalist expansion in the emergent *metaphorical* frontier of the country's industrial economy, these institutions would not have existed without prior efforts to conquer the *literal* frontier. Furthermore, early industrial capitalism, in the form of mechanized agriculture, new technologies of resource extraction, and manufacturing plants, still required the material land base that emerged from the histories of colonial accumulation that preceded it. Thus, the perceived need for knowledge produced in higher education in order to perpetually conquer metaphorical frontiers rests on the attempted conquest of the literal frontier, and these colonial foundations continue to have violent material implications.

The frontier trope has been adapted throughout US higher education history. For instance, scholarly work is evaluated largely according to its perceived novelty and individual innovation, which can encourage the erasure of preceding genealogies of thought as well as collaborative thinking. This framing elevates the individual and disavows the historical, political, and economic contexts and relationships in which they are embedded. The prototypical academic is often conceptualized as a lone thinker, celebrated for "pioneering" or "discovering" this or that innovation in their field. Manu Karuka (2019) observes that such framings "actually proceed from and renew the logic and relations of the Doctrine of Discovery" (p. xv).

Beyond these general patterns, direct evocations of the frontier were revived in the post–World War II era by Vannevar Bush in his 1945 report *Science—The Endless Frontier: A Report to the President on a Program for Postwar Scientific Research*, which advocated for increased federal support for basic research on health, national security, and economic prosperity (Crow & Dabaras, 2012). For Bush, science represented the next frontier as a means to ensure US military advantage and economic expansionism, a dynamic that I consider further in chapter 4. Today, frontier language often circulates in discussions about universities' internationalization. Some land-grant schools have even declared themselves to be aspiring "world grant" or "global land-grant" institutions. The growth of land-grant institutions' international engagements is often articulated in relation to a concern about growing competition and fear that the US populace lacks sufficient education to conquer new "frontiers" of knowledge within the "knowledge economy" (Simon, 2009). This fear echoes concerns from 160 years ago about threats to US economic competitiveness and assertions of the role of higher education in ensuring national success, concerns that helped secure support for the first Morrill Act.

If we take the colonization of North America to be a condition of possibility for US democracy *and* capitalism, then US public higher education has always unfolded within a globalizing horizon premised on a colonial imaginary of inevitable expansion, possession, and dominance. The land-grant universities make this visible, and this is not just a matter of a distant past. As Byrd (2011) asserts, "The continued colonization of American Indian nations, peoples, and lands provides the United States the economic and material resources needed to cast its imperialist gaze globally" (p. 58). The shape-shifting frontier logics of the colonial US state, capital, and higher education are rearticulated over time, successively opening up new lands and communities for extraction, yet always requiring ongoing Indigenous dispossession "at home." In this sense, we should not be surprised that US universities today are being subject to, as well as subjecting others to, economic logics that seek to minimize costs and maximize profits, often in the name of the public good (Slaughter & Rhoades, 2004). This can be understood as only the most recent moment in a much longer history of public universities' dependence on *and* vulnerability to the dynamics of capital accumulation.

The Colonial Template of US Public Higher Education

In this chapter, I argue that a decolonial reading of land-grant historiography offers one way to reconsider the foundations of US public higher education that both challenges romanticized notions of a democratic past and invites us to consider the possibility of futures not premised on ongoing colonial relations. Reflecting on the contrasting and polarizing stories that are told about land-grant history, Peters (2013) suggests that, too often, people either lionize or demonize land-grant institutions. He suggests that both of these narratives have an element of truth but are in themselves insufficiently nuanced. Regarding the latter narrative, he suggests that "many who have condemned the land-grant system as an anti-democratic tragedy of colonialist oppression and environmental and cultural destruction will not believe that it has sometimes functioned in ways which were both democratic and democratizing. However, evidence supports the claim that it has (and still does)" (p. 349). While I agree with Peters's assertion that history is rarely simple, we cannot merely understand the benefits of land grants as occurring at the same time as its harms. We must rather understand that their greatest harm was the cost of their gifts. Specifically, these benefits were enabled through the granting of Indigenous lands that were stolen and redistributed by the US government at the expense of Indigenous communities. In this way, it is not so much that land grants were simultaneously destructive *and* democratic, but rather that the vision of democracy that underlay the grants was premised on destructive colonial violence. Then, as now, the sacrifice of certain human communities and the commodification of land itself were calculated as justifiable with regard to the public good that this sacrifice was perceived to produce.

This chapter is an effort to "story" the history of land grants in a way that challenges assumptions about the benevolence of public higher education and reframes commonsense analyses about the root causes of the contemporary predominance of capitalist logics in higher education.

The imperative of capital is to perpetually seek novel "frontiers" for exploitation, expropriation, and extraction in order to ensure continued growth, expansion, and circulation. Today, some of those new frontiers target the wealth and entitlements of the US middle-class and those who aspire to it, people who are increasingly subject to, in Harvey's (2005) terms, accumulation by dispossession. Many of these contemporary modes of accumulation are premised on the privatization of what was once deemed public—including higher education. However, these "public goods" also have a colonial history.

As David Lloyd and Patrick Wolfe (2016) suggest, the "public patrimonies of the modern liberal state that emerged from an earlier moment of enclosure and dispossession represent vast storehouses of capital, resources, services and infrastructure" (p. 109). On one hand, it makes sense that people would rush to defend public goods. Yet public goods, no less than private, were produced and are arguably still sustained through processes that violently commodified Black, Indigenous, and other colonized lives and lands. These lives and lands were transformed into white settler property, all of which has an exchange value and is still tradeable within the capitalist market. Thus, not only do these "public goods" themselves remain under perpetual threat of privatization in the service of capital accumulation, but they are also premised on the continued occupation of Indigenous lands and subjugation of Black lives. Each new frontier of capital does not replace but is rather layered on top of earlier and ongoing modes of racialized dispossession that have largely yet to be acknowledged, let alone interrupted and redressed in substantive ways. If this is the case, then it may not be sufficient to simply resist novel forms of capitalism in higher education. We will also need to consider the colonial relations at the root of existing institutions, and the underlying extractive economic logics that have always governed and subsidized our institutions.

While the narratives often told about the historical public good purpose of higher education and its relationship to the promises of US liberal democracy may be effectively mobilized for achieving immediate gains, they are inadequate for identifying, interrupting, and repairing the colonial harms that have been the cost of these promises. Tracing contemporary developments in US higher education back to a colonial template is only the first step in a much longer process of reimagining how those of us working and studying in higher education can challenge contemporary forms of economic rationalization. As part of this work, we will need to learn to identify and distinguish between different modes and intensities of violence, and to discern between the different possible efforts to interrupt and redress that violence.

In particular we might ask: If higher education is understood to be in the service of the "public good," but that public good is premised on dispossession and assimilation, then what does this say about the possible horizons of justice that the framing of "higher education for the public good" allows? How can we critique and contest current efforts to dismantle the "public good" of higher education without invisibilizing the colonial foundations of that "public good"? How can we link, for example, the explosion of student debt and the increased precarity of faculty to the foundational colonial logic of accumulation, while also recognizing that previous funding for students and faculty security was obtained largely at the expense of marginalized communities and the environment? Can we imagine a public good of higher education that does not presume the continuity of the United States as a colonial state? What might the public good look like after the restitution of stolen lands and lives? None of these questions has neat or easy answers; rather they invite us to hold space for the complex considerations and contradictions that arise in any efforts to imagine decolonial futures. In the following chapter, I consider these questions in relation to US higher education in the post–World War II era.

Chapter Four

The "Golden Age" of Higher Education and the Underside of the American Dream

Colleges and universities . . . give substance to the idea that anything is possible to those with talent, energy and motivation. This sense of society with limitless possibilities for all, largely (though not exclusively) through higher education, is what is usually meant by "the American dream."

—Martin Trow, 2000, p. 312

The itineraries of war would—along with civil rights gains—help to produce the conditions for expanding student-body populations.

—Roderick Ferguson, 2012, p. 49

The university was not free, people have always been paying for it, it was always being paid for. . . . Should the tuition be zero? Yes. Should we fight in support of the people fighting for the tuition to be free? Yes. But that's not the same as saying it was free, or public.

—Fred Moten, 2015

No era of US higher education is more celebrated than the post–World War II "golden age," which is usually dated from the mid-1940s to the mid-1970s. Some refer to the university of this era as the "Cold War university," not only because it was somewhat contemporaneous with the Cold War itself but also because the Cold War was a driving force in higher education during this time. Another candidate for naming is the "welfare state university," as Jeffrey J. Williams (2006) suggests, "because it instantiated the policies and ethos of the postwar, liberal welfare state" (p. 159). The United States emerged from World War II an unrivaled global economic and political superpower alongside the Soviet Union, as Europe was decimated by war and much of the rest of the world was still struggling for independence from colonialism. Cohen and Kisker (2010) describe the United States at this time as plainly "the most powerful nation on earth" (p. 187). A booming postwar economy resulted in growing opportunities for social mobility. Alongside strong economic growth, there was popular support for high taxes to fund social services, a holdover from two world wars and the New Deal. Close associations between higher education and the American Dream were cemented during the post–World War II era.

Jim Cullen (2003) identifies several interrelated varieties of the American Dream that have shifted over time but that all rest on the basic ideals of maximizing personal freedom, social mobility, and individual success. Stephen McNamee and Robert Miller Jr. (2005) emphasize the centrality of individualism in the Dream, according to which "we are 'masters of our fate.' We 'go our own way' and 'do our own thing.' For Americans, 'it all comes down to the individual'" (p. 5). They suggest that this Dream entails not only a general investment in progress, economic stability, and a secured futurity but also the fulfilment of specific goals, generally including "home ownership, improved life chances for children (especially defined now as sending children to college), opportunities to get rich, and a secure and comfortable retirement" (pp. 11–12).

Higher education is often understood as a central site for facilitating achievement of the American Dream. Brint and Karabel (1989) contend that by the early twentieth century, "vast inequalities of wealth, status, and power though there might be, the ladders of opportunity created by the new educational system helped the United States retain its national identity as a land of unparalleled opportunities for individual advancement" (p. 5). Simon Marginson (2016) suggests that by the postwar era, it was "widely agreed that the fairest and best means of sorting the continuing competition for social position and success were higher education and the nexus between education and professional occupations" (p. 15). The promise of higher education as a means of social mobility became a central part of the postwar social contract between (certain) US citizens and the US nation-state (Heller, 2016).

For many people, this era is understood as the high point of US higher education history. Within many contemporary critical higher education narratives that are oriented by the promise of continuous progress, the neoliberal present is understood as a temporary interruption of an otherwise linear path of perpetual improvement and expansion of opportunities. Boggs and colleagues (2019) note that "even when the tone or intentions are not explicitly nostalgic, the midcentury university exerts a powerful normative force on virtually all discourse about U.S. universities" (p. 6). Some mainstream texts do address the shortcomings and unfulfilled promises of this era, and historians are not necessarily shy about the role of US hegemony in enabling the expansion of higher education. For example, Cohen and Kisker title their chapter on this era "Mass Higher Education in the Era of American Hegemony." Yet most of these narratives fail to critically engage with the colonial conditions for or the imperial manifestations of US global power and its implications for higher education. Thus, for many the "golden age" continues to serve as a source of inspiration and proof that other funding models are possible—in particular, models through which publicly subsidized higher education serves as an equitable and accessible pathway to achieve (or at least pursue) the American Dream. This framing forecloses a more thorough examination of the *true* costs of postwar US abundance, including the costs of social mobility and the American Dream itself, which is what I offer in this chapter.

Examining these costs through a decolonial historiographic approach prompts a rethinking of common critical narratives about the neoliberal present and a reconsideration of contemporary efforts to "reclaim" and reinvigorate the American Dream. After all, regardless of the exact proposal, there is a general consensus that this dream is worth reclaiming and that higher education should have a central role in reclaiming it. Even as many admit that access to higher education alone is not enough to address growing inequality and diminishing job prospects, they remain deeply invested in defending higher education's position as a uniquely accessible pathway to social mobility and the American Dream.

For instance, Sara Goldrick-Rab (2016) acknowledges that "college alone will not conquer inequality. But this doesn't mean that we shouldn't be doing more to realize the ideals of meritocracy and equal opportunity" (p. 20). Recently, the Gates Foundation sponsored a series of articles in the *Chronicle of Higher Education* about the relationship between higher education and social mobility. In one such article, Karin Fischer (2019) writes, "Colleges may be an imperfect vehicle for ending inequality, a flawed agent of social mobility, a shaky ladder to the middle class. But it's the one we've got." From these perspectives, the American Dream is increasingly difficult to achieve but it remains an unmitigated good, and higher education is still the best, albeit an imperfect, pathway to achieve it.

Yet there are other ways of conceptualizing the American Dream. Kim TallBear (2019) analyzes the American Dream using a Dakota onto-epistemology that centers reciprocity.

She argues that the American Dream is "ever-constituted with deadly hierarchies of life" premised on ongoing violence, or what we might call the Colonial Nightmare (p. 25). According to TallBear, these hierarchies preclude and in fact are premised on denial of the Dakota imperative of "being in good relation" (p. 26). In her reading, racial subjugation, colonial expropriation, and ecological destruction do not occur *in spite of* the Dream but rather are what enables its realization. If this is the case, then, as TallBear suggests, "the American Dream in any form, whether White supremacist or 'progressive,' cannot be our guiding hope" (p. 36). She contrasts "American Dreaming," which is the promised expansion of colonially secured individual entitlements, with "caretaking relations" across species and generations (p. 26).

TallBear's analysis invites a deeper examination of the costs of the American Dream within US borders, as well as within a broader global context. In this chapter, I trace these two threads of the largely invisibilized costs of the American Dream (the local and the global) as they relate to higher education during the postwar era. I argue that high levels of public funding during higher education's "golden age" depended on a nationalistic militarism that sought to ensure the United States' political economic hegemony abroad (Labaree, 2016) and on a shallow promise of formal equality and inclusion at home that functioned to "explain (away) the inequalities of a still-racialized [and colonial] capitalism" (Melamed, 2006, p. 9). A decolonial reading of this era challenges the imperative that the American Dream must be the orienting horizon of hope and justice for higher education. For those still enchanted by the American Dream, the violences that subsidize it are generally either disavowed or acknowledged but understood to be the result of certain communities' *exclusio*n from the Dream. In contrast, a decolonial analysis suggests that violence is itself constitutive of the Dream and its accompanying promises. Thus, the primary crisis of the present is not "the unfinished business of the American Dream" (Beach, 2007, p. 149) but rather continued investment in the Dream itself, especially at a time when its sustainability may be increasingly untenable and harmful.

What were the conditions of possibility for the American Dream during the "golden age" of higher education? To answer this question, I first review mainstream narratives of the postwar era of US higher education, especially the narratives' emphasis on the expansion of higher education access and the accompanying promise of merit-based social mobility. Next, I address the limits of the "interest convergence" that structured the expansion of higher education access and social mobility (Bell, 1980). I do so by addressing how liberal inclusion efforts and progress narratives during this era offered an alibi for ongoing racialized socioeconomic hierarchies at home and for US political and economic hegemony abroad. In this way, a primary means of reproducing social and economic hierarchies during the postwar era became the *conditional inclusion of difference*, rather than the *outright exclusion of difference*, as it had been in previous eras. Conditional inclusion is a means by which access (including access to higher education and to the American Dream) is offered to formerly excluded groups, but only if they adhere to existing (whitestream) institutional norms and are not perceived to pose a threat to the continuity of business as usual. Beyond the domestic implications, I consider how the expansion of access, mobility, and opportunity "at home" was contingent upon the United States' commitment to ensuring its political and economic hegemony abroad. This commitment appeared in US higher education not only through Cold War–related funding priorities but also through universities' role as agents of international development initiatives. I also argue that, because it was rooted in the promise of infinite economic growth on a finite planet, expansion of the American Dream in this era was made possible only through intensified ecological destruction. From there I ask how things have shifted from the postwar era to the present, and address the limits of critiques of the present that are premised on romanticization of the so-called golden age and its promise of distributed affluence. I conclude by asking what other horizons of hope might be possible for higher education beyond the American Dream.

Mainstream Readings of the Postwar Era of US Higher Education

Growth is a primary theme of mainstream historical narratives about the "golden age" of higher education. As Cohen and Kisker (2010) write: "Enrollments, finances, institutions—all aspects of the system expanded" (p. 187). Lucas (2006) argues, "No mind-numbing litany of statistics . . . could do justice of itself to the growth of American higher education in the post-War period" (p. 252), but these statistics can nonetheless help illustrate it. For instance, "during the 30 years between 1949 and 1979, enrollments increased by more than nine million students, a growth of almost 400%" (Labaree, 2016, p. 110). By 1980, more than 11 million people were attending higher education institutions (more than one-third of the total youth population), in comparison to less than 1.5 million in 1940 (less than one-twelfth of the total youth population) (Kim & Rury, 2007). Access was expanded first for war veterans through the Servicemen's Readjustment Act, or GI Bill, and later for a much broader swath of students. The immediate postwar expansion of access to higher education was most dramatic among white men, but especially by the 1960s there was a significant increase in enrollment of white women and racialized men and women (Kim & Rury, 2007). The latter expansion was thanks in part to the US Supreme Court's *Brown v. Board of Education* ruling in 1954, which outlawed segregation in schools, and the *Florida ex Rel. Hawkins v. Board of Control* case in 1956, which formally extended the *Brown* ruling to higher education (Cohen & Kisker, 2010; Lucas, 2006).

Growth was also enabled by a significant expansion of federal funding, the colonial costs of which I elaborate later in this chapter. First came the GI Bill. Later, higher education research, construction of facilities and physical plant, and student scholarships and loans were expanded through the National Defense Education Act of 1958, as well as programs of the National Science Foundation and National Institutes of Health that same year, the Higher Education Facilities Act of 1963, and the Higher Education Acts of 1965 and 1972 (Lucas, 2006; Vandenberg-Daves, 2003). Ultimately, "overall federal funding during the Cold War for research of all types grew in constant dollars from $13 billion in 1953 to $104 billion in 1990, an increase of 700%" (Labaree, 2016, p. 110). As Lucas (2006) notes, following significant government support for higher education during World War II, "governmental policy was to continue and extend research grants and training contracts in the postwar period" (p. 252).

While much of this spending targeted specific goals, overall federal funding was broadly "defended by the argument that in strengthening colleges and universities, the government was bolstering the nation's defenses and helping to advance vital national policy objectives" (Lucas, 2006, p. 253). This notion of serving the US national interest by supporting the expansion of its global political and economic power was used not only to rationalize federal funding for research in higher education but also to enable more students to enroll. As Labaree (2016) notes, it was thought that universities "would educate the skilled workers needed by the Cold War economy, produce informed citizens to combat the Soviet menace, and demonstrate to the world the broad social opportunities available in a liberal democracy" (p. 101). In addition to federal funding, state governments also invested in the expansion of higher education, which resulted in an explosion in the number of community colleges (Thelin, 2004) and enabled schools to charge state residents little to no tuition.

Postwar Promises of Progress and Social Mobility

According to Christopher Newfield (2008), higher education was central to the postwar "vision of publicly funded social development [that] resulted in the creation of the first mass middle class in the United States" (p. 4). In Newfield's reading, conservative social and economic forces eventually led to today's privatized "corporate university" and interrupted postwar progress toward achieving a "multiracial mass democracy" (p. 23; see also Newfield, 2016). As Newfield suggests, higher education was framed in this era as a key site and driver of human progress and equality (see also Wellmon, 2021).

As Thelin (2004) points out, however, the growth in higher education access during this era was not solely the result of clearly coordinated policy decisions and progressive ideological commitments, or of a strong commitment to achieving racial and economic justice. For instance, the GI Bill came about not primarily from an effort to ensure access to education, but rather as a strategic means to "first . . . adjust wartime production to a peacetime economy, and second . . . to avert the civil strife of disgruntled military veterans who arrived home without good jobs or good prospects" (Thelin, 2004, p. 262). Enrolling returning soldiers in higher education was understood as just one prong of a comprehensive strategy to allow factories time to shift from manufacturing war provisions to making cars and other consumer goods. The economy could not yet absorb returning veterans as workers (Labaree, 2006). One projection warned that unemployment rates might reach 25 percent (McClanahan, 2017). The GI Bill included unemployment insurance, medical care, and counseling; covering tuition, books, and living expenses for higher education was more of an afterthought (Cohen & Kisker, 2010). Actual uptake of the educational dimensions of the GI Bill well exceeded the planners' expectations. In addition to absorbing returning soldiers who could not be immediately employed, universities also received surplus military supplies and buildings through the Surplus Property Act of 1944 (Lucas, 2006).

Ultimately, access to higher education came to be linked to social mobility in this era more than ever before. As Labaree (2016) notes, by the time high school enrollments became universal in 1940, for working-class families "the new zone of social opportunity became higher education" (p. 110). In the decades after World War II, popularity of the idea of merit-based socioeconomic sorting by way of higher education depended on two primary narratives: (1) the presumption that education was a form of human capital, which meant that more education meant both higher individual incomes and more society-level economic growth; and (2) the promise of equality of opportunity to compete for socioeconomic mobility (Marginson, 2016). Together these two narratives "told the public that higher education had a great role in making a just and efficient society in which merit conquers all" (Marginson, 2016, pp. 15–16).

These narratives contained some truth. According to Thomas Piketty, after the war, "inherited wealth lost much of its importance, and for the first time in history, perhaps, work and study became the surest routes to the top" (as cited by Marginson, 2016, p. 16). But while, according to Marginson (2016), the "meritocratic vision of equity and economy advancing together was irresistible to educational leaders" (p. 16), especially as it became a useful means to advocate for public funding and other forms of public support, in reality higher education alone was hardly so powerful. Social mobility was enabled not only through expanded access to higher education but also through a larger social context of economic growth and a corresponding increase in the quantity and quality of opportunities.

In this sense, higher education was as deeply dependent on and entangled with the expansion of liberal industrial capitalism and its violent underpinnings in the past as it is with neoliberal financial capitalism in the present, albeit in different ways. For instance, as Manuel Souto-Otero (2010) points out, "advances towards the meritocratic ideal . . . have not been the result of education alone but have depended upon the expansion in the number of highly paid jobs" (p. 399). Apart from a robust economy, the effects of two world wars and New Deal reforms were such that many previous fortunes were lost and higher taxes were in place to fund public services, all of which facilitated socioeconomic mobility (Marginson, 2016). The relative immobility of labor and capital during this time, as compared to the present, also meant employers were more likely to compromise with workers (and their unions) in relation to wages, benefits, and working conditions. These compromises were in many cases facilitated by state policy and enabled the expansion of positions within the middle class, which in turn meant expanded purchasing power in the era's commodity-driven capitalism (Mahmud, 2012).

Economic opportunities ultimately became closely tied to having a higher education credential. According to Jodi Vandenberg-Daves (2003), by the 1950s "college was beginning to become a crucial pathway to middle-class economic success in an economy increasingly characterized by corporations and large public bureaucracies" (p. 60). Indeed, the number of well-paid positions for credentialed professional workers grew during this time, and the "education premium" (i.e., the lifetime economic benefits of having a university degree) was strong (McClanahan, 2017). Nonetheless, in the first two decades after the war, the middle class (based on income levels) still included blue-collar, service, and trade workers (Newfield, 2008). Unions also bolstered the middle class (Harvey, 1990), and thus college was not the only viable means to achieve the American Dream (Goldrick-Rab, 2016). According to Newfield (2008), it was during the late 1970s, with the intensification of US deindustrialization, that college became "a dividing line between those who would succeed in the new postindustrial economy and those who, lacking the appropriate college credentials, would and should fail" (p. 4). And it was precisely around this time that public support for higher education began to falter.

Rather than examine the reasons for this declining support, which many others have analyzed in depth, in the remainder of this chapter I consider the underlying limits and costs of US higher education's postwar prosperity and the horizons of justice that guided it.

The Limits of Interest Convergence

Derrick Bell Jr. (1980) famously argued that the expansion of civil rights and the incorporation of Black people into whitestream institutions during the postwar era was only possible because of "interest convergence." Bell argued that the *Brown v. Board of Education* decision, which declared racial segregation unconstitutional, "cannot be understood without some consideration of the decision's value to whites, not simply those concerned about the immorality of racial inequality, but also those whites in policymaking positions able to see the economic and political advances at home and abroad that would follow abandonment of segregation" (p. 524). In this dynamic, rather than an authentic and enduring commitment to interrupt and redress systemic, historical, and ongoing harm, limited concessions toward racial justice are granted "from time to time" when it is "counted among the interests deemed important by the courts and by society's policymakers" (p. 523). While the question of what constitutes a community or social group's "interests" is hardly straightforward, homogenous, or uncontested, Bell's concept is useful for making sense of the US state's rationales and strategies for granting certain conditional concessions to Black and other marginalized peoples in the postwar era.

Viewed from the lens of interest convergence, those in power extended access to higher education and diversified its fields of study at least partly because they perceived these measures would serve US political and economic hegemony. Ferguson (2012) describes this shift as a "new ethical project for the American nation-state, one that would try to administer difference for the expansion of national power and territory" (p. 24). Thus, the price the US state exacted for granting civil rights and equal opportunity to Indigenous, Black, and other racialized peoples was their simultaneous inclusion in its Cold War agenda, including what can be described as its global imperialist designs. This agenda encompassed higher education as well. According to Labaree (2016),

> The government needed top universities to provide it with massive amounts of scientific research that would support the military effort. And it also needed all levels of the higher education system to educate the large numbers of citizens required to deal with the ideological menace [of communism]. We needed to produce the scientists and engineers who would allow us to compete with Soviet

technology. We needed to provide high-level human capital in order to promote economic growth and demonstrate the economic
superiority of capitalism over communism. And we needed to
provide educational opportunity for our own racial minorities
and lower classes in order to show that our system is not only effective but also fair and equitable. (p. 109)

Making the promise of inclusion in the American Dream conditional upon allegiance to US "interests" by those who were
"being included" in turn rationalized the disciplining of those
who were deemed "un-American." Many who rejected conditional inclusion and sought more radical changes "at home," as
well as those who challenged the United States' domineering
foreign policy abroad, were punished or even murdered by the
state (Ferguson, 2012; Mustaffa, 2017).

For Bell, the "gains" that result from changes rooted in interest convergence are always limited because the basic structures
of political and economic power do not shift and only changes
that do not fundamentally challenge those structures are enacted. And these already-limited gains can be reversed when
no longer deemed necessary—as started to occur by the end
of the "golden age."

The US nation-state's postwar embrace of conditional inclusion also functioned to further naturalize settler colonization by vindicating the supposed benevolence of the colonial
nation-state (Byrd, 2011). Framing justice as formal equality
functioned to include Indigenous peoples as an internal ethnic minority of the US state, rather than as sovereign political
nations seeking to end their occupation by the US state. In
fact, the postwar era saw significant federal efforts to further
the assimilation of Indigenous peoples. According to Dunbar-
Ortiz (2014), following World War II, "attitudes among the ruling class and Congress regarding Indigenous nations turned

from supporting autonomy to their elimination as peoples with a new regimen of individual assimilation" (p. 173). This policy change included the Termination Act of 1953, which ended federal recognition of more than one hundred tribes and thus also ended financial support for vital services such as health care, education, and fire departments (Dunbar-Ortiz, 2014). In 1956, the Indian Relocation Act encouraged Indigenous peoples to leave their reservations for cities, a program motivated largely by the desire to privatize millions of acres of still–collectively held lands.

From a decolonial perspective, the postwar era's "nonredistributive antiracism" served as ideological cover for the expansion of US political and economic power at home and abroad (Melamed, 2006, p. 4). This strategy, in turn, "enabled the normalizing violences of political and economic modernity to advance and expand" (p. 5). To the extent that access, rights, and opportunities were expanded for Black, Indigenous, and other racialized people, it required that they demonstrate their allegiance to the United States' colonial capitalist political and economic system and consent to be complicit in its violence. In higher education, Ferguson (2012) points to "the itineraries of war [that] would—along with civil rights gains—help to produce the conditions for expanding student-body populations" (p. 49). This close relationship between the expansion of war abroad and the expansion of rights "at home" severely limited the possible futures and imaginaries of justice that were legible to and sanctioned by whitestream institutions, including universities.

The Promise of Social Mobility as a Horizon of Justice

The promise of social mobility dominated the available horizons of justice in the postwar era, and apart from the fact that access to social mobility remained deeply racialized and classed, its limits and costs were largely obscured. While there is more than one way to define "equality of opportunity," according to Silva (2016), the most prevalent definitions conceptualize it as the "freedom to enjoy social mobility—not to be discriminated against in situations of competition" (p. 192). In other words, equality of opportunity is a promise that people's social and economic worth, power, and position will be determined by how well they can compete within an inherently stratified system—rather than being determined by other factors, such as one's race or the class into which one is born. In relation to higher education during the post–World War II era, there was an assumption that expanded access would create a more just society "because when individuals have equal opportunities to gain access to various avenues of employment and to participate more fully in the polity, the background from which they sprang becomes a weaker influence" (Cohen & Kisker, 2010, p. 294). In other words, more people would have the ability to pursue the American Dream. However, there were limits to the kinds of justice that such a system could enable, and its internal logic entailed damaging costs and consequences.

The postwar promise of merit-based social mobility as a horizon of justice posed no challenge to social and economic hierarchy itself—only a challenge to the notion that one's position in that hierarchy should be inherited (as it had been previously) and an assertation that one's position in that hierarchy should instead be based on hard work and talent, that is, merit (Baez, 2006). Within a capitalist system, the only way to achieve or maintain a middle- or upper-class socioeconomic position is to participate in and benefit from forms of exploitation and dispossession that are harmful (whether directly or indirectly) to both humans and other-than-human beings. In fact, the promise of equal opportunity to compete for mobility through one's merit and hard work justified, rather than challenged, the continuity of the hierarchical structure of the US system (and of the global system as well), since higher socioeconomic positions were ostensibly now earned, rather than inherited.* In this way, according to Marginson (2016), privilege was "modernized" or "meritified" (p. 17).

As a horizon of hope and justice, "equality of opportunity to compete for social mobility" is distinct from horizons premised on transforming the basic structures of societies and institutions in ways that might dismantle, redress, or otherwise radically reimagine existing racial and economic hierarchies and regimes of accumulation on both local and global scales. While many have demonstrated that the US system of meritocracy is imperfect, and others have sought to reimagine what counts as merit (Guinier, 2015), few question the basic premise of a merit-based distribution of unequal social positions and rewards. As Benjamin Baez (2006) points out, one reason is the general belief that the only alternative is a system in which one's position and status are inherited (i.e., a hereditary system). The promise of social mobility through meritocracy also rests on the assumption "that social inequality is an unavoidable consequence of a complex society" (Liu, 2011, p. 391), and thus the best that one can hope for is greater opportunity to compete for mobility within it.

In this way, the promise of achieving merit-based rewards through higher education helps to legitimize US society's high degree of stratification and the persistence of poverty and exploitation within it: inequality appears acceptable given the

---

* Indeed, this was a primary critique of Michael Young, who coined the term "meritocracy" in his satirical 1958 book, *The Rise of the Meritocracy, 1870–2033: An Essay on Education and Society*, as an effort to foretell the ways that supposedly objective measures of "merit" would become the new means through which to reproduce and rationalize social inequality.

possibility of social mobility. For instance, Brint and Karabel (1989) argue that part of what makes inequalities of wealth and power tolerable in the United States is widespread adherence to the claim that everyone has "a chance to advance as far as his ability and ambition would take him" (p. 9). Thus, Trow (2000) writes, "through its role in fostering social mobility and the belief in a society open to talents, American higher education legitimates the social and political system" (p. 313).

Indeed, the postwar formalization of the promise of equality of opportunity can be understood through a decolonial lens as an effort to legitimize the US social and political system on both a domestic and a global stage. In the post–World War II era, it was no longer tenable for the United States to continue condoning formal inequality and racial segregation. The nation-state sought to both distance itself from Nazism and position itself as a more righteous and egalitarian global superpower than its competing superpower, the Soviet Union (Bell, 1980; Dudziak, 2011; Ferguson, 2012; Labaree, 2016; Melamed, 2006). Various antiracist and anticolonial social movements, both local and global, sought to transform or dismantle white, Western geopolitical and economic power (Melamed, 2006). The desires and strategies of these movements varied, ranging from those more focused on the expansion of civil rights and democratized economic opportunity, to those more committed to deeper forms of societal transformation, sometimes articulated as liberation and decolonization. The promise of equality of opportunity to compete for social mobility sought to appease at least some of these demands, especially antiracist demands in the domestic context, while neutralizing the more radical ones and ultimately re-entrenching white and US supremacy and capitalist forms of political economy. In the context of US higher education, this approach became a matter of "trying to redirect originally insurgent formations and deliver them to the normative ideas and protocols of state, capital, and academy" (Ferguson, 2012, p. 8).

Racial Liberalism and "Minority Incorporation" in Higher Education

While certain rights and forms of access were expanded in the postwar United States, Jodi Melamed (2006) argues, "racial privilege and discipline evolve[d] to take on new forms" (p. 2), because the promise of "racial equity was not an end in itself" but rather a means to secure white and US political and economic interests (p. 6). By framing racial injustice as a failure to include certain communities, rather than as endemic to the political, economic, and epistemic structure of the US nation-state, the government could shift away from more blatant forms of white supremacy and toward what Melamed (2006) calls "racial liberalism." Racial-liberal approaches to racial injustice claimed to repudiate racism but without doing much to redress or transform the accumulated effects of centuries of colonialism, slavery, and segregation. Racial liberalism was enacted through formal recognitions of existing racial inequalities without substantive accompanying commitments to interrupt those inequalities by redistributing power and resources within existing institutions or enacting restitution and reparations for legacies of racial and colonial violence in ways that could lead to entirely different social and economic structures.

Racial liberalism was also underpinned by an effort to link antiracism with nationalism so as to produce "a liberal symbolic framework for race reform centered in abstract equality, market individualism, and inclusive civic nationalism" (Melamed, 2006, p. 2). When the US nation-state declared itself to be officially *against* racism, it paradoxically made it difficult for further antiracist critiques or demands for alternative forms of social, political, and economic organization to be viewed as legitimate (Silva, 2014). Within this dynamic one can identify the paradox of looking to the state to secure rights and justice, as "the state guarantees liberal capitalism and, therefore, the racialized exclusions on which it depends, assuring that there will be widespread exploitation in the midst of opportunity" (Ferguson, 2012, p. 170). Sara Ahmed (2012) critiques the "non-performativity" of formal commitments to antiracism that result in little or no substantive changes to systemically racist institutions. These nonperformative postwar commitments to antiracism allowed the continuation of racist, colonial, and extractive modes of social organization and education to be slipped in the back door of institutions, including institutions of higher education, despite the "welcome" sign now hanging out front.

By the 1960s, there was a "promise of minority incorporation into social, political, economic, and academic realms" (Ferguson, 2012, p. 4), but this promise was hardly straightforward or operationalized without strings attached. By ensuring that a greater number of Indigenous, Black, and other racialized students could formally access higher education, universities could disavow their legacies of racism, white supremacy, and colonial expropriation while often effectively reproducing and even naturalizing race-based differences and outcomes (Ferguson, 2012; Melamed, 2006; Silva, 2001). Social and economic hierarchies in higher education were thus reproduced through the conditional inclusion of difference, which replaced the reproduction of hierarchies through the outright exclusion of difference. Ferguson (2012) describes the Second Morrill Act (1890) and the subsequent founding of several Black land-grant institutions in the South as an early effort to "designate the American university as the location to resolve national contradictions over the inclusion and exclusion of minoritized subjects" (p. 86); in the postwar era, this contradiction-resolving role of the university was amplified.

For instance, while the report *Higher Education for American Democracy* (President's Commission on Higher Education, 1947), commissioned by President Harry Truman, recognized the problem of racial inequality, it also touted a proud narrative of continuous national improvement toward "equity, justice, and freedom for all" so that more people might eventually become "participants in the benefits of social and cultural progress" (pp. 12–13). "The only possible solution" to educational inequalities, the president's commission suggested, "is . . . to raise economic and cultural levels in our less advanced areas" (p. 32). This progress-oriented approach to education repeated colonial narratives of pathologization and deficiency in racialized and Indigenous communities and made their inclusion in universities and other whitestream institutions conditional upon adherence to a developmental path of "acculturation" or "racial uplift" into a supposedly universal (i.e., white middle-class) realm of culture and knowledge. It reproduced the notion of whiteness as the height of human development. From this perspective, people found themselves in lower economic positions because they lacked skills and capacities, rather than because of capitalist exploitation and expropriation. Thus, responsibility for racism and poverty was displaced from those who benefited from them to those who were harmed.

Postwar racial liberalism framed racism as the result of ignorance, which had significant implications that reproduced the presumption of white peoples' cultural and epistemic supremacy. "Ignorance" in this framing was understood as the lack of supposedly universal knowledge on the part of racialized peoples (because it had been previously denied to them) and the lack of nonbiased knowledge about cultural difference on the part of racist white people (Melamed, 2006). If ignorance were the primary problem, then the solution to both sides of this equation would be more (higher) education. Contrary to this assumption, decolonial analyses find that white supremacy and coloniality are not primarily attributable to a lack of knowledge or information, but are rather built into the grammar of the modern onto-epistemological system and its subjectivities (Silva, 2011; Wynter, 2003). If this is the case, then inviting more racialized people into this system is unlikely to interrupt white supremacy, and providing more information about racialized communities to white people will not interrupt colonial violence.

This line of thinking was not lost on Indigenous, Black, or other racialized students and faculty who were increasingly granted access to higher education by the early 1960s. Not satisfied with simply being included, some fought to transform universities to be more relevant to their experiences and communities. In particular, the convergent impact of student movements and wider social coalitions led some institutions to permit the institutionalization of interdisciplinary ethnic and gender studies as a means to signal their commitment to equity and universality. In this way, racial liberalism and its promise of conditional inclusion did create some strategic opportunities for institutional transformation, but they also meant that "student movements and student demands had to negotiate with and appeal to prevailing institutional structures" (Ferguson, 2012, p. 16). For example, Mitchell (2011) notes, "Yale's BSA [Black Student Alliance] had found a strategy to trap universities within the rhetoric of their putative universality. If it was the task and the responsibility of the liberal university to produce universal knowledge, then the failure to include blacks fully within the scope of universality could only be seen as its institutional failure" (p. 102). The limit of this tactic is that universality was then framed as part of the solution to racial injustice, and thus it became more difficult to see how it was also part of the problem. In general, white social, political, and epistemological norms continued to be deemed "universal" by the university, and anything outside these norms was considered "particular" and therefore devalued. Roderick Ferguson (2012) describes this as a "constitutive contradiction within the student movements—their simultaneous estrangement from and appeals to institutional power" (p. 16). Decolonial critiques suggest that the institutionalization of ethnic studies fields was therefore not evidence of universities' benevolent nature, but rather proof of their eagerness to co-opt radical critiques as part of their "instrumentalizing calculus of 'diversification'" (Mitchell, 2015, p. 86). The resulting curricular changes were thus both "disruptive *and* recuperative of existing institutions" (Ferguson, 2012, p. 17), as "minoritized subjects and practices" were permitted to enter "on the condition that they be regulated" (p. 190).

Postwar racial liberalism formed the foundation upon which contemporary mainstream diversity, equity, and inclusion (DEI) efforts are formulated in higher education, albeit today with a multicultural neoliberal (rather than racial liberal) orientation (Melamed, 2006). The mainstreaming of racial liberalism was hardly a threat to the continuity of white advantage as the expansion of access to previously excluded communities was accompanied by an underside of new mechanisms for racialized stratification. Yet the racial dimensions of this stratification could be denied because it was established under the banner of equal opportunity and merit. This expansion of stratification is clearly evident in the widely celebrated California Master Plan and its three tiers of higher education access (community colleges, state colleges, and universities).

Clark Kerr, who served as the chancellor of the University of California at Berkeley and president of the University of California, was one of the key developers of the California Master Plan for Higher Education, released in 1960. Kerr (1978) argued that expanded opportunity to access higher education could "create a base for social gradations in a democracy that reduce the sharp distinctions (and potential resentments) between the educated classes and the uneducated masses, that help to soften class distinctions and class antagonisms" (p. 266). At the same time, Kerr noted that the Master Plan was never intended to diminish social differences or eliminate inequality of outcomes. He firmly defended the merit-based hierarchy that was built into the plan and its three tiers of higher education access. He argued that those with more merit should be given better training, as "elite higher education is needed by and useful to society ... even in a Rawlsian world of more perfect 'justice'" (p. 269). Kerr clarified:* "I considered the vast expansion of the community colleges to be the first line of defense for the University of California as an institution of international academic renown. Otherwise the University was either going to be overwhelmed by large numbers of students with lower academic attainments or attacked as trying to hold on to a monopoly over entry into higher status" (p. 267).

For Kerr, the California Master Plan was thus designed to maintain social hierarchy.[†] Brint and Karabel (1989) similarly argue that it was the growth of community colleges that "introduced a new tier into the existing hierarchy" of US higher education and US society in general (p. 6). While Kerr does not directly invoke race in the above statement, his claim about the need for "defense" against the threatening figure of

---

*I thank Amy Scott Metcalfe for bringing my attention to this passage.

[†] The irony is that Kerr was eventually ousted by then–California governor Ronald Reagan, who viewed him as too radical.

the "overwhelming" masses of undeserving, underprepared, and thereby polluting students is an implicitly racialized and classed one. The Master Plan was designed such that, as overall access to higher education increased, so did institutional stratification, resulting in revised hierarchies that were now rationalized through the notion of merit-based social and economic rewards (Marginson, 2016).

Kerr's evocation of the need for the "defense" of elite higher education echoes the era's rationale for expanding funding of higher education in the name of *national* defense. In fact, the golden age's shine was largely subsidized through efforts to defend US global hegemony. In this way, in addition to the preservation of racial disparities at home, it is important to consider how the postwar era intensified global disparities between the United States and the rest of the world—disparities that US higher education institutions both benefited from and were called upon to reinforce.

The Cold War University as a Site for Securing US Hegemony

The fact that the promise of social mobility in the postwar United States was conditional upon economic growth points to a considerable cost of this promise: in order for the United States and its citizens to benefit from economic growth, it had to ensure its continued political and economic hegemony within a global capitalist system, which entailed both continued (racialized) economic exploitation at home and continued assertation of US political and economic power abroad. Charisse Burden-Stelly (2020) notes that the expansion of US empire from its domestic to a global context, especially after World War I and even more so following World War II, produced benefits and luxuries for US citizens—especially poor and middle-class white citizens—that would otherwise have been unavailable to them.

Paul Kramer (2016), citing Rosenberg, notes that even before World War II, the United States had developed "many of the state-corporate arrangements" that would enable its postwar global economic dominance, including: "a promotional state oriented toward aiding US corporate expansion into foreign markets, American companies abroad as instruments of US foreign policy, and developmentalist ideologies that fused capitalism and social evolution under the banner of American exceptionalism" (p. 335). The United States was uniquely positioned to enter previously closed or saturated markets in Europe and elsewhere, as well as to import raw materials from (former) colonies. Economic hegemony was also cemented through US leadership in establishment of the International Monetary Fund (IMF) and World Bank in 1944 at Bretton Woods.

According to Sam Gindin and Leo Panitch (2012), the United States "succeeded in integrating all the other capitalist powers into an effective system of coordination under its aegis" (p. 13). This led some to designate the United States as the new global imperial and neocolonial power, which remained at the same time dependent on the ongoing colonization of Indigenous lands "at home" (Byrd, 2011; Morgensen, 2011).

However, especially for white US citizens, the postwar global division of labor appeared natural within the persistent colonial hierarchy of humanity that placed white people at the top (Silva, 2015). The United States' presumptive benevolence, exceptionalism, and moral leadership were also thought to justify its position (Melamed, 2006). In 1953 Kerr called on US universities to support the "continuing upward movement of our Western civilization" (as cited by Wellmon, 2021, n.p.).

While Williams's (2006) designation of postwar higher education as the "welfare state university" is appealing, decolonial critiques might describe it instead as a "welfare-warfare state university." This would follow Ruth Wilson Gilmore's (2007) description of the "welfare-warfare state" in this era, in which the more democratized but still racialized capitalist production and distribution of wealth depended on white colonial supremacy at home and imperial militarism abroad. According to David Stein (2016), "From 1946–1974, defense spending never dipped below 30% of the [US] federal budget and reached almost 70% in some years" (p. 82). This spending can be understood in relation to the development of what Senator William Fulbright (1972) called the "military-academic-industrial complex" during this era, connecting universities' involvement in the production of military technologies, weapons, intelligence, and capitalist profits (Cohen & Kisker, 2010).

Must We Love the Bomb?

Labaree (2016) writes, "If World War II was good for American higher education, the Cold War was a bonanza" (p. 109). For instance, as Cohen and Kisker (2010) report, "in 1950 federal support for research totalled around $140 billion, most of it for projects related to the nation's war-making capacity, a sizeable portion going to the universities, and much to faculty members soliciting support for their own studies" (p. 274). Cohen and Kisker suggest that the Cold War was fought primarily not with traditional armies or weaponry but with "inventions and new technologies" that depended on the kinds of scientific expertise and innovations that many universities were happy to sell (p. 275). And Henry Heller (2016) argues that public spending on military research had significant spillover effects, generating "a constant flow of new knowledge and techniques that fostered the productivity and competitiveness of American industry" (p. 29).

While much military-focused research was located in science and technology fields, social sciences and humanities disciplines also supported the US Cold War apparatus of knowledge and power (Barkan, 2013; Cumings, 1997; de Wit, 2002; Kamola, 2014; Paik, 2013). According to Heller (2016), it was in these disciplines "that hegemonic ideologies and knowledges were created which justified continued dominance of the capitalist system under overall American command" (p. 42). These efforts also continued the colonial tradition of knowledge production oriented toward "mak[ing] the whole of the world coherent for the West by bringing all we knew of it within the imperial order of things" (Willinsky, 1998, p. 11). This knowledge could then be instrumentalized to serve US national interests.

The creation of "area studies" exemplifies the entanglements between universities' knowledge production and the imperial ends of the US nation-state. Nominally focused on different regions of the world, area studies "developed out of the recruitment of intellectuals in the service of the state" starting during World War II (Paik, 2013, p. 5). The National Defense Education Act of 1958 included federal funds for area studies (Paik, 2013), and several major foundations, including Carnegie, Ford, and Rockefeller, also provided funding for area studies research. The idea was for researchers to "collect and analyze information and data which may bear on national security" (Cumings, as cited by Paik, 2013, p. 6). Despite claims that its researchers maintained a formal separation from the state and its interests, many area studies scholars and centers had various ties with the FBI, CIA, and the military, and its areas of focus and paradigms of study were significantly shaped by US military interests (Paik, 2013).

Certainly, there was criticism of and resistance to the mobilization of scholarship toward militarized ends (Paik, 2013), just as there was resistance to universities' conditional, nonredistributive approaches to antiracism. Often, scholars, students, and social movements articulated these two sets of critiques together as they made connections between historical and ongoing racial and colonial violence at home and abroad (Ferguson, 2012). This was perhaps most clearly evident in the student movements that arguably reached their zenith in 1968, especially the Third World Liberation Front (Paik, 2013). However, scholarship that made these connections was disciplined, devalued, and underfunded by universities, the federal government, and private foundations (Chatterjee & Maira, 2014; Paik, 2013), and demands rooted in these critiques were often met with force or were compromised and deradicalized in the process of their institutionalization (Ferguson, 2012; Mitchell, 2016).

If the post–World War II iteration of the American Dream depended on US global political and economic hegemony, this reliance was assured not only through deterrence, the generation of "global goodwill," and the production of knowledge in the service of expanding and shoring up US power, but also through various US military and political interventions, particularly in countries that either openly criticized the United States or established some form of communist or socialist government. Such intervention entailed influencing elections in Indonesia, Lebanon, and Chile and covertly supporting coups and assassinations in Iran, Chile, Guatemala, the Congo, Indonesia, Brazil, and elsewhere, as well as waging outright "hot" wars in Korea and Vietnam and various military actions and campaigns in locations throughout Asia, Latin America, and the Middle East (Dunbar-Ortiz, 2014; Grossman, n.d.).

Even those mainstream higher education history narratives that link high levels of public funding to the Cold War rarely attend critically to the war's harmful effects, especially outside the West. For instance, Cohen and Kisker (2010) describe the postwar era as one characterized by "the search for

security in a world made unstable by collapsing colonial regimes; the rise of the Soviet Union as a military power; the
increase in nationalist expectations among ethnic and linguis-
tic groups in Europe, Africa, and the Pacific; and the fearsome
new military capabilities, headed by atomic weaponry"
(p. 187). While they do not directly condone this "search for
security," they also do little to problematize how security was
used as justification for US militarism in the era. For instance,
"the fearsome new military capabilities, headed by atomic
weaponry," were spearheaded by the United States' own development and use of that weaponry. Arguably, the United States'
efforts to "search for security" during this era—aided in many
cases by research produced in universities—tended to make
the rest of the world (especially non-Western nations) more
insecure.

Newfield (2016) suggests that federal funding for military
research in higher education in this era was driven by a concern
for the public good: "Universities lost money on this research, . . .
[but] this was a public service that they were expected to per-
form, and public universities could afford to subsidize it with
Cold War levels of state funding" (p. 40). This framing down-
plays how the United States subsidized the domestic public
good through US militarism abroad. "Ironically," Sheila Slaughter and Gary Rhoades (2004) note, "the 'social contract' between university science and society, of which research was
the cornerstone, was built on military funding that flowed
from the cold war" (p. 47). From a decolonial reading, however, this postwar funding structure aligns with the historical
tendency for US higher education funding to be enabled
through state and state-sanctioned violence. This structure appears ironic only if one starts with a baseline assumption of
higher education's benevolence and exceptionalism.

Also acknowledging the central role of the Cold War in prompting generous federal higher education funding in this era, Labaree (2016) actually critiques nostalgic narratives about the golden age in arguing that there is likely no going back to similar levels of public funding. He therefore suggests, "We should just say thanks to the bomb for all that it did for us and move on" (p. 115). Although Labaree's use of "the bomb" here serves as a metonym for the Cold War as a whole and makes wry reference to the dark comedy *Dr. Strangelove or: How I Stopped Worrying and Learned to Love the Bomb*, this statement nonetheless papers over the ethical and political accountability that exists in relation to the very real violence of the Cold War in general and of nuclear bombs in particular. Notably, many university researchers were involved in the development of the atomic bomb (Cohen & Kisker, 2010). Hundreds of thousands of Japanese people were killed or otherwise harmed by the dropping of atomic bombs in Hiroshima and Nagasaki at the end of World War II; Diné (Navajo) peoples continue to live with the toxic legacy of uranium mining in their territory; and enduring environmental contamination from nuclear testing throughout the Pacific Ocean has resulted in high levels of cancer and other harmful health outcomes in the Marshall Islands and elsewhere (Cornum, 2018).

US Universities as Agents of International Development

Postwar US higher education also played a key role in securing US global hegemony through "international development" projects. As part of the nation-state's self-appointed global leadership role, universities offered conditional political and economic support in the form of technical assistance and educational "capacity building" programs in the Global

South as a form of development aid. These programs not only presumed a universal, teleological, Western-led vision of human progress and social change; they were also largely driven by US self-interest—even as the programs were often framed as examples of the US benevolence. Kramer (2016) suggests that these efforts' intended effect was to create, often undemocratically, large-scale social, political, and economic transformations in recipient countries to ensure the alignment of "foreign states and societies with U.S. geopolitical and political-economic goals" (p. 338).

According to Gilbert Gonzalez (1982), by 1967 the US Agency for International Development (USAID) "established 134 contracts with 71 universities and institutes to carry out research and planning for the implementation of reform in 40 countries" (p. 332). He cites the 1961 Atcon Report, prepared for the US State Department, which analyzed education in Latin America, with a specific focus on university reforms. The proposed reforms echoed some of the views of US higher education reformers like Kerr who believed that (Western-style) universities were necessary to ensure continuous progress, which in turn was rooted in depoliticized notions of liberal governance, a narrow focus on scientific and technical knowledge, and capitalist economic growth (Wellmon, 2021). However, the US government did not support broad higher education public funding in other countries, instead advocating forms of privatization that it only later began to implement at home.

The Atcon Report suggested that universities in Latin America (1) were "incapable of producing the social prerequisites for development" and were responsible "for producing agents whose actions led to the reproduction of an underdeveloped and politically unstable society" (Gonzalez, 1982, p. 335); (2) needed to become depoliticized institutions (especially in relation to student political activism); and (3) had to reorient their curricula in order to emphasize the training of managers and technicians to run economic projects. To illustrate the effect of the Atcon Report, Gonzalez shows how the "Basic Plan for Colombian Higher Education," developed at the University of California Berkeley, sought to ensure that Colombia's educational system "would provide a support system for the hemispheric division of labor" that benefited the United States (p. 341). The Basic Plan sought, among other things, to implement tuition fees, decrease public funding, and make the university increasingly indebted to banks and other financial lenders. Gonzalez describes these shifts and the plan itself as a form of "imperialist modernization" that for many years was nonetheless successfully resisted by Colombian students and professors.

Another example of universities' direct implication in securing US hegemony is the US State Department–funded anticommunist operations in South Vietnam run by Michigan State University professors and researchers from 1955 to 1962 (Kuzmarov, 2009). The project was funded as part of an aid package from the United States to South Vietnam (Michigan State University Vietnam Group Archive, n.d.). Jeremy Kuzmarov (2009) argues that these programs "were conceived as mechanisms for advancing American strategic interests" and, among other effects, "resulted in the spread of political repression and violence" by developing intelligence networks that were then used to target and repress dissenters, militarizing the South Vietnamese police, and demonizing political dissent, especially communism and grassroots mobilization (p. 192). At times the researchers collaborated directly with the CIA (Johnson, 2018).

The other side of the US goal of stemming the spread of communism was expanding capitalist (specifically US) markets

(Kramer, 2016; Silva, 2015; Wynter & McKittrick, 2015). Recruitment of international students was considered a form of development aid that would prepare future leaders of recently decolonized nations while ensuring their sympathies with the United States specifically and with capitalism more generally (Kramer, 2009). These recruitment efforts were largely directed at political and economic elites with no guise of ensuring "equal opportunity" in the selection process (Kramer, 2009) and often without covering the cost of their studies (Boggs, 2013). Nonetheless, within the frame of American exceptionalism this was characterized as a form of charity—by enabling the spread of the West's supposedly universal values, prosperity, and enlightenment. The export, imposition, and naturalization of the capitalist economic system had more than social implications. Below I review the ecological implications of ensuring capitalist economic growth at the expense of exploiting and polluting the environment.

The Ecological Costs of Economic Growth

US higher education's promotion of postwar economic growth through international development and other means had considerable ecological implications. Following formal decolonization in much of the world, many newly independent nation-states were incorporated into a still-Western-dominated global political economic system through the promise of industrial development. As Sylvia Wynter writes (in Wynter & McKittrick, 2015), within the framework of development, the economic poverty of newly decolonized nations was viewed not as the product of centuries of slavery and colonization that in turn warranted forms of restitution or reparations from European powers, but rather as the product of a "lack" of development. Within this framework, Wynter further argues, the only way to "become *un-underdeveloped*, was by following the plans of both their and our economists," most of the latter of whom had been educated in Western institutions of higher education (p. 20; emphasis in original).

The dominant idea of development attributed so-called developing countries' poverty to their earlier position on a Western-led evolutionary path toward prosperity and universal knowledge (Rostow, 1960). Emphasis was thus placed on following the example of "developed" countries such as the United States. According to Ilan Kapoor (2014), this relationship of tutelage was premised on the notion of a clean break with the most recent histories of colonialism: "Cold war politics demanded the construction of a strong and irreproachable West, cleansed of any suggestion of complicity in Third World 'underdevelopment'" (p. 1127). The idea also crowded out possibilities for alternative imaginaries of development, including socialist or grassroots development, or alternatives to development itself (Santos, 2006).

Given the rhetoric of freedom surrounding World War II as well as varied antiracist and anticolonial movements, formal exclusion of non-European peoples and unfettered resource extraction was no longer tenable. Much as racial liberalism offered a means of US domestic racialization by other means, development offered a mode of US global imperialism by other means. But in addition to reproducing colonial relations, development also supported not only the reproduction but also the expansion of a global capitalist economic system built on industrialization, unending economic growth, and extraction of so-called natural resources—and, thus, ecological destruction.

Wynter posits that the adoption of developmentalist frameworks by newly independent nation-states—in particular, through industrialization—is linked to a spike in the acceleration of global warming. Indeed, several scholars describe the onset of the "Great Acceleration" in 1950 as leading to increases in economic growth, population, petroleum consumption, international travel, urbanization, and consumption (Steffen et al., 2011). The impacts of this acceleration on production and consumption and, thus, resource use were enormous (Steffen et al., 2015). The post–World War II era therefore marked a turning point for the planet's ecology.

Will Steffen and colleagues (2011) note that the Great Acceleration was fueled in part by the establishment of US-dominated supranational institutions (such as the World Bank and IMF) that supported post–World War II economic recovery and growth and reorganized the global economic system. From 1955 to 1970, "the world witnessed the fastest period of economic growth ever" (United Nations, 2017, p. 26). Alongside these rapid economic shifts came the growth of new technologies (alongside growing numbers of university-educated scientists who could develop them), most of which required "the cheap energy provided by fossil fuels" (Steffen et al., 2011, p. 850). The expansion of wealth that the Great Acceleration enabled, Jason Hickel (2019) argues, "has come at the expense of an extraordinary depletion of the living world" (p. 64). These ecological consequences have included rising "carbon dioxide levels, mass extinctions, and the widespread use of petrochemicals including plastic" (Davis & Todd, 2017, pp. 763–764), alongside radioactivity from atomic bombs.

Steffen and colleagues (2011) also note that with the Great Acceleration, "partnerships among government, industry and academia became common, further driving innovation and growth" (p. 850). Thus, it is not unreasonable to deduce that the economic growth that allowed for the expansion of US higher education, and that US higher education in turn supported, has had considerable ecological costs. Furthermore, although postwar development meant that many other (predominantly nonwhite) nations were producing more carbon, the whiter, wealthier subsets of humanity have made a disproportionate ecological impact by externalizing the costs of their particular way life and development onto other humans and other-than-human beings.

In fact, the United States is calculated to have produced far more carbon throughout history (since 1750) than any other nation-state (Carbon Brief, as cited by Brasuell, 2019). Still, today, "the ever-increasing energy consumption habits of the United States present a threat to the planet's ability to sustain collectively human life, and are located in infrastructures of expropriation and encroachment on Indigenous lands in North America and beyond" (Karuka, 2019, p. 33). Beyond attending to the unevenly distributed responsibilities that those in the United States—especially white settlers—bear for the contemporary climate crisis, including the responsibilities of universities themselves for contributing to this crisis (Stein, 2020), Wynter suggests we can no longer afford to rely on the same mode of knowing and being that "has led to our now major collective human predicament: the ongoing process of global warming, climate instability, and economic catastrophe" (in Wynter & McKittrick, 2015, p. 20). Thus, the postwar university does not offer a viable model for a more just and sustainable higher education future.

Crumbling Postwar Promises

Williams (2006) refers to the university of today as "'the post–welfare state university' because it carries out the policies and ethos of the neo-conservative dismantling of the welfare state" (p. 159). According to Williams, whereas "the welfare state university held a substantial role in redistribution; the post–welfare state university holds a lesser role in redistribution and a more substantial role in private accumulation" (p. 198). Following

Gilmore's (2007) designation of the contemporary state as a "workfare-warfare" state, a move away from the preceding "welfare-warfare" state, we might consider the university of the present as a "workfare-warfare university." Gilmore notes that the welfare-warfare state "began to lose its legitimacy to manage crisis, and thus reproduce itself and endure, . . . in the mid-to-late 1960s" (p. 79). This delegitimation led to a shift away from economic redistribution; lowering tax rates, for example, reduced the funds available to be redistributed. Despite the shift away from welfare provisions, including higher education funding, the warfare piece remained in place—both domestically, through a massive expansion of prisons and related carceral institutions, and globally, through the perpetual expansion of the United States' military presence and its accompanying enormous annual budgets.

While the Cold War may be over, the War on Terror has continued for over twenty years. If US global militarism and imperialism were part of the price of public support for higher education during the golden age, we can see the extension of this legacy in universities following 9/11 (Paik, 2013). Horace Campbell and Amber Murrey (2014) note that, for example, the production of social science knowledge for US national security departments today, "and the use of such knowledge to refine and inform intelligence missions on the African continent" (p. 1461), is a continuation of strategic research in the region since the decolonization era. Meanwhile, scholars who critique US imperialism are still subject to reprisal and repression (Chatterjee & Maira, 2014).

Despite the abiding military entanglements of higher education, federal funding for military-related research and training today tends to take the form of more targeted investments. In contrast to the Cold War era, broad public investments in higher education are not understood as necessary to winning the War on Terror or to bolstering the "nation's defenses" or "advanc[ing] vital national policy objectives" (Lucas, 2006, p. 253). Students are expected to pay for more of their own educational costs. It was precisely at the moment when college became increasingly necessary to maintaining or obtaining a place in the US middle class that states started to spend less on their public higher education systems, tuition started to rise, and federal funding started to shift from student grants to student loans. These changes reflected the shift from a "welfare" to a "workfare" state, even as the "warfare" remains constant.

As it was during the golden age, socioeconomic stratification continues to shape US higher education. For instance, Tressie McMillan Cottom (2017) argues that elite institutions benefit from the expansion of the "subsector of high-risk postsecondary schools and colleges," such as for-profit institutions, that "absorbs all manner of vulnerable groups" (p. 11). She argues that this arrangement preserves the guise of educational opportunity as an engine of social equality while it frames unequal outcomes as the product of individual talent and effort (i.e., merit). Disproportionate numbers of low-income and racialized students attend for-profit institutions, with low graduation rates and some of the highest student loan default rates (Soederberg, 2014). Rising tuition increasingly affects middle-class families, too (Goldrick-Rab, 2016). Yet Philip Brown, Hugh Lauder, and David Ashton (2010) suggest that, even as we "confront the prospect of a high-skill, low-wage work force" (p. 147), higher education is nonetheless "a necessary investment to have any chance of fighting for a decent standard of living" (p. 12).

The stakes of this gamble continue to grow as social safety nets continue to diminish. Despite the persistent rhetoric that more education will inevitably lead to more and better jobs, those jobs have not appeared even as more people have obtained higher education. This means that more people are competing for the same number of (or fewer) "good" jobs (Brown et al., 2011). Further, this competition is increasingly global. Given the increased ease of mobility for those deemed "skilled" laborers and the ease of relocating businesses, there is now a "global war for talent" (Brown & Tannock, 2009) and a race to lower labor costs. This, in turn, has fueled resentment among those in the United States who have come to believe (thanks in part to decades of US hegemony) that the world owes them a living (Brown et al., 2011).

Chad Wellmon (2021) suggests that the contemporary idea of the student consumer that has emerged with the "post-welfare" or "workfare-warfare" state is in fact not incompatible with the orienting logic of the "welfare-warfare" university. This logic held that "higher education was not just efficient at expanding the national GDP, but also constituted a profitable investment in individuals." Another way of saying this is that higher education is both a public and private good. We might therefore understand the contemporary decline in public higher education support to indicate not a fundamental shift in the perceived value or purpose of higher education but a revised calculation that it is no longer compellingly beneficial to capital accumulation or national political power for the US state to underwrite or ensure affordable access to higher education.

Expanded higher education access in the postwar United States was imprecisely understood as a benevolent and progressive shift from what preceded it, because, at the time, it also served the interests of industrial capital. Universities trained laborers who would produce greater value for their employers and who would also buy and consume the commodities industries produced. However, the economic system has now shifted from being oriented by the imperatives of industrial capital to being oriented by the imperatives of financial capital. Financial capital is much more mobile and less nationally bound than industrial capital. At the same time, claims about a growing "knowledge economy" notwithstanding, many of the jobs in the fastest-growing economic sector since the late 1980s—the service sector (Soederberg, 2014)—do not require bachelor's or higher degrees. Thus, public subsidies for education may no longer be prioritized, particularly as many individuals have thus far proven willing to invest in their own education in order to compete for the few remaining "good jobs."

With the fall of the Soviet Union and the decline of many socialist governments throughout the world, there have been fewer levers through which to compel the United States toward more socially just policies. In other words, as the viability of other possible political economic systems appeared to diminish, it was no longer in the interest of the US state to dedicate significant resources and political will toward ensuring more racially equitable opportunities that made capitalism appear as the "best" or "better" option. Thus, the "interest convergence" that emerged and offered (limited and conditional) gains in the postwar era has been significantly weakened. Some have also suggested that public funding for social welfare services like higher education has declined, at least in part, because of a racist backlash and subsequent disinvestment by white citizens and lawmakers who perceived growing numbers of racialized people as benefiting from these services (Chun & Feagin, 2021).

To Defend, Expand, or Disinvest from the American Dream?

Even though public funding for higher education has significantly declined, the postwar promise of achieving the American Dream by way of higher education is not easily abandoned—

even by many to whom it was never really promised. Further, the decline of the American Dream has not meant the decline of the Colonial Nightmare that has subsidized it. If anything, the Nightmare continues to grow: we are moving toward its increased generalization, which is still visited with much more severity upon already-subjugated communities. However, holding on to the promise of achieving the Dream by way of higher education may foreclose other possibilities and keep us invested in pursuing untenable outcomes that incur a huge social and ecological cost.

As higher education remains a significant site in which people invest their desires for the future promised by the American Dream, some have questioned these desires (e.g., Boggs & Mitchell, 2018; Joseph, 2015; Marez, 2014). For instance, for Lauren Berlant (2011), "a relation of cruel optimism exists when something you desire is actually an obstacle to your flourishing . . . when the object that draws your attachment actively impedes the aim that brought you to it initially" (p. 1). The cruelty Berlant describes lies in the fact that the object of one's desire—higher education, for example—fails to deliver on its promised outcome—in this case, the American Dream (or at least, its associated promises of middle-class financial stability). Berlant's concept of cruel optimism is in many ways fitting for an analysis of contemporary US higher education, as she asks, "Why do people stay attached to conventional good-life fantasies . . . when the evidence of their instability, fragility, and dear cost abounds?" (p. 2).

Yet, as Byrd (2011) points out, when Berlant describes the "cost" of conventional good-life fantasies, she is primarily speaking of the cost of unfulfilled promises to the fantasy haver. If we emphasize only this cruelty, we may lose sight of another, deeper cruelty, which is the driving concern of this chapter: the constitutive (and often disavowed) colonial costs of the *ful-*

filled promises of the imagined good life itself. This then raises a different question: For whom is the American Dream the good life, and at whose expense is their good life fulfilled? To ask this question does not require that we dispense with concerns about the losses (real and perceived) of the fantasy haver; rather it emphasizes that these are not the only losses, and generally not the most severe losses. Even at its best, the American Dream rests on harm—the continued occupation of Indigenous land, racialized mechanisms of state securitization that rationalize the use of violence against those positioned as threats (in the United States and abroad), continued ecological destruction effected by unending economic growth, and ongoing military aggression and other efforts to maintain US global political and economic hegemony.

Because the promise of socioeconomic mobility as a horizon of justice depends on perpetual economic growth and accumulation, the promise breaks down when economic growth slows—as indeed it has in recent decades. Slower economic growth can lead not only to a sense of broken promises and stalled progress but also to a perceived need to place blame for it. While some people point the finger at governments or at capitalism itself, others prefer to scapegoat already-marginalized communities. Donald Trump's 2016 campaign promise to "Make America Great Again" affirmed the anxieties of white voters in all income brackets that the American Dream was under attack, and pledged to restore it. While this was read by some as a not-so-subtle commitment to "Make America White Again," many critiques of Trump were articulated in *defense* of the American Dream as well. At least three primary narratives and associated slogans emerged at the time: (A) the American Dream is being taken away from those who are rightfully entitled to it (in particular, white men), and this dream must be reclaimed at any cost ("Make America Great Again");

(B) we must preserve America's noblest ideals and democratize and expand the Dream ("The American Dream is big enough for everyone"); and (C) existing problems are getting worse and affecting more people, but are still disproportionately affecting Black, Indigenous, and other racialized peoples who have borne the costs of the Dream from the start ("America Was Never Great") (see: Stein et al., 2017). From the perspective of narrative A, the existing system is ideal and universally valuable, but its greatest benefits should be reserved for certain exceptional, deserving, meritorious people and protected from encroachment by others. From the perspective of narrative B, the best parts of the system are under threat (from narrative A) and must be expanded to benefit more people. From the perspective of narrative C, both A and B are invested in a system that isn't "broken" but rather was built to operate this way.

TallBear (2019) poses Indigenous, and in particular Dakota, forms of "making kin" as a means to "undercut settler (property) relations" (p. 38) that characterize the American Dream as imagined by both narratives A and B. One possible way to end this chapter would be to suggest this as a path forward, and there is no doubt that there is an urgent need to "right relations gone bad" (p. 37)—that is, to address the breach of the "relational tipping point" that was "crossed long ago through systems of colonialism, capitalism, and industrialization" (Whyte, 2020, p. 3). Yet, as TallBear (2019) herself notes, "US exceptionalism, though it has suffered hard blows [during the Trump presidency], will not be let go easily" (p. 36). Shotwell (2016) argues that precisely because it is so difficult for those socialized within modern systems and institutions to imagine the world other than it is, Westerners, especially white Westerners, often "turn, sometimes in colonial or orientalist ways, toward 'other' cultures, which show that things are very different elsewhere than they are here" (p. 186). While this can indeed be an important reminder that things could be "otherwise," for white settlers like myself to appropriate Indigenous forms of making kin as a way out of nearly 250 years of American Dreaming would be an escapist and extractive move that fails to redress our systemic complicity in harm or to challenge our ongoing investment in the promises the Dream offers. We will need to start, rather, by honestly confronting the depth, complexity, and magnitude of the challenges involved in unraveling the hold that the Dream has on us and on the institutions we inhabit.

Confronting the Costs of the American Dream

As the US middle class continues to shrink, along with public funding for higher education, it may seem risky or even irresponsible to ask for anything but a reinvigoration of postwar promises, using the familiar language of equal opportunity (within capitalism) and engaged citizenship (within the nation-state). In this context, can one advocate an abdication of the fight to maintain or expand existing institutional commitments to justice conceived within the framework of the American Dream?

King (2016) argues that "temporarily resuscitating the subject [of civil rights], specifically within the context of the neoliberal university, may be necessary even to those interrogating the very terms and existence of the subject" (p. 134). Engaging in this kind of situated and strategic rhetoric and action is particularly crucial if doing so reduces harm, enables more people to access a living wage, and generally makes life more liveable in the present. As Mitchell (2016) points out, even most demands of student movements in the 1960s "were not fundamentally at odds with the form of Keynesianism that was present within the US military liberalism of the time." Their entanglement with and use of mainstream logics underscores how deeply political strategies and desires are shaped by context, including the mainstream discourses, subjectivities, and frameworks that are available and legible.

It is possible to advocate for higher education as a public good in the short term while simultaneously committing ourselves to tracing the true externalized costs of that good and to asking precisely what is meant by both "public" and "good" so that in the long term we might desire and imagine something entirely different and less harmful. As Fred Moten (2015) has observed, the public university "wasn't 'free,' it cost something." To recognize that the golden age of higher education came at great cost does not require giving up on public higher education entirely or dismissing the possibility of radical transformations within existing institutions. However, it may prompt us to do more than simply try to resuscitate the university's imagined role as a pathway to the promises encapsulated by the postwar American Dream. We might also question the imaginaries of justice and change within which this golden age was produced, the horizons of hope it made possible in practice, and the horizons it excluded or denied.

What kind of higher education could "sustain good relations among all beings that inhabit these lands" (TallBear, 2019, p. 38)? And how can we develop the necessary stamina, capacities, and dispositions to do the difficult work of disinvesting from the American Dream and its promises so that other forms of higher education might become possible?

Inclusion Is Not Reparation: Reckoning with Violence or Reproducing Higher Education Exceptionalism?

Because of the presumed inevitability of reconciliation and the centering of settler futures, interpretive lenses are already circumscribed by categories of forced harmony, and thus, the possibility of noncolonial futures is foreclosed.

—Dallas Hunt, 2018, p. 85

Educators are called upon to play a central role in constructing the conditions for a different kind of encounter, an encounter that both opposes ongoing colonization and that seeks to heal the social, cultural, and spiritual ravages of colonial history.

—Rubén Gaztambide-Fernández, 2012, p. 42

Your rent is due, Higher Education.

—Megan Red Shirt-Shaw, 2020, p. 8

It has been said that we are living in an "age of apologies," as various governments and social institutions have offered apologies "for certain kinds of historical wrongs" (McElhinny, 2016, p. 53). The meaning of the term "apology" here, as Bonnie McElhinny (2016) notes, "ranges widely, across expressions of regret or remorse, admission of wrong-doing, 'acknowledgements,' etc." (p. 53). Universities are no exception, and by now several US institutions have offered some form of apology for their complicity in slavery. While fewer have reckoned with their complicity in colonization, a slow shifting is under way. Yet critical and decolonial scholars have also pointed out that contemporary apologies often ring hollow when they are not accompanied by efforts to substantively redress the harms done and reckon with countries' and institutions' complicity in both historical *and* ongoing forms of systemic violence (Al-Kassim, 2008; Coulthard, 2014; Povinelli, 2002; Simpson, 2011; Somani, 2011; Walcott, 2011). In most cases, universities' apologies are not spontaneous but are offered in response to research and public pressure from activists, academics, students, and community members. Some of these same groups have also pressed institutions to extend and elaborate their initial apologies toward deeper forms of accountability (e.g., Desai, 2019; UCARE, 2012).

One of the earliest efforts to bring attention to universities' complicity in slavery was a study produced by a group of Yale University graduate students in 2001 (Dugdale, Fueser, & de Castro Alves, 2001). In 2003, the president of Brown University appointed a steering committee to study the history of slavery at Brown; the committee's report was released in 2006. Since then, the list of institutions engaged in efforts to address their legacies of slavery and colonialism has continued to grow, as has steady pressure to extend this work beyond mere apologies that recognize harms done toward deeper forms of accountability, including not just increased representation of historically and systemically marginalized communities but also redistribution, reparation, and restitution to those communities for harms done to them by the institution.

The consortium Universities Studying Slavery (USS), led by the University of Virginia, "allows participating institutions to work together as they address both historical and contemporary issues dealing with race and inequality in higher education and in university communities as well as the complicated legacies of slavery in modern American society" (von Daacke, 2013).

While most of the USS's thirty-plus member institutions are located in the United States, a handful are in the United Kingdom, Canada, and Ireland, which speaks to the transnational nature of Western higher education's implication in slavery and colonization (Pietsch, 2016).

In this chapter, I consider the recent wave of efforts among US universities to address their institutional legacies of racial and colonial violence, as well as responses to these efforts that suggest the importance of going beyond tokenistic efforts that can be deemed mere window dressing. I examine a handful of telling examples of apologies and related institutional actions in order to examine their orienting horizons of justice and ask whether and how they either enable or foreclose substantive engagements with individual and collective responsibilities related to the anti-Black and settler colonial foundations of US higher education. I suggest that many institutions that have embarked on this work adopt a liberal approach to justice that is largely symbolic and thus inadequate for identifying, interrupting, and redressing systemic colonial harm.

Different approaches to justice have different orienting assumptions, desires, and directions. Liberal theories of justice generally presume that injustice is a product of the betrayal of or exclusion from otherwise universal and benevolent economic, political, and educational systems. Thus, their reparative move is to reform or revise and expand these systems, often by offering more inclusion and access to those who have been systemically excluded. Because it ultimately seeks to preserve these systems, liberal justice cannot identify, let alone interrupt, the violence that is constitutive of these systems in the first place. By contrast, decolonial critiques contend that these systems are themselves primary sources of contemporary injustice, because the existence and ongoing maintenance of those systems is subsidized by inherently harmful and unsustainable processes. By offering a decolonial reading of liberal approaches to institutional legacies of violence, I do not dismiss them. Despite their many limitations, these approaches can result in important changes that reduce harm and create more opportunities to engage in initial conversations about deeper forms of social and institutional transformation. However, I draw attention to the ways that liberal frames of justice often allow for the circular reproduction of colonial patterns. It will be necessary to identify and interrupt these frames and patterns in order to imagine and practice more accountable ways of responding to ongoing colonial legacies.

Addressing the Colonial Past, Obscuring the Colonial Present

Decolonial scholars emphasize that settler colonial and anti-Black violence are ongoing and structural in ways that are coded into the basic DNA of all US institutions, including colleges and universities. Yet many institutional apologies single out a specific era or event of higher education history as the primary site of violence. By locating violence in a particular moment, colleges and universities can disavow their complicity in ongoing harm and can protect their public images as institutions that are fundamentally benevolent and innocent. In this way, a shameful but apparently isolated chapter of history can be opened and briefly acknowledged, only to be closed again so that a proud organizational saga and path toward linear progress can be reaffirmed—and so that the institutional brand can be protected from further criticism.

For instance, Taylor (2020) finds a common pattern among institutional reports about historical entanglements with slavery in which the mere creation of the report is understood to constitute the act of reckoning itself, instead of just the beginning of a long-term, difficult practice of acknowledging and accepting ongoing responsibility, redressing harms done, and building generative relationships. "For most reports," Taylor writes, "the very attempt to undertake truth-telling research is seen as redress. All the reports point toward extensive public display of their truth-telling with detailed and attractive websites" (p. 312). Perhaps this is because institutions worry that, if they were to actually address the full extent of their entanglement with processes of slavery and colonization, they would undermine the very legitimacy of their continued existence. Perhaps they worry that if they were to attempt to actually pay all of their colonial debts, they would go bankrupt. Yet if apologies and "truth-telling" efforts about historical wrongs are not accompanied by deeper efforts to reckon with the contemporary implications and ongoing accountabilities that accompany these truths, these efforts risk renaturalizing and invisibilizing an institution's continued complicity in harm.

In some cases, an institution's efforts to reckon with its past have even been mobilized to justify the continued need for the institution—in its now revised, more ethical and socially responsible state. The perceived imperative to ensure university futurities in the context of efforts to address legacies of racial and colonial violence is evident in certain dimensions of *Scarlet and Black*, Volume 1: *Slavery and Dispossession in Rutgers History* (Fuentes & White, 2016), which was produced on the 250th anniversary of Rutgers's founding. The edited volume brings together contributions solicited by the university's Committee on Enslaved and Disenfranchised Populations in Rutgers History.

One of the book editors suggests in the introduction that the institution's "anniversary should be, and is, a time of celebration, but the writers of this first volume on African and Native Americans in Rutgers's history also want it to be a time of reflection—reflection on Rutgers's past as a way to improve its future" (White, 2016, p. 4). The editor further suggests that history should not be used to "tear down or weaken this very renowned, robust, and growing institution but rather to strengthen it and help direct its course for the future" (p. 5). This theme is echoed in the foreword by the university's chancellor, who suggests that, "to truly praise Rutgers, we must honestly know it; and to do that, we must gain a fuller understanding of it" (Edwards, 2016, p. ix). Here, arriving at a place where we can once again "praise Rutgers" appears to be a key driver behind the institution's inquiry into its history. Thus, from the very outset, the text affirms the imperative of institutional preservation and improvement; the university's futurity itself is never under question. These affirmations may speak to an underlying anxiety that honestly and unreservedly exhuming the violence of the past could unravel the whole institutional fabric in the present, or at least generate a great deal of uncertainty that is deemed too much of a risk.

As I discuss in the following section, a primary means of securing institutional legitimacy and futurity in the wake of an apology is committing to the inclusion of more Black and Indigenous people within the institution, emphasizing the need for representation. This inclusion tends to happen in two ways: (1) writing Black and Indigenous people—usually individuals deemed exceptional—into the history of the institution by updating existing organizational sagas; or (2) promising greater access to the contemporary institution for Black and Indigenous people, especially as students and faculty. The assumption that inclusion equates to justice also affirms the institution's presumed exceptionalism, reinscribing both the desirability of its educational offerings as well as its ability to be reformed and redeemed. Below I examine the limits of this assumption before considering alternative approaches to justice in higher education.

The Limits of Inclusion as a Form of Redress

In his foreword to *Scarlet and Black*, the university chancellor writes that he formed the Committee on Enslaved and Disenfranchised Populations in Rutgers History because of the need "to seek out the untold history that we have ignored for too long" (Edwards, 2016, p. viii). He continues, "I believed it was time that we began to recognize the role that disadvantaged populations such as African Americans and Native tribes played in the university's development" (p. viii). He closes his statement by reflecting on the story of an enslaved person, Will, who helped construct the university's first building, which now houses the chancellor's office, and whose story is recounted in a subsequent chapter of the book. Yet rather than reflect on the violence of the enslavement of Will and others, and the university's complicity in that violence, Edwards ends by noting how pleased he is that students will finally know Will's story. This way of framing the work of the committee sets the tone and terms on which histories of institutional violence at Rutgers can be addressed, analyzed, and translated into action (or not).

In addition to uncritically positioning the institution itself as a suitable actor for addressing its own wrongs, the chancellor's framing of the issues in the foreword suggests that "disadvantaged populations" were always part of Rutgers's development, even as their role has unfortunately gone unrecognized for centuries. To remedy this erasure, Black and Indigenous peoples are to be retroactively recognized and included as contributors to the university's important legacy and organizational saga. The decision to describe these communities as "disadvantaged" is significant, as it views them as having merely been denied the advantages that were afforded to white people. While this is certainly true, it is only one part of the story. First, it assumes that these peoples sought inclusion in the whitestream higher education institution, as opposed to seeking the self-determination to choose that or to create or regenerate their own forms of education that many universities have been complicit in suppressing. Second, it elides a more explicit acknowledgment of the racial and colonial violence by which the institution sub-jugated Black and Indigenous peoples *as the price* of the white population's "advantages." That is to say, this analysis elides the fact that racial, colonial, and ecological violence is not simply an unfortunate footnote to the university's otherwise unblem-ished and benevolent history, but rather an underlying condi-tion of possibility for the university's very existence.

If the primary historical injustice of slavery and colonization is exclusion—that is, certain populations' historical exclusion both from the institution's organizational saga and from access to its promised benefits—then the primary remedy is inclusion in the form of increased representation of historically and systemi-cally subjugated communities. This inclusion often takes the form of amended and revised institutional narratives that in-clude "exceptional" individuals from those communities in the past, as well as efforts to make the institution more wel-coming to those communities in the present. I address the former approach first.

Several institutions engaged in the work of addressing their historical complicity in slavery have selectively acknowledged and even celebrated the role of enslaved people in building their institution. These acknowledgments tend to center the (in-voluntary) "contributions" of the enslaved people, rather than confront the ways the institution forced that contribution. This can be read as a means to deflect deeper examination of institu-tional culpability. For instance, the University of Virginia (UVA) placed a plaque on university grounds in 2012 to com-memorate Henry Martin, who labored on the UVA campus first as an enslaved person and later as a freedman, a path not uncommon for formerly enslaved persons who had few post-Emancipation options for employment (Wolfe, 2013). According to a UVA visitor brochure, "Martin made a strong impression on generations of students and was remembered as a man of 'intelligence, firmness, and diligence'" (University of Virginia, 2013). Another story in the same brochure features William and Isabella Gibbons, who were enslaved at UVA and "were able to maintain family connections and become literate despite the constraints of slavery." In 2015, a new residence hall was named after the Gibbonses. In this way, UVA retroactively integrated Henry Martin and Isabella and William Gibbons in the official narratives of the school's institutional history (Stein, 2016).

However, as former UVA professor Corey D. B. Walker notes, "we have to remember, these people were enslaved. No matter how much we want to romanticize it, they did not control their destiny. . . . The problem of making the assertion that [Henry Martin] was wonderful and a beloved figure belies the very violence of the institution of chattel slavery" (as cited by Graves, 2012). This is the drawback of granting institutional "recognition" to Martin and others enslaved by and at universities: it reaffirms the value of the institution and reduces enslaved peoples' complex lives to the labor they involuntarily gave to the institution. As Theodor Adorno (2009) suggests, celebrating something someone has done as a "contribution" presupposes "the merit of the order to which one is supposed to contribute something" (p. 161). Instead, he argues, "it is precisely the merit of the order that is to be questioned" (p. 161).

Writing about recent historical novels, Christina Sharpe (2014b) suggests that many contemporary portrayals of slavery are "engaged in constructing a useable past out of which a post racial present and future might be understood to have been always already coming into existence—even under the

most brutal of systems" (p. 194). Similarly, by including carefully crafted accounts of certain enslaved individuals' stories,
UVA crafts a "useable past" that can be mobilized to reassert
its own benevolence and refuse "in the present to account for
the persistence, necessity, and instrumentalization of black
suffering" (p. 197). Framing inclusion as a means to make up
for violent pasts is not limited to UVA. For instance, the College of William and Mary made "a multifaceted and dynamic
attempt to rectify wrongs perpetrated against African Americans by William & Mary through action or inaction," which it
named the Lemon Project, after one of the persons the institution enslaved, who was known as Lemon.

Beyond Inclusion

There are significant limits to efforts to address legacies of
slavery and colonialism through inclusion alone—particularly
forms of inclusion that instrumentalize marginalized peoples
and their stories in the service of a revised organizational saga
and restored public image. The paradigm of inclusion as a means
of redress presumes the underlying value and desirability of
the thing in which something or someone is being included.
Indeed, most whitestream institutions in settler colonial
societies claim to be universally valuable and relevant. Institutions use this supposed universality to explain their hegemony
and justify their suppression or devaluation of other, "particular" forms of knowing, being, and relating. In turn, universities
often mobilize conditional inclusion as a strategy to demonstrate the university's generosity, and protect themselves and
their claims of universality and benevolence against criticism.
Inclusion is therefore framed as a concession, rather than
as an (insufficient) effort to address colonial debts. In other
words, rather than respond substantively to critiques that question their presumed universality and benevolence, institu-

tions selectively include difference as a means to reassert that universality and inoculate themselves from being further challenged about their implication in harm (Ahmed, 2012). In this framing, whereas an institution once excluded difference, now it embraces difference, thereby not only redeeming itself but also becoming all the more universal and benevolent in the process. Thus, selective and conditional forms of inclusion can become a strategic means to avoid facing the full extent to which the institution is entangled with historical and ongoing brutality, let alone accepting responsibility for redressing that brutality in the present.

In addition to including previously excluded stories of enslaved people in a revised organizational saga of the institution, some universities' efforts to address legacies of slavery develop a forward-looking approach by pledging to increase the representation of Black students in their student bodies. One example comes from Georgetown University, whose early operations were funded by a Jesuit-owned plantation where enslaved Black people were forced to labor. The sale and subsequent separation of 272 of these enslaved people in 1838 saved the institution from financial ruin. In 2016, following the recommendations of its Working Group on Slavery, the university offered preferred admissions to the descendants of those 272 people, alongside commitments to create an institute for the study of slavery and its relationship to the university. Georgetown also renamed two campus buildings, previously named after the presidents who brokered the sale, after one of the enslaved men who was sold to benefit the university, Isaac Hawkins, and a free Black woman who started a school for girls who lived in the area surrounding the university, Anne Marie Becraft (Duster & Kwak, 2017).

In response to this announcement, some labeled Georgetown's effort—which at the time was one of the more substantive

institutional responses—reparations. Refusing this characterization, McMillan Cottom (2016) wrote that preferred admissions for the 272 enslaved people's descendants did not constitute compensation for stolen lives and labor: "The idea that
preferred admission equals payment stems from the American ideology that opportunity, especially educational opportunity, is a 'fair' form of recompense. Opportunity has a moral
basis: It will only be valuable for those who deserve it and will
not inconvenience or harm those who already have the opportunity (whether they deserve it or not). Our society likes
opportunity because it does not demand redistribution of resources acquired through harm." The suggestion that preferred access to Georgetown itself equates to recompense is
rooted in, and thereby reproduces, the presumed value and
desirability of a Georgetown education. McMillan Cottom
further notes that, even if we lay aside all the limitations of
educational opportunity as a mode of justice, "preferred admission doesn't equate to much of an opportunity." She thus
argues that this promise of inclusion is not only highly conditional but also decidedly *not* a substantive form of redress for
institutional complicity in the violence of slavery. Even the offer of both admission and free tuition would not equate to
restitution to descendants for Georgetown's profits from slavery. McMillan Cottom concludes, "If universities want credit,
spiritual and political capital, for doing reparations, they
should actually have to *do reparations.*"

McMillan Cottom's analysis suggests that the conditional inclusion offered through preferred admissions offers a limited
horizon of justice and an impoverished approach to institutional redress. Georgetown's own students agreed, and in 2019
voted overwhelmingly to create a fund from additional student
fees for the descendants of the enslaved people who were sold
in order to fund the early institution (Desai, 2019). This sig-

naled a demand for the university to go beyond its public recognition of harm and promise of increased representation toward at least some form of economic redistribution, if not full restitution. The university later announced that instead of relying on student fees, it would raise $400,000 in donations each year in order to create a fund to support health clinics, schools, and other community projects that would benefit the descendants (Swarns, 2019). Meanwhile, some descendants of the enslaved people sold by Georgetown are seeking $1 billion from the university for a foundation to fund health care, housing, and other community needs and services.

Virginia Theological Seminary (VTS) was one of the first higher education institutions to create a fund with which to pay reparations to individual direct descendants of those Black people who labored on the campus during slavery, Reconstruction, and segregation. The fund draws income from VTS's endowment fund to make annual payments to the descendants, whom the school is still working to identify (Redden, 2021). The institution announced its plans to create the fund before the Virginia governor signed legislation in March 2021 that directed five of the state's public universities, including VTS and UVA, to "annually identify and memorialize, to the extent possible, all enslaved individuals who labored on former and current institutionally controlled grounds and property" and to "provide a tangible benefit such as a college scholarship or community-based economic development program for individuals or specific communities with a demonstrated historic connection to slavery that will empower families to be lifted out of the cycle of poverty" (as cited by Redden, 2021).

It is increasingly difficult for universities to entirely ignore the growing critical attention that has been brought to their histories of slavery and colonization. Yet some observe that more substantive possibilities for transformation and redress are being minimized in the translation from public calls for accountability to the institutional actions taken in response. Brophy (2018) argues that over time, efforts to address universities' institutional violence have been deradicalized. "That may explain why," he suggests, "the movement has gained such popularity among administrators" (p. 231). "If the movement is radicalized again, it will be by expanding the discussion of reparations. Of course, if that happens, it will likely lose popularity among administrators, if not faculty and students" (p. 232). It is difficult to say for certain which came first—deradicalization, which sparked the interest of administrators, or administrative interest, which led to deradicalization. Regardless, this dynamic raises questions about what is potentially lost in the mainstreaming of conversations about institutional complicity in slavery and colonialism, particularly as institutions seek to accumulate "spiritual and political capital" without giving anything up or disrupting the continuity of business as usual.

The False Promise That Knowledge Leads to Institutional Change

In addition to inclusion, another common institutional response to colleges' and universities' legacies of violence is to emphasize how well suited they are to address these legacies through their own commitment to education, the pursuit of truth, and the production of knowledge. On the surface, this appears to be a fitting and potentially fruitful response. Max Clarke and Alan Fine (2010) observe, "The structure and goal of the university are uniquely able to facilitate a process of apology. Unlike other institutions, the academy claims to be a center of discussion and debate. The professed goal of the academy is to arm students with tools of analysis—tools that can be put to use asking questions, observing, and creating conclusions about the world" (p. 85). Brophy (2018) hopes "that at some point the University and slavery movement will begin asking large questions such as how did Universities contribute to the institution of slavery—and to the Civil War—and what would be the appropriate response to those contributions? That response should draw on what Universities specialize in: knowledge production and dissemination" (p. 232). Brophy's hope exemplifies both a general promise within modernity about the redemptive capacities of knowledge and a particular promise that more knowledge about institutions' complicity will lead to substantive institutional transformation. In turn, this presumes that the primary barrier to justice is ignorance. Similarly, Cambridge University's vice chancellor Stephen Toope (2019) notes, "Understanding our past and shaping our future are not separate projects. The University of Cambridge is exceptionally well placed to undertake both of them. The legacies of enslavement form a part of who we are today, and inform what we wish to achieve. We can never rewrite history, or do away with our heritage, but we can try to address prevailing inequalities. This process begins through greater self-knowledge and self-reflection."

There is indeed much transformative potential in greater knowledge and self-reflection. In fact, it is likely impossible to move toward change without first reckoning with the full truth of institutional and individual complicity in racial and colonial violence. Yet it is also important to consider how investments in the power of knowledge to facilitate justice often fail to account for the role of knowledge in maintaining and reproducing *in*justice. In particular, there is a failure to address how universities' knowledge was and continues to be used to naturalize colonial domination in the first place (Mustaffa, 2017; Patton, 2016; Wilder, 2013; Wynter, 2003). As Sharpe (2014a) notes, an anti-Black "death-dealing episteme continue[s] to be produced in 'think tanks' and in the university, by teachers, lecturers, researchers, and scholars, and then reproduced by the students who have been educated in the classrooms and institutions where [Black people] labor" (p. 61). This enduring "death-dealing episteme" is not merely contained in explicitly white-supremacist knowledge, or even in today's more blatantly pathologizing and damage-centered strains of mainstream social science research (Tuck, 2009). Instead, according to Wynter (1994), "both the issue of 'race' and its classificatory logic" are built into the basic ordering logics of the modern systems of knowledge that continue to dominate most corners of US higher education institutions (p. 47).

At UVA, an alumni-commissioned catalog of institutional initiatives centered on slavery has justified further research on the topic by invoking the university's founder and enslaver, Thomas Jefferson, who once said, "This institution will be based on the illimitable freedom of the human mind. For here we are not afraid to follow truth wherever it may lead, nor to tolerate any error so long as reason is left free to combat it" (as cited by Faulkner, 2013, p. 17). From a strategic perspective, invoking Jefferson's words to seek support for further study of institutional complicity in slavery is clever. Yet this invocation also obscures the ways that commitments to freedom, truth, and reason have all been mobilized in the service of racial and colonial hierarchy and domination, including by Jefferson himself (Silva, 2007; Stein, 2016; Wilder, 2013; Wynter, 2003). This framing also fails to consider the violence instituted by claims of universal Western "truth" (Grosfoguel, 2013; Santos, 2007). Without attending to these dynamics regarding the racial-colonial politics of knowledge in both the past and present, any effort to address UVA's institutional legacies of slavery and segregation will remain incomplete, as any new knowledge produced about these legacies risks reproducing colonial epistemic frames.

One way to start attending to these dynamics is to unpack "the difficulty many of us have reconciling slavery, an institution now universally reviled as unnatural and abhorrent, with the ideals and values that we associate with universities—with progress, enlightenment, the unfettered pursuit of knowledge" (Harris, Campbell, & Brophy, 2019, p. x). While examining such cognitive dissonance can be a means to sit with hypocrisy, contradiction, or a failure to live up to stated individual or institutional values, we might also push further. For instance, it is also to important to consider how "progress, enlightenment, the unfettered pursuit of knowledge" were historically employed to rationalize and defend slavery, even as some also used these to critique slavery (Lowe, 2015). The profits of slavery were also used to fund "the unfettered pursuit of knowledge" by white men. We might further ask how our pursuit of knowledge today is still entangled with racialized systems of exploitation and expropriation.

Emphasizing the primacy of knowledge in institutional change can also further "disqualify" and invisibilize the existing knowledge about institutional violence that is held by the communities that have been subject to that violence (Taylor, 2020). As Taylor (2020) notes, the communities that have been most harmed by higher education institutions "have kept alive the memory of our complicities" (p. 313), even though institutions themselves have chosen to forget. This critical community knowledge has long been delegitimized or outright ignored by the institutions that are implicated in harm (Stein, 2016). Thus, to suggest that producing more knowledge about systemic violence will interrupt or end it both disavows and reproduces the colonial politics of knowledge in which certain sanctioned voices are valued and viewed as legitimate and objective, and others are not. That is, this framing fails to consider how universities have sought to suppress knowledge about their own harm and are still invested in ensuring that any new knowledge produced can be oriented toward ensuring their own futurity.

Making the production of knowledge about injustice central to achieving justice is common in liberal discourses of apology. Yet many critical scholars reproduce similar patterns. For instance, Mitchell (2015) challenges the "confidence" among critical ethnic studies scholars (in, e.g., Black studies, Indigenous studies) "that it is through knowledge that racial justice, in one or another measure, can be done" (p. 88). He further notes that the common phrasing of the righteous imperative to speak truth to power "indexes such a fantastic arrangement in which the intellectual is at once distant enough from the dominant apparatuses of power not to be identified with them, yet at the same time proximate enough to them for her speech to be heard" (p. 91). Mitchell suggests that this "fantasy" can at times generate important intellectual and practical interventions, but he reminds us of the need also to confront "the extent to which we are made by that which we oppose" (p. 91). That is, even those who critique the university and may be marginalized by it are complicit in its violences and, in many cases, are still deeply invested in its continuity. This involvement ultimately shapes both the actual knowledge we as scholars produce and our investment in the notion that it is primarily through knowledge that change will happen, as opposed to other theories and strategies of change. I return to this issue later in the chapter when I review possible alternatives to liberal approaches to apology.

Sanctioned Ignorance of Institutional Complicity

Beyond the failure to interrogate the politics of knowledge, institutional responses that frame education and knowledge production as the sole or primary means to address their own legacies of violence also tend to overlook the affective desires, material investments, and presumed exceptionalisms that contribute to the reproduction of harmful systems and their modes of education—even when critical knowledge about these systems is available and engaged.

As Shotwell (2016) notes, one way to understand the endurance of colonial relations is to assume "a kind of benign ignorance—people just haven't been taught the facts of the situation, and so they can't be held responsible for not understanding how race, poverty, indigeneity, and more, are present in their lives. If this were the problem, just giving people more and better information would correct their knowledge problem" (p. 38). Yet, as Shotwell suggests, the overwhelming failure to confront the full extent of higher education's implication in violence is due not merely to a lack of available information about that violence. Certainly, this lack of information is part of the problem in many cases, but it is not the whole story. Much of this information is already out there, even though many more stories are still to be written, read, and heard. Instead, the failure to confront the violence of whitestream higher education institutions is due also to an ongoing investment in the exceptionalism, ownership, certainty, comfort, control, autonomy, and authority that these institutions promise (even if they do not always deliver). This investment, in turn, feeds an "epistemology of forgetting" (Boggs & Mitchell, 2018, p. 442) or a willful, socially sanctioned ignorance of colonialism that characterizes white settler memory *and* futurity (Alcoff, 2007; Mills, 2007; Vimalassery, Pegues, & Goldstein, 2016).

In this process of "forgetting," the violence required to establish and maintain one's position of systemic advantage is partly or even wholly concealed. Willful ignorance often extends to denying the full implications of our complicity in violence *even when we are confronted with clear information about it that is intellectually impossible to deny.* Denial of the implications of one's complicity in harm, even when that harm is recognized, is often evident in the land acknowledgments that are increasingly undertaken by settlers in higher education institutions and elsewhere. In these acknowledgments, generally offered at the beginning of public events, local Indigenous communities are named and sometimes thanked by settler speakers. There are numerous thoughtful discussions about both the recolonizing risks and decolonizing possibilities of settler land acknowledgements (e.g., Cornum, 2019; Red Shirt–Shaw, 2020; Stewart-Ambo & Yang, 2021; Vowel, 2016; Wark, 2021), but in practice these acknowledgements are often treated by settlers as "tick the box" exercises that are not necessarily accompanied by deeper forms of accountability to Indigenous peoples and lands.

In my own experience teaching and speaking about colonial violence, there is no clear correlation between, on one hand, exposure to and even acknowledgment of the veracity of information about individual and institutional complicity in violence and, on the other hand, accepting and acting on the responsibilities that follow from that complicity. The latter requires disinvesting from perceived entitlements to power, resources, and authority and being willing to give up colonially subsidized social and material advantages. Without doing so, no amount of information can interrupt, redress, and transform colonial patterns of knowledge production and relationships. Further, I have often found that even white people like myself who agree that decolonial change is necessary feel entitled to maintain control over, and seek certain outcomes from, the process of change itself. This effectively forecloses the possibility of substantively different, noncolonial social and institutional arrangements, as white people continue to defend the advantages that we have accumulated through intergenerational colonial processes.

Thus, it is no doubt important for higher education institutions and scholars to continue to produce and disseminate knowledge about their deep entanglements with slavery and colonization. However, it is also unlikely that producing more knowledge alone will be sufficient for interrupting harm and enacting reparations and restitution for stolen lands and lives.

If the problem is not merely a lack of knowledge about racial, colonial, and ecological violence but also active (and often unconscious) investments in and desires for the promises that this violence enables, then in addition to intellectual work, there is a need for affective and relational work that invites people to sit with and sense the true costs of those investments and their political, economic, and ecological implications, and to accept responsibility and pursue redress for those costs without reproducing colonial patterns in the process (such as seeking innocence, absolution, or white settler futurity, authority, and control). I elaborate further on how to this work in the concluding chapter, but now I consider how moments of apology can become moments of reproducing rather than interrupting colonization.

The Reproduction of Higher Education Exceptionalism

The examples reviewed above have something important to teach about the difficulties of interrupting white settler memory and futurity in higher education—and the related difficulties of imagining and enacting decolonial futures. Institutional apologies tend to be carefully crafted to admit to past wrongs while nonetheless disavowing the realities of the ongoing colonialism that enables universities' continued existence. Institutional apologies rooted in frames of liberal justice commonly mobilize *higher education exceptionalism*. These apologies significantly narrow the scope of responsibility and bypass alternative avenues for redress for racial and colonial violence. In the process, they also tend to reconstitute the primary promises of US higher education, in particular those related to the institution's intrinsic benevolence and perpetual progress. In doing so, the institution presents itself as already having all the necessary knowledge and tools to address its own injustices. In other words, rather than an interruption, the apology can serve as a deflection against challenges to institutional legitimacy and innocence. According to Brophy (2008), "We live in an age of apology and of redemption as well" (p. 1095). Indeed, it seems that many acknowledgments of institutional complicity in violence are structured largely by a desire to secure redemption rather than to accept responsibility.

Many university apologies and similar institutional efforts to address legacies of slavery and settler colonialism can be understood through what Dallas Hunt (2018) calls a "hermeneutics of reconciliation." Speaking in the wake of the Truth and Reconciliation Commission of Canada, which confronted the legacy of residential schools for Indigenous peoples, Hunt describes this hermeneutics of reconciliation as "the way in which settler critics, scholars, artists, and the broader public cannot seem to conceive that the relations of (and between) Indigenous and non-Indigenous peoples are indeed fraught, or imagine a world in which societal problems are not easily resolvable for the sake of civil, social, or political expediency" (p. 84). The concept of a hermeneutics of reconciliation points to the teleological approach often taken in engaging with difficult, complex, and contentious relational issues, with the assumption that they can be neatly resolved and, further, that this resolution will enable the smooth continuity of existing systems. By contrast, when engagements with racism and colonialism are articulated in ways that challenge these assumptions, they are often either discredited or outright ignored.

A hermeneutics of reconciliation is rooted in a temporality in which isolated past harms have ceased and there is a call to "move on" toward a more peaceful future. In these framings, Rachel Flowers (2015) asserts, there is no "commitment to changed behavior in response to recognizing the structures and systems that are predicated on violence and permit it to occur in the first place" (p. 47). Such approaches exonerate settler individuals, governments, and institutions for their role in continued colonization; in many cases, they also exonerate people for past harms without actually enacting restitution for those harms. Consequently, according to Tuck and Yang (2012), as it is commonly mobilized by settlers, "reconciliation is about rescuing settler normalcy, about rescuing a settler future" (p. 37), rather than interrupting and undoing colonization. In some cases, there is a fantasy that it is possible to do both at the same time.

Of course, settler refusal of responsibility for historical and ongoing colonial harm has not stopped people from challenging the colonial status quo and seeking to create space for other possibilities. For instance, the Indigenous-led #LandBack movement seeks to restore Indigenous peoples' relationships to their traditional and ancestral territories, including by reclaiming Indigenous nations' jurisdiction over those territories. This project is understood as a continuation of centuries of Indigenous anticolonial resistance. #LandBack advocates for settler individuals, institutions, and governments to enact restitution for colonialism, by, for example, respecting Indigenous governing authority and legal orders, unraveling the coloniality of settler law, and returning all lands to their Indigenous caretakers (Yellowhead Institute, 2019). Yet these demands and change efforts are often dismissed as unrealistic, overreaching, or simply unintelligible. Those who persist in raising the issue are deemed to be impediments to progress (Coulthard, 2014). As Hunt

(2018) observes, "Within a hermeneutics of reconciliation, alternative relationships and societal formations are impossible to imagine because their potential is already made a conceptual impossibility, a void, and the necessary process of working through how to enact ethical relations 'outside of' colonialism is pre-empted" (p. 85).

When one approaches US higher education's historical and ongoing complicity in racism and colonialism from a hermeneutics of reconciliation, as is often the case within liberal frames of justice, one presumes that existing institutions can and should be reformed and restored to a position of innocence. As well, unless one offers a guarantee of reform and redemption that ensures institutional futurity, conversations about complicity in violence are generally nonstarters. Thus, the typical cycle of institutional apologies forecloses, or at least significantly circumscribes, the kinds of conversations that can be had and, thus, the conceivable possibilities for interrupting, rethinking, and moving away from the continuation of violent relationships (Stein, 2020). The desire for a quick and painless resolution is linked to the promise of US higher education's presumed intrinsic benevolence and to investments in its continuous progress.

Taylor (2020) draws attention to the ways that reconciliatory apologies for slavery in higher education are often approached as transactional processes in which a specific harm is identified and then redressed (usually in limited ways), with the assumption that the institution will be redeemed once this "transaction" is complete. He describes this as "a kind of moral or theological two-step. First there is confession of sin or moral wrong; then, second, some repentance and/or consideration of redress. The rhythm often appears as between courageous 'truthtelling' about institutions' entailment in slavery, and then 'reconciliation' as somehow restorative" (p. 311). As long as institutions' perceived interests drive apologies, those interests will delimit how legacies of violence can be redressed. This is because those offering the apology are always making a utility-maximizing calculation about what they will get out of it in relation to what it will cost them. For instance, when an institution pursues an apology out of a desire to restore its public image, those offering it will often do just enough to ensure that it results in good PR coverage, effectively making the apology merely symbolic.

Apologies are therefore often mobilized as a means to reaffirm institutional legitimacy, or what Elizabeth Povinelli (2002) describes as "the self-evident good of liberal institutions and procedures" (p. 16). Ahmed (2004) also points out that when an institution takes on the mantle of shame, it often suggests it has failed to "live up to its ideals"; this admission ultimately serves a redemptive purpose as "evidence of the restoration of an identity of which we can be proud." In this way, the exceptionalism of higher education can paradoxically be reaffirmed in the very moment it comes under question, and efforts to confront institutional and individual complicity in violence can be mobilized to ensure the continuity of business as usual. Moves to address the violence of institutions' extraction of value through slavery and colonization become sites of extraction themselves. These efforts do little to shift the ongoing colonial practices of the institution or its relationships to Black, Indigenous, and other marginalized communities. None of this is to say that transactional apology efforts are entirely meaningless or unimportant; rather there is a need for vigilance regarding their limits, especially in the way they may help rejuvenate higher education exceptionalism and extractive relationships.

Alternatives to Liberal Justice

Those who problematize commonsense liberal theories and practices of justice are frequently asked the question that orients the remainder of this chapter: "If not this, then what?" Rather than offer a universal prescriptive answer to this question, I review some different possible approaches to justice in higher education that go beyond institutional acknowledgments of harms done and tokenistic and conditional forms of inclusion. To review these possibilities, I consider what they assume, what they enable, what they foreclose, and how they relate to one another. These include critical approaches that seek not only deeper forms of representation and recognition than those offered by liberal approaches but also redistribution of power and resources within existing institutions, as well as "beyond reform" approaches that seek reparation and restitution and look toward the possible "end of higher education as we know it" (which may or may not mean the end of existing institutions). In this analysis, "recognition" refers to the acknowledgment and affirmation of (cultural) difference; "representation" refers to the inclusion of individuals and knowledges from different communities (particularly systemically marginalized ones) in mainstream organizations (e.g. universities); and "redistribution" refers to the (limited) transfer of material and other resources, generally to more marginalized groups.

Critical approaches to justice are often articulated within student demands for institutional transformation. This approach seeks forms of change that will interrupt enduring racial inequalities and exclusions that characterize contemporary campuses. For instance, in 2015–2016, a wave of student movements across the United States demanded such changes as hiring more Black, Indigenous, and racialized faculty; transforming and decolonizing curricula; admitting and offering more scholarships for Black, Indigenous, and racialized students; requiring mandatory education for all students and staff regarding issues of racism and colonialism (including the institution's own complicity in either or both); and providing more funding and institutional support for ethnic studies and gender studies departments (or creating such departments if they didn't already exist). The implication of such demands is that transformation will ensue through including more Black, Indigenous, and other racialized people and knowledges in the institution (representation), emphasizing the value of their contributions to their institution and to humanity as a whole (recognition), and increasing the available funding and other resources for members of those communities (redistribution).

Without dismissing these demands and while commending the students on their organizing efforts, Robin D. G. Kelley (2016) suggests that, much like the liberal apologies rooted in a desire for redemption, desires for representation, recognition, and redistribution still generally presume that the university "is *supposed* to be an enlightened space free of bias and prejudice, but the pursuit of this promise is hindered by structural racism and patriarchy. Though adherents of this perspective differ in their assessments of the extent to which the university falls short of this ideal, they agree that it is perfectible" (emphasis in original). These critical approaches recognize the tangible realities of racism and colonialism and, in response, demand that institutions finally prove that they are in fact as benevolent and progressive as they have always claimed. Yet, Kelley argues, this is an impossible aspiration, as "the fully racialized social and epistemological architecture upon which the modern university is built cannot be radically transformed by 'simply' adding darker faces, safer spaces, better training, and a curriculum that acknowledges historical and contemporary oppressions."

Kelley (2016) suggests that another, less common strain of student demands understands these limitations of higher education as we know it and "promotes and models social and economic justice." These demands seek more substantive institutional redress for historic, systemic, and ongoing institutional wrongs, often emphasizing the need to address the economic dimensions of ongoing settler colonialism and anti-Blackness (see, for instance, "A Collective Response to Anti-Blackness" authored by UNC students in 2015). They include free tuition (especially for Black and Indigenous students) (see, e.g., Red Shirt–Shaw, 2020), institutional divestment from prisons, living wages for all campus workers, and the disarming or removal of campus police.

However, for Kelley (2016), ultimately both kinds of student demands, which I categorize as critical approaches to addressing institutional complicity in racial and colonial violence, are asking universities to "change in ways that we cannot expect them to change. The first group asks universities to deliver on their promise to be post-racial havens, but that will not happen in a surrounding sea of white supremacy. The second sees universities as the leading edge in a socially revolutionary fight.... I think that universities are not up the task." Kelley suggests that these approaches are asking the impossible of universities that remain deeply rooted in the racial capitalist and settler colonial logics and systems of the wider US society.

Sandy Grande (2018) builds on Kelley's analysis by foregrounding Indigenous critiques of the ways that recognition-based justice renaturalizes the power of dominant groups. In practice, "the terms of accommodation usually end up being determined by and in the interests of the hegemonic partner in the relationship" (Coulthard, 2014, p. 17), and the marginalized partners often become preoccupied with currying the "good favor" of the hegemonic partner. Generally, good favor is granted only if the hegemonic partner senses that it can grant it without actually giving anything up, or if the good favor garners the partner something equally desirable in return—a calculation of interest convergence (see chapter 4). None of this exchange fundamentally challenges or interrupts existing relations of unequal power. As Grande (2018) notes, in "the liberal academy, discourses of recognition garner wide appeal as they provide a means for neatly bracketing what are fundamentally complex and ongoing sets of power relations" (p. 56). She suggests that such demands can even impede the struggle for other possibilities, as they offer the false impression that substantive changes have occurred and injustice has been redressed.

Through their engagements with existing efforts to achieve justice in higher education, Grande (2018), Kelley (2016), and a handful of others (e.g., Andreotti et al., 2015; Boggs et al., 2019; Boggs & Mitchell, 2018; Moten & Harney, 2004) raise the possibility that existing institutions of US higher education might be "beyond reform"—that true justice would require the end of higher education as we know it. This analysis is informed by the traditions of Black and Indigenous struggles that have sought not "equal opportunity in a burning house" but rather "to build a new house" (Kelley, 2016). However, there is no consensus about what this new house might look like (or whether it should indeed be a house, rather than some other possible form of shelter), how it should be built, who should live there, or how, for as long as the burning house continues to stand, we should relate to it. Some people offer a clearly articulated vision of alternative futures "with guarantees," while others suggest that even for those who sense this alternative future is necessary, it remains inconceivable from where we currently stand and, thus, we must move toward that direction without predetermined maps.

Kelley emphasizes the importance of political organizing and educational practice outside whitestream higher education institutions, citing the Mississippi Freedom Schools of the 1960s as one example. The Dechinta Centre for Research and Learning offers a contemporary example of an effort to imagine a shelter different from the colonial system's "burning house." Dechinta is a land-based educational initiative with deep connections to local Indigenous communities in what is currently known as northern Canada (Simpson & Coulthard, 2014). Dechinta centers Indigenous knowledges and practices while also working with the University of Alberta and the University of British Columbia to offer accredited courses. This educational approach is not entirely disentangled from settler colonial institutions or independent of present economic and political constraints, but it seeks to mobilize those institutions' resources in order to experiment with place-based and Indigenous-centered decolonial possibilities that do not presume the long-term continuation of those institutions (Ballantyne, 2014).

Some people operating in the "beyond reform" space emphasize the need for institutions to enact restitution for the expropriation of lands and lives. This need includes calls to offer reparations to the descendants of enslaved peoples, which are often supported or even led by students, including those at Georgetown University and the over 80 percent of Brown University students who voted in support of their institution paying reparations to the decedents of enslaved people who were "entangled with and/or afflicted by the University and Brown Family and their associates" (Richardson, 2021). There are also calls for the rematriation (return) of expropriated lands and wealth to the appropriate Indigenous nations (Red Shirt–Shaw, 2020). Others suggest that universities should at least institute genuine forms of shared governance or cogovernance with local Indigenous nations (Gaudry & Lorenz, 2018) or pay a land tax or rent to those nations. For many people, especially white settlers, who work and study in higher education, these actions are unimaginable, and indeed they would likely make existing whitestream institutions unrecognizable from their current structure. However, examples of similar efforts outside the higher education context do exist. For instance, the land tax initiated by the Indigenous organization Sogorea Tè Land Trust seeks to return land to Ohlone Lisjan people by requesting donations from settlers who live in the area. The Real Rent Duwamish fund in Washington State operates according to a similar principle of taxing local residents. As Meghan Red Shirt–Shaw (2020) puts it, "Your rent is due, Higher Education" (p. 8).

One beyond-reform approach comes from the emergent Abolitionist University Studies group. In "Abolitionist University Studies: An Invitation," Boggs and colleagues (2019), propose a "left abolitionist approach to universities" that has two dimensions: "reckoning with universities' complicity with a carceral, racial-capitalist society while creating an alternative, abolition university" (p. 2). The authors suggest that while critical or abolitionist histories of US higher education can help to contextualize contemporary struggles, these histories offer "neither a blueprint for what to do nor a horizon for understanding what an abolitionist relation to the university might look like in practice and execution" (p. 28). Thus, they argue for the need to collectively develop the latter.

Some of the first contemporary scholars to point toward an abolitionist approach to universities were Fred Moten and Stefano Harney (2004), through their now-well-known theorization of "the undercommons." Moten and Harney initially used this concept to describe those who are "in but not of" the university, though some have suggested that this disidentificatory framing can serve as a means to deflect responsibility for complicity by externalizing it. For instance, Mitchell (2016) writes, "It almost feels like, 'I get to have my cake, I get to take home my paycheck, and also to claim that I am not part of the dominant logic of the institution, that it does not articulate itself through me.'"

With my collaborators Vanessa Andreotti, Cash Ahenakew, and Dallas Hunt, I have also identified three different possible responses to the diagnosis that higher education as we know it is "beyond reform," without endorsing one over the others (Andreotti et al., 2015; Stein et al., 2021): walking out, hacking, or hospicing. Those who "walk out" of the university are generally seeking alternative forms of education, and there is much to be learned from these efforts. However, alternatives pursued with a desire for personal purity from complicity, and for guaranteed outcomes, may still be rooted in at least some colonial investments (in, for example, certainty, progress, innocence), and we may romanticize these alternatives to the point that their inevitable mistakes and contradictions are ignored (Amsler, 2019). Further, the ability to choose whether or not to walk out is unevenly available, as many are structurally excluded to begin with, while others have no other viable livelihood.

"Hacking" responses seek to capture and redirect institutional resources toward nurturing other educational possibilities, whether inside or outside institutional walls. This approach requires that one "play the game" of the institution to an extent while also trying to bend the rules toward ends other than "winning." Important, especially redistributive work can be done through this approach, but it is sometimes difficult to know when one is playing the system or being played by it. Some who operate in this space may also position themselves outside implication in systemic harm (that is, the "in but not of" framework).

Finally, "hospicing" responses to a beyond-reform diagnosis suggest facing the inevitable end of fundamentally unethical and unsustainable modern systems and institutions, including universities. The goal of this approach is to foster conditions for a "good death," so that as these systems and institutions are dying, the lessons from their mistakes can be learned, integrated, and applied as we witness and help to provide prenatal care for the birth of something different and potentially wiser. Hospicing also entails disinvesting from the harmful promises of the dying system so that they are not carried over into the new, emerging system, thereby overdetermining and smothering it before it even has space to breathe. Thus, while these responses support alternative forms of higher education, they also understand them as experiments that do not provide universal solutions but rather are important and generative opportunities for learning from successes *and* failures (see chapter 6). Finally, apart from merely learning from previous mistakes, hospicing approaches emphasize the need to enact restitution for those mistakes—particularly harms done to communities that have been dispossessed by existing institutions. The idea is that we cannot enable truly different forms of higher education if we do not take the necessary steps to enact repair for the form we are hospicing. Further, it is understood that the learning and unlearning that take place in the process of envisioning and enacting repair and restitution alongside affected communities as equal partners will also help to ensure that those mistakes will not be repeated, even as new mistakes might arise.

Much more could be said about each of these alternative approaches to addressing universities' legacies of racial and colonial violence, but I summarize each in table 2. These approaches to legacies of violence are *not* mutually exclusive. In practice, they are often combined or mobilized in strategic ways, depending on what is possible in any given context. Rather than advocate for a single path forward based on one or another of these approaches, I propose developing a deeper sense of where they each come from (i.e., what their orienting assumptions are, what their social and intellectual genealogies

Table 2. Possible alternative approaches to institutional legacies of violence

Orienting approach	How does this approach conceptualize the racial and colonial violence of higher education institutions?	What institutional responses to complicity in violence does this approach propose?	What is this approach ultimately seeking?
Liberal	Historical exclusion of Black, Indigenous, and other racialized peoples and knowledges from the institution	Formal apologies; individual inclusion (e.g., recruit more racialized students and faculty; incorporate racialized people into the organizational saga)	Redemption; a return to "business as usual"; good PR
Critical	Historical and ongoing exclusion, exploitation, and expropriation of Black, Indigenous, and other racialized peoples and knowledges	Deeper forms of inclusion and reallocation of resources (e.g., more scholarships or free tuition for Black, Indigenous, and other racialized students; more funding for ethnic studies departments; living wages for campus workers)	Representation, recognition, redistribution
"Beyond reform"	The institution would not be viable in its current form without historical and ongoing systemic racial and colonial violence	Working to reduce harm within existing institutions, without investing in their futurity or assuming they can or should be redeemed; experimenting with alternative forms of higher education; enacting repair for harms done	Restitution and repair (e.g., reparations, rematriation); "the end of higher education as we know it"

are), what they enable (what they make possible in practice, which direction are they moving toward), and what their limitations are (what harmful patterns they might unintentionally reproduce).

In addition to thinking through the prospects and limitations of each approach, I argue that it is important for students, staff, and others who are interested in unraveling the colonial foundations of US higher education to develop the stamina and capacities to do this work in sustainable, strategic, contextually relevant, relationally rigorous, and socially and ecologically accountable ways—regardless of their chosen approach.

I review these capacities in more detail in the concluding chapter. However, first I consider the possibilities and complexities of a strategic rather than static approach to enabling change in practice, and then review some of the circularities that tend to emerge within all of the possible approaches to justice reviewed above.

Navigating Opportunities for Engagement

The distinction between different approaches to justice offered in this chapter can be useful for identifying the different promises, investments, and assumptions that underlie any particular effort to address the constitutive racial and colonial violence of existing higher education institutions. For instance, the limits of liberal justice are made visible in many institutional responses to acute incidents of racism on campus, statements of institutional support for wider social movements such as #BlackLivesMatter, or public responses to racist legislation like the Trump travel ban (Ahmed, 2012; Cole & Harper, 2017; Daigle, 2019; Davis & Harris, 2015; Squire, Nicolazzo & Perez, 2019; Stein, 2018). As Ahmed (2012) notes, these institutional responses often pledge commitments to antiracism or equity, yet rarely do they translate into substantive efforts to transform the ongoing racist and colonial conditions of everyday campus life. Hence, much as many universities treat their apologies as if they constitute redress, many also treat the act of *saying* that they are committed to antiracism (or equity or justice) as if the statement itself were equivalent to actually *enacting* institutional change. Ahmed describes these kinds of statements as "non-performative": they do not do what they say they do.

As important as understanding these institutional dynamics and different possibilities for conceptualizing and enacting justice is, strictly aligning oneself with one approach and engaging only from that space—that is, seeking a position of moral or political purity (Shotwell, 2016)—can result in lost opportunities for engagement and responsible experimentation (without guarantees). At the same time that we challenge the naturalization of colonial futurities of higher education (Daigle, 2019), we can recognize opportunities to mobilize change. Some opportunities might simply allow for harm reduction, while others might open up avenues for deeper transformation in both direct and indirect ways. In my arts and research collective, Gesturing Towards Decolonial Futures, we have identified the generative potential of asking ourselves the following question in any given context: "What is the next, most responsible small thing I can do to try to interrupt harm and invite deepened accountability?"

To engage these opportunities in ethical and effective ways that do not compromise our integrity or the possibility of more substantive long-term change, we would need to map our accountabilities alongside what is both possible and responsible for us to do within any given context—which depends not only on the context itself but also on our own positionalities, vulnerabilities, complicities, and capacities for engagement. This approach also requires us to recognize that however we decide to engage will likely be incomplete, problematic, difficult, and contradictory and offer no guaranteed outcomes. It may be that some engagements require a bracketing of certain important questions, nuances, or concerns, which we would need to address at another time. Some might require strategic use of institutional language that we might otherwise critique. In many cases, we cannot know in advance how things will move as a result of our engagement; or we might simply recognize that a particular intervention can reduce immediate harm and alleviate suffering, even if it does not necessarily lead to deeper change. Thus, it is important to develop discernment for identifying and prudently assessing the possibilities and risks of different opportunities for engagement.

For instance, the fact that liberal inclusion is a limited framework does not mean that all efforts that fall under this approach are not worthwhile. Particularly because this is the dominant paradigm of institutional efforts to address legacies of colonial violence, it is important to consider its potential for reducing harm and protecting limited spaces for critical conversations and knowledges in the short term. These efforts can also be used to leverage or at least create more opportunity and legitimacy for seeking deeper forms of dialogue and transformation. When strategic engagements with liberal justice efforts are oriented by commitments to a decolonial horizon, rather than by an earnest investment in the forms of justice offered, new possibilities emerge that may not have been visible before. At the same time, these engagements should work to keep visible their own limitations and complicities and be vigilant about their potentially harmful impacts. We remain accountable to the concerns and critiques that we might have strategically bracketed in order to make our interventions intelligible and consequential.

Meanwhile, it may make little sense to advocate for the "end of higher education as we know it" to administrative leaders of an existing institution of higher education, as this is likely to be quickly dismissed, be deemed unintelligible, or result in retribution. However, it is nonetheless important for the critiques and propositions offered within this approach to justice, such as calls for #LandBack and reparations for slavery, to be present in the context of universities' discussions about the wider ecology of possible approaches to redressing institutional complicity in systemic, historical, and ongoing violence. Indeed, the mere presence of these seemingly impossible demands can help push "mainstream" conversations further than otherwise would have been possible if only those demands already deemed viable and fully intelligible by the institution were present. As Cutcha Risling Baldy notes, "The more work that we do with decolonization and reconciliation, the more you start to realize there is no reconciliation without the return of stolen land. It doesn't work otherwise," and thus, "we have to start with this discussion of what could that look like" (as cited by Lee & Ahtone, 2020).

Regardless of where and how one intervenes, it is important to learn to discern the contours and edges of different conversations and sensibilities in order to better map and understand, approximately, how one's argument, proposal, or critique might be received—including how it might be weaponized or instrumentalized to further institutional violence, and how those offering the critique might be read as further contributing to the problem. This work is multidimensional. For instance, one can work toward achieving the return of institutional lands to the appropriate local Indigenous nations while identifying opportunities to redirect and redistribute institutional resources to Indigenous staff and students and to fund research led by local Indigenous nations in order to support Indigenous resurgence.

In sum, any intervention that is legible in an existing institution will likely present some contextually relevant opportunities for change, but it will also contain significant limitations in terms of its transformative potential. Further, no matter how critical, careful, or self-reflexive we may seek to be, there is always a considerable chance that our efforts to enact decolonial change will circularly reproduce harmful colonial patterns. Below I review some of these patterns.

CIRCULAR Patterns in Approaches
to Decolonial Change

With the Gesturing Towards Decolonial Futures collective, I developed the acronym CIRCULAR to support members of the collective and others in identifying and deconstructing common patterns that emerge when decolonizing work is not accompanied by the interruption of colonial desires, perceived entitlements, and exceptionalisms (Stein et al., 2020). The intention behind outlining these patterns is not to condemn or shame people for reproducing them or to assert a moral high ground. Instead, it is an invitation for people to reflexively observe their own actions, analyses, and responses in relation to these patterns so as to more quickly identify and potentially interrupt them when they emerge, and open up new possibilities for knowing, being, sensing and relating. Strong *dis*identification with any of these patterns may be an indication that we have more work to do in that area, as most of these patterns are deeply socialized within us, even when we have a critique of those patterns. For those of us who have been socially rewarded for reproducing these patterns, instead of transcending them entirely we likely can commit only to continuing to grapple with them over the long term.

When these CIRCULAR desires or perceived entitlements are not met, it can lead to feelings of frustration, hopelessness, and betrayal, which can in turn result in outward displays of various fragilities, resentment, or even violence. This can happen even among those who are otherwise deeply committed to decolonization work; and these patterns can emerge among those who take liberal, critical, and beyond-reform approaches to the realities and responsibilities that follow from the debts of slavery and colonization. Attending to these patterns can help either avoid or interrupt efforts to address harm that

Table 3. CIRCULAR Patterns in Approaches to Decolonial Change

Continuity: Seeking the perpetuation (and perhaps expansion) of the existing system and its promised securities, certainties, and entitlements. This pattern leads people to approach change in conditional ways wherein they calculate the perceived benefits of change against potential losses and generally do not make choices (or renounce choice in ways) that compromise their own position of advantage. E.g., *"I want to transcend colonialism without giving anything up."*

Innocence: Positioning oneself outside complicity in violence, often because of one's stated commitment to oppose violence. This pattern erases how our implication in harm is largely the product of our structural positions within harmful systems and institutions, and our learned, often-unconscious habits of being, rather than a product of active choices to hurt others. E.g., *"Saying that I am against violent systems means I am no longer complicit in them."*

Recentering: Privileging the feelings, experiences, and perspectives of oneself or the majority group, nation, or other entity, rather than looking at systemic dynamics of inequality and violence and discerning from there what actions are needed in order to work toward developing healthier possibilities for coexistence. E.g., *"How will this change affect me or make me feel?"*

Certainty: Desiring (and demanding) fixed, totalizing knowledge, simple and guaranteed answers to complex, power-laden problems, and predetermined outcomes before taking action. This pattern denies that all knowledge is situated and contextually (rather than universally) relevant, and that all solutions are partial, imperfect, and may reproduce the problems they seek to address, or create new ones. It therefore refuses possibilities for movement or change that do not have a guaranteed destination. E.g., *"I am entitled to know exactly what is going to happen, when, and where."*

Unrestricted autonomy: Placing primacy on one's free choice and independence at the expense of honoring interdependence and responsibility. This pattern envisions responsibility as an intellectual choice, often based on a cost-benefit, utility-maximizing analysis, as opposed to an imperative to do what is needed in order to develop and maintain respectful reciprocal relationships premised on trust, respect, reciprocity, accountability, and consent. E.g., *"I am not accountable to others unless I choose to be."*

Leadership: Framing oneself, *or* another person or community, as uniquely worthy and deserving of the power to determine the approach and direction of decolonial change. This pattern positions the exceptional person or group above critique and outside complicity, thereby imposing unrealistic expectations that in turn make it difficult to acknowledge the complexities and the good, the bad, and the broken in everyone. E.g., *"I, or the person or group I designate, am exceptionally qualified and entitled to direct and determine the character of change for everyone."*

Authority: Appointing oneself as the moral and political authority with the right to arbitrate justice, or the epistemological authority with the right to adjudicate the truth and the most desirable path toward change. Generally, this pattern re-silences those who are systemically ignored, and imposes one's own desires and expectations on others' existence. E.g., *"I should be the one to decide who and what is valuable and deserving of which rights, redress, and punishments."*

Recognition: Seeking affirmation of one's righteousness, redemption, and exceptional-ism. Often recognition is sought by curating (and trying to control) one's public image and attempting to ensure that one is seen and heard as being and doing "good." This circular pattern serves as a distraction from focusing on the work that is needed in order to interrupt harmful systemic behaviors and desires in oneself and others. E.g., *"But don't you see that I'm one of the 'good' ones?"*

ultimately reproduce or otherwise do little to transform underlying structures of individual and institutional violence.

Disinvestment as a Possible Decolonial Pathway

In this chapter I emphasize the limitations of liberal approaches to the apologies and associated efforts to address
institutional legacies of slavery and colonialism. These approaches tend to relegate violence to a historical era, rather
than identifying it as a systemic and ongoing condition of
possibility for the institution's continuance. These approaches
also tend to reaffirm the underlying benevolence and inevitable futurity of existing institutions. This is achieved through a
hermeneutics of reconciliation that offers an apology for
harm done with the expectation of receiving moral redemption in return, without necessarily committing to the difficult
and uncomfortable work of enacting restitution for that harm
and transforming relationships to interrupt its reproduction
now or in the future. In addition to reviewing examples that
illustrate these common patterns of absolution seeking, I also
consider alternative approaches to redressing legacies of
harm, which in turn are not immune from naturalizing colonial investments in and desires for the continuation of higher
education as we know it.

Especially for white settlers, decolonizing our institutions
would require us to disinvest from the perceived entitlements
that have been promised to us by a harmful system and secured
at the expense of Black, Indigenous, and other racialized communities, as well as other-than-human beings and the planet
itself. This includes entitlements to epistemic, political, and
moral authority and arbitration; a sense of superiority; unrestricted autonomy; and certainty, comfort, and security at any
cost. The transformational work that is required to address and
redress centuries of colonial structures and desires—work

that is at once intellectual, affective, relational, political, economic, and ecological—cannot be done quickly, and much of it may not be feasible within the institutions we currently have. Despite these possible limitations, I also emphasize the importance of, in the short-term, identifying opportunities to strategically and accountably intervene in our institutions in ways that might reduce harm, and, in the long-term, developing our capacity to engage in difficult conversations about the need for deeper forms of individual and institutional responsibility, and ultimately, restitution and repair, in the context of today's considerable complexity, volatility, fragmentation, polarization, and uncertainty.

In the following chapter, I further consider the importance of refusing to let what is currently imaginable dictate what is possible, and of creating the conditions in which alternative possibilities can become viable. That is, I address both the necessity and the difficulty of imagining higher education otherwise, which may be possible only at the end of higher education as we know it.

Chapter Six

Imagining Higher Education Otherwise

How might we, as scholars whose lives and livelihoods are entangled with institutions of higher education, address these institutions in this moment and moving forward? How do we need to understand the histories of such institutions in order to do so? What forms of knowledge and what types of tools are available for scholars who hope to work in, through, and on these institutions? Toward what ends do we labor?

—Abbie Boggs & Nick Mitchell, 2018, pp. 437–438

There is no way we are going to intellectually reason our way out of coloniality, in any conventional academic sense. There is no way we are going to publish our way out of modernity. There is no way we are going to read our way out of epistemological hegemony.

—Anders Burman, 2012, p. 117

Throughout this book, I draw on decolonial critiques to examine how celebrated eras of US higher education history were subsidized by racial, colonial, and ecological violence. I have also tried to emphasize the importance of attending to the systemic and ongoing impacts of this violence as we consider possible responses to the challenges that have developed in the wake of decades of neoliberal reforms and public defunding, and in the context of various ongoing and emerging global crises—including health pandemics, climate catastrophes, biodiversity loss, economic precarity, and political volatility.

An emergent paradox characterizes the current moment. On one hand, neoliberal hegemony has narrowed the purposes of US higher education and crowded out possibilities for alternative higher education futures. On the other hand, the future of our existing institutions also appears highly unstable, complex, and uncertain, and the continuation of business as usual (including the fulfilment of higher education's promises) appears increasingly unlikely. As a result, anxiety about the future is growing, and the concepts and vocabularies that existing scholarship of higher education has made available appear increasingly inadequate for making sense of the present and for enacting both ethical and strategic interventions toward different futures.

In this book, I question both the desirability and feasibility of the continuity of modern/colonial higher education. It is commonly expected that when one challenges the presumed continuity of the existing order of things, one will offer an alternative order in its place. Therefore, readers might expect me to conclude by proposing my vision for a decolonial future of higher education, and a plan for how we might arrive there. However, I cannot meet this expectation. First, no future that is decolonial could be imagined by one person, and a white settler at that. But, more substantively, if the problems that we face are a product of our existing systems, any alternatives that we formulate from where we currently stand within those systems are likely to reproduce colonial patterns.

Thus, in consideration of a colonial past that seeps into and shapes the colonial present, and in the face of overlapping contemporary crises, instead of proposing an alternative higher education future, I conclude this book with an invitation to face the limits of the mode of higher education that we have inherited and to compost the colonial desires, fragilities, and perceived entitlements that reproduce it, so that we might nurture the soil for the "possibility of possibilities" (Barnett, 2014) from which different, perhaps decolonial futures and formations of higher education might ultimately emerge. In taking this approach, I also caution against immediate, feel-good solutions driven by a rush to "reform" or even "revolutionize" higher education, even as I recognize the imperative of systemic change and the importance of taking immediate action to reduce harm. I suggest that at the same time as we ask what needs to be done in the short-term in order to make our institutions more liveable, we also need to develop the stamina to engage the difficult, unsettling, long-term work of imagining higher education otherwise—and to learn from our inevitable mistakes along the way.

Enduring Attachments to the Modern/Colonial University

Addressing the colonial foundations of US higher education—at least in nontokenistic ways—has always been difficult, but it can be particularly difficult in an era when higher education is perceived to be in crisis, under threat, and therefore in a vulnerable position requiring defense.

Historically, public funding for higher education has helped secure middle-class investment in the United States' colonial nation-state and capitalist system by offering the egalitarian promise of equal opportunity to compete for social mobility. While this promise has always been more readily available to white people, many nonwhite people have also fought for access to it. Yet over the past several decades, as a result of capitalism's perpetual search for new "frontiers" of profit, many goods and social services previously categorized as public, including higher education, have become targets of private accumulation (Melamed, 2015), which can be understood as part of a larger systemic transition from the hegemony of industrial to financial capitalism (Lloyd & Wolfe, 2016).

Critical scholarship and activism has portrayed higher education as both a victim of and an active contributor to contemporary forms of capital accumulation. Changes associated with this shift have been variously described as privatization (Fisher, 1992); marketization (Chan & Fisher, 2009); corporatization (Aronowitz, 2000; Newson, Polster, & Woodhouse, 2012; Rhoads & Rhoades, 2005); commercialization (Bok, 2003); commodification (Harkavy, 2006; Soederberg, 2014); financialization (Beverungen, Hoedemaekers, & Veldman, 2014); rationalization (McMillan Cottom & Tuchman, 2015); academic capitalism (Slaughter & Rhoades, 2004; Metcalfe, 2010); and enclosure of the academic commons (Kamola & Meyerhoff, 2009; Sumner, 2009). Although these terms are not synonymous, they all gesture to what Brian Pusser (2014) describes as "a rare degree of consensus in the scholarly community on the power of market ideology in shaping the contemporary politics and practice of higher education" (p. 80).

The numerous impacts of these shifts are impossible to canvas here, but one of the primary effects has been a shift in higher education funding from public to private sources, resulting in rising tuition fees for students and their families, and increasing student debt (Williams, 2006). Although white people and middle-class people are not immune to this trend, patterns of student debt reproduce and exacerbate existing racial wealth disparities (Soederberg, 2014). Meanwhile, poorer people are more likely to take on often-risky securitized debt in the form of student loans (McMillan Cottom, 2017; van der Zwan, 2014). Black families rely more heavily on student debt than white families and are compelled to take on riskier forms of debt (Kahn, Huelsman, & Mishory, 2019).

Novel forms of capital accumulation have also resulted in shifts in the position of faculty, including a decline in autonomy and influence in university governance (Beverungen, Hoede-maekers, & Veldman, 2014; Lea, 2009; Olssen & Peters, 2005; Preston & Aslett, 2014; Suspitsyna, 2010), and massive growth in the numbers of non-tenure-track and non-full-time faculty (Bousquet, 2008; Newfield, 2008; Posecznick, 2014), leading to what some refer to as the "precariatization" or "casualization" of faculty (Bousquet, 2008; Kamola & Meyerhoff, 2009; Thorkel-son, 2015; Ty, 2011). As is the case with student debt, white women, and Indigenous and racialized people of all genders, are disproportionately affected by these shifts in comparison to their male, white counterparts. For instance, white women and racialized faculty of all genders hold a greater proportion of lower-rank and part-time positions than white men (Martínez-Alemán, 2014; Marez, 2014; Metcalfe & Slaughter, 2008).

Despite these and many other shifts that have led to a qual-itative change in US higher education over the past several de-cades, the assumption that colleges and universities are or at least *should* be a primary site in which the American Dream can be realized, and that modern promises can be fairly and efficiently distributed, still has a significant hold on both the popular and scholarly imagination. As Boggs and Mitchell (2018) note, "The university increasingly assumes the social function of embodying, enabling, and managing social inse-curities of various forms" (p. 440). That does not mean that higher education actually *solves* these insecurities, but the promise is that it will (McMillan Cottom, 2017).

Thus, investments in the university's continuity do not just involve the institution itself but are also tied to its perceived role in validating and perpetuating our wider socioeconomic system. Boggs and Mitchell (2018) go so far as to suggest that, "because higher education has been the dominant mechanism of so many of our most long-standing ameliorative discourses, from antipoverty to racial and gender justice, for it to appear in the frame of crisis cannot but be understood as an assault on the possibilities of progressive social change" (p. 411). I have found this to be the case even when people are aware of the university's colonial origins; even when they know that the post–World War II "golden age" was subsidized by militarism and the expansion of US-led global capitalism; and even when they grasp that the shift from Keynesian industrial capitalism to financialized neoliberal capitalism has meant growing disinterest on the part of capital to purchase social peace in ways that would cut into its profits and a growing disinterest by the state in showing a benevolent face that is invested in social welfare and the public good (including by funding higher education).

At the end of the day, most critiques of the contemporary university are rooted in an enduring investment in its futurity, however much this may be accompanied by the desire for it to be perpetuated in either a slightly or even significantly transformed state (Boggs & Mitchell, 2018). Colleges and universities become prime sites where hope in the continuity of existing systems is rearticulated and reanimated, including through the research and development of social and technological innovations to improve those systems.

This hope is also evident in the theories of change that many scholars of higher education offer. Most of these theories of change involve a basic formula: a *description* of the primary problem with the existing higher education system, followed by a *prescription* that purports to solve that problem. Descriptions of the problem vary. As noted at the outset of this book, many identify the primary problem of contemporary US higher education as public defunding and privatization, and therefore prescribe an increase in public investment as the primary means to address that problem. A few, such as those working in abolitionist university studies, describe the problem as not that the US university is broken but that it is working as designed within "a carceral, racial-capitalist society." Their proposed response is to dismantle that university model and create "an alternative, abolition university" (Boggs et al., 2019, p. 2).

But whatever problem is diagnosed, there is generally hope for a predetermined solution that can resolve it, either by "fixing" or reforming existing higher education in some way, or by developing a different, better higher education to replace it. Regardless of their specific content, most theories of change that follow the description-prescription formula are premised on the assumption that they represent the most desirable path forward for social and educational transformation. But to what extent does a description-prescription approach enable us to respond deftly and responsibly to the volatilities, complexities, and uncertainties of our current context? Can any prescription premised on establishing a "single forward" be accountable to the various communities that would be affected by it? And who should decide where that forward should be oriented, in whose name, for whose benefit, to what end, and at whose expense? I consider these questions in the following section.

The Insufficiency of Description-Prescription in Today's Complex World

Theories of change rooted in the description-prescription formula may be starting to lose their efficacy not only in shifting political economic conditions but also in a contemporary context within which we are producing more information than humans have the capacity to process and absorb (Bauman, 2001, 2011). This flood of information is paired with enduring challenges from across the political spectrum to established forms of authority, including epistemic authority. While these shifts have the potential to open up more substantive, equitable forms of epistemic pluralism, what we largely find instead is that many people are increasingly encased within their own personalized knowledge bubbles. These knowledge bubbles are even more individualized than collective echo chambers, wherein there is at least some sense of shared meaning, values, and sense making. Within their own personalized knowledge bubbles, people tend to build virtual realities around what is convenient and affirming. Thus, the approaches to knowledge that are engaged from within these virtual realities eschew established conventions of intellectual depth, and certainly make consensus difficult if not impossible within even relatively small communities, let alone across whole institutions or societies.

Change also happens today faster than our existing theorizations and strategies can generally keep up with. Zygmunt Bauman (2011) reflects on the temporal shift from previous eras of modernity to the present by using the metaphor of ballistic missiles versus smart missiles. The former must determine their path before they start moving, and neither their target nor their flight path can change as they move; a smart missile, in contrast, can change its direction mid-flight to keep up with a moving target. In this sense, "smart missiles, unlike their ballistic elder cousins, learn as they go. So what they need to be supplied with initially is the ability to learn, and learn fast" (p. 17). While we might take issue with Bauman's choice of militaristic metaphors, the fact remains that it is increasingly difficult to predict and plan for the future as we once did; this includes the difficulty of determining which kinds of knowledge—if any—will be most useful in any given moment or setting, in light of this constant change. In that case, there is a need to develop capacities to learn fast, adapt on the move, and discern the relevance and potential impact of possible interventions in complex, volatile contexts.

Given that we face an overwhelming amount of information, an impossibility of achieving consensus as people construct their own virtual realities, and an unprecedented speed and complexity of change, even gaining peoples' attention, let alone sustaining it, is a difficult challenge, and one often gamed most skillfully by those who seek to profit from it. We can therefore sense a looming impossibility of establishing epistemic hegemony and consensus about what constitutes the "public good" and the most desirable way forward. Yet many of us who study higher education, and many others who work in higher education institutions, still think that if we describe the problem accurately and convincingly enough, we can determine and prescribe an ideal solution, and people will absorb this description-and-prescription and subsequently change their behaviors. Even if scholars, practitioners, and policy makers could agree on such a framework—an unlikely prospect—at this point it seems almost fantastical to approach the future of higher education from a universal, normative set of ideas, practices, and values and to expect this to lead to our predetermined desired outcomes.

Beyond questions about the feasibility of establishing a "single forward" for higher education, we can also draw on decolonial critiques to ask about its desirability. The attempt to establish a consensus that could restore a sense of order, predictability, and certainty is often rooted in an attempt to restore stable hierarchies of knowledge, authority, and cultures. While for some this may be a reactionary desire to reestablish previous hierarchies, others understand it as a revolutionary desire to create new hierarchies. In both cases, however, the idea is that there is an exceptional, deserving, righteous individual or group that should prescribe a universal pathway forward, and others who should follow this prescription. This is captured in the Five E's, reviewed at the beginning of this book: exceptionalism, exaltedness, entitlement, ego empowerment, and externalization of culpability. Theories and strategies of change that are rooted in the Five E's tend to repeat colonial patterns that orient our currently dominant systems in their search for universality, authority, certainty, and innocence.

None of this means that knowledge produced within a description-prescription theory of change, or an approach to institutional transformation rooted in the Five E's, has lost all value. Indeed, both approaches can lead to many important conversations and practical interventions. However, responses to current challenges that are articulated from within these frames alone may be inadequate for preparing us to navigate the complex contemporary landscape of higher education and to address ongoing settler colonization, the afterlife of slavery, US imperialism, and ecological destruction.

So, what is to be done? I propose that those of us who work and study in colleges and universities might consider both the prospects and limitations of existing descriptions and prescriptions of current problems, and supplement those description-prescriptions (1) by connecting contemporary challenges to persisting colonial legacies of violence and unsustainability in higher education; (2) by approaching the future in ways that do not presume either the continuity of higher education as we know it (through various kinds of reform) or its replacement with a universal alternative with guarantees; and (3) by confronting increasing volatility, uncertainty, complexity, and ambiguity with more individual and collective reflexivity, accountability, and discernment. Throughout this book, I address the first task on this list. In the following two sections, I address the second and third.

The End of Higher Education As We Know It

A sense that higher education is in crisis often leads to responses rooted in a reactive defense of existing institutions, without always asking whether substantively different kinds of higher education might be both possible and desirable (Boggs & Mitchell, 2018). For instance, institutional responses to the COVID-19 pandemic suggest not only that most colleges and universities are unprepared for social and ecological crises, but also that when these crises do arise, they seek to restore business as usual, as quickly as possible. They devote little time or institutional will to questioning whether a return to "normal" is either desirable or feasible—and, if so, for how long and at what cost. Some suggested that COVID-19 presented an opportunity to "resurrect the public university" (Robin, 2020). The *New York Times* Editorial Board, for example, recited a romantic history of the Morrill Act, rooted in white settler memory, in a piece about the need to ensure that "the United States has a chance to emerge from this latest crisis [COVID-19] as a stronger nation, more just, more free, and more resilient" (2020).

According to Whyte (2020a), these kinds of responses can be understood as a reflection of colonial "epistemologies of crisis," which "make some people believe that it is possible to make transformation in the world in ways that ensure societies can bounce back to some current state of affairs." That state of affairs is one in which colonial practices and relations continue uninterrupted. To challenge hope for this "bounce back" is to invite dismissal and be deemed irrelevant, defeatist, or even dangerous: perceived either as aligning with decades of efforts to privatize and dismantle public higher education, or as propagating despair. While there is widespread agreement that *naïve* hope is bad, we are told that critical hope or radical hope or educated hope is needed, perhaps now more than ever. To even consider that one possible outcome of current crises is the end of higher education as we know it is to be understood as calling it into being; one may be doubly rebuked if one does not propose a predetermined system in its place. I have been warned, for instance, that raising this issue with university students will cause them undue stress and burst their hopes and dreams. This assertion dubiously assumes that students are not already considering this possibility, and that it is in their best interest for us to offer certainties and promises about the continuity of existing systems and institutions rather than prepare them to responsibly navigate inevitable challenges, complexities, and uncertainties.

If, as Denise Ferreira da Silva (2014) suggests, decolonization requires "the end of the world as we know it," the decolonization of higher education may entail "the end of higher education as we know it" (Stein, 2019). However, rather than frame this thought as a prescription for where we should go, we might understand it as one possible description of the current state of things. That is, we might be facing the end of higher education as we know it, whether we like it or not. Given this possibility, throughout this book I articulate the ethical and practical imperative of imagining higher education otherwise, while registering my reluctance to imagine otherwise *before* we have begun the difficult work of disinvesting from modern/colonial institutions and the promises they offer—lest we continue to imagine more of the same.

I use the term "disinvesting" here in contrast to "divesting," inspired by Anna Agathangelou and colleagues (2015). In this articulation, disinvestment does not entail removing oneself from a situation by searching for some place that is not compromised; rather, it means facing the fact that complexity and complicity form the "constitutive situation of our lives" (Shotwell, 2016, p. 8). Disinvestment would mean recognizing that those of us who have benefited from whitestream institutions and their promises, and thus from the racial, colonial, and ecological violences that made them possible, are implicated in wrongs that we may never be able to right, harms that we may never be able to heal, and debts we may never be able to pay. At the same time, it means recognizing that we have no choice but to try anyway.

In the introduction to this book, I suggested thinking of responsibility in three layers: (1) *attributability*, or recognition that the privileges and benefits we enjoy are rooted in historical and ongoing colonial, racial, and ecological harm; (2) *answerability*, or recognition of one's role in the systemic dimensions of harm; and (3) *accountability*, or recognition that one is both systemically culpable and individually complicit in harm and that there is thus both an individual and collective obligation to interrupt the reproduction of harm, enact restitution, and repair harms already done. Many higher education institutions in the United States have not yet arrived at the point of attributability; those that have are still grappling with what it means, and their institutional efforts to respond to this attributability are often enacted in superficial and nonperformative ways. Some individuals in these institutions are also starting to ask what answerability might entail. But for most people it remains unclear what accountability, defined as restitution and reparation for complicity in harm, could actually look like in higher education, because most people—especially white settlers like myself—have not yet even registered that this is a possible future, let alone a desirable one. Considerable work remains to be done to make the possibility of decolonial futures legible, both within universities and beyond.

However, this work cannot even begin if we remain invested in colonially subsidized promises, or if we are motivated by the search for immediate redemption and resolution rather than a sense of ongoing responsibility. Disinvesting from the continuity of "higher education as we know it" does not mean that we should not work to make life more livable and equitable in existing institutions for as long as they stand. However, it might mean not placing hope in their futurity, and instead committing to learn from past mistakes so that we might not continue to repeat them. This commitment will require us to confront the collective mess we have (unevenly) made, without looking for an easy exit or prefabricated alternative.

This work is unlikely to go in a straight, predictable line. No amount of information or planning can prepare us to respond to every specific situation, crisis, or conflict that might arise in the process of honestly grappling with the extent to which our institutions of higher education, and we ourselves, are implicated in harm. Instead of trying to plan for every possible contingency, we might instead develop the stamina and capacities that would enable us to "stay with the trouble" (Haraway, 2016) and have difficult conversations without relationships falling apart. This commitment will likely entail learning to engage in the messy, challenging work of individual and collective transformation that has no clear end or predetermined outcome; to sit with uncomfortable truths about the full extent of our individual and institutional complicity in harm, without becoming irritated, overwhelmed, or immobilized and without seeking premature resolution; to discern the challenges, complexities, tensions, uncertainties, failures, and contradictions that will inevitably arise in efforts to fully accept and act on our individual and institutional responsibilities; and to respond to the aforementioned difficulties in more grounded, dexterous, responsible, and critically informed ways that support continuous movement away from harm and toward greater accountability, humility, and maturity.

Development of the above capacities and dispositions cannot be taught in a course, or transmitted through a book such as this. Intellectual work might enable us to get to the edge of what it is currently possible to imagine within dominant modern/colonial frames and institutions, and to more clearly discern their internal limits and harmful effects—but it cannot, in itself, transport us somewhere different or lead us to interrupt and rearrange colonial desires (Spivak, 2004). As Elwood Jimmy (2019) writes, "Thinking is what got us where we are. Thinking will not get us where we need to be. We need practices of feeling, practices of humility, practices that regenerate and recalibrate exiled capacities that will allow us to really see and sit with each other for the long-term. These practices are not a sprint. They are a marathon—a lifelong one." Thus, we might consider the uses *and* limits of intellectual critique (e.g., reading and writing articles and books like this one, giving lectures, raising awareness, disseminating information), and ask what other kinds of work need to be done not just to acknowledge but also to interrupt and accept responsibility for the violence and unsustainability that characterize the higher education institutions we have inherited. We would have to also discern what kinds of work can be done in existing institutions and what needs to be done elsewhere; how we can do this work with integrity, given institutional limitations and issues of intelligibility, as well as own our complicity and tendency to reproduce colonial circularities; how we can recognize the urgency of this work while not rushing but instead moving at the speed of trust; and how we can distribute this work in ways that do not re-create uneven patterns of labor in which Black, Indigenous, and racialized peoples are expected to bear most of the burden for change (Jimmy, Andreotti, & Stein, 2019).

Disinvesting from higher education as we know it and imagining higher education otherwise thus involves not only intellectual work but affective and relational work as well, which can ultimately enable us determine what forms of political and economic restitution are needed (Andreotti, et al., 2018; Jimmy, Andreotti, & Stein, 2019; Stein, 2019; Stein et al., 2022). Affective and relational work might entail, for instance, learning to look beyond our stated and conscious ethical and political commitments so that we might learn to notice and ultimately interrupt often-unconscious harmful defenses, deflections, and desires. We would need to learn to ask and stay with the question of "whether what I desire . . . is what I should be desiring. Whether what I desire is going to help or hinder in living my life well, with others, on a planet that only has a limited capacity for meeting our desires" (Biesta, 2020). It might also mean learning how to interrupt the colonial tendency to calculate, consume, and instrumentalize relationships for individual or institutional self-interest. This change would require activating a sense of accountability that is not contingent on what is convenient or self-serving, but rather is rooted in our interdependence on a shared finite planet. In doing this work, we might learn how to foster relationships that are premised on trust, respect, reciprocity, accountability, responsibility, and consent (Whyte, 2020b), and collaborations that are not oriented by predetermined outcomes but rather by the quality and integrity of the process (Whyte, 2020a) and by a recognition of the responsibility to repay colonial debts and repair harms done.

So What? Now What?

If the dominant forms of higher education are increasingly unlikely to continue, yet truly different futures also appear out of reach, how might we proceed with imagining and engaging higher education otherwise? One way to approach this question is to accept that there is much difficult intellectual, affective, and relational work to do, work I describe in the previous section. In addition to these different layers of work, we also need to consider that different kinds of interventions are needed in the short, medium, and long term.

In the short term, we can continue to engage in institutional change strategies usually categorized as "diversity, equity, and inclusion" (DEI). We can advocate for more institutional spaces, resources, and opportunities for those whose communities have been structurally excluded from higher education, especially Indigenous and Black communities. Institutions can recruit and retain more Indigenous and Black students and faculty, include more non-Western knowledges in courses of all kinds, and offer free or greatly reduced tuition for Indigenous and Black students. While these efforts are important in their own right and can serve as initial steps toward opening up and leveraging other, more thoroughly transformative higher education futures, they are insufficient for addressing the enduring coloniality of our institutions. There is also a need to cultivate a deeper understanding of the responsibilities that follow from institutions' complicity in slavery and colonization. Doing so would require supplementing the common analytic that emphasizes *exclusion* of marginalized communities from the promises offered by modern/colonial institutions with an analytic that emphasizes that those promises are made and fulfilled at the *expense* of marginalized communities, other-than-human beings, and the planet itself. In the short term, we might also focus on developing more stamina and capacities to stay with this work over the long haul, especially when it becomes difficult and conflicts and discomfort inevitably arise.

In the medium term we might support efforts to create alternatives that are possible under existing conditions, such as the Dechinta Centre for Research and Learning (see chapter 5).

Educational experiments like Dechinta gesture toward different futures. Even though constrained by present conditions, they can generate possibilities for education and existence that exceed what is currently available. Rather than treat innovative institutions like Dechinta as *universally applicable models* for what should be done, they can be understood as *contextually relevant experiments* to imagine and practice education otherwise that have both gifts and limitations and thus have much to teach (Stein et al., 2020). Efforts to be taught by these kinds of experimental examples should interrupt the tendency to romanticize alternatives or seek immediate solutions, and instead be rooted in respect for the work that has been done to imagine and enact education differently, as well as a commitment to learn from the paradoxes, mistakes, and possibilities.

Long-term efforts are perhaps the trickiest to engage, as they are necessarily open-ended. At most, this kind of work can only gesture toward alternative horizons. From this perspective, hope for different futures does not rest in any particular vision or promise but rather in the learning and unlearning that can arise from continuous efforts to move away from the harmful and unsustainable horizons that are currently enabled by the relational, political, economic, and epistemological systems of modernity/coloniality. This work is not focused on specific changes to policy, practice, or curricula, but rather emphasizes the importance of ongoing individual and collective practices of disinvesting from the modern/colonial desires for innocence, exceptionalism, entitlement, supremacy, certainty, mastery, and universality that narrowly circumscribe the possibilities for existence, so that we might clear space for the "possibility of possibilities" (Barnett, 2014). It is not just about doing or thinking differently, but rather learning to *be* differently. There is no one way to interrupt the hegemony of higher education as we know it; redress systemic, historical, and ongoing racial, colonial, and ecological violence; regenerate broken relationships; and imagine substantively different futures. However, it is unquestionable that this work will require us to face today's challenges in ways that recognize past mistakes, denaturalize present colonial circumstances, and engage other ways of knowing and being without instrumentalizing difference as a form of escapism (Tuck & Yang, 2012).

Here, I bookend the questions asked in the introduction by offering another set of questions that might encourage us to continue deepening this work in the long term:

- What has allowed higher education institutions, and many who work and study in them, to disavow the role of racial, colonial, and ecological violence in their foundations for so long?
- Why are institutional legacies of violence being increasingly visibilized now, and in the particular ways that they are? How can we ensure that, in the process of addressing these legacies, we do not renaturalize the violence that continues to structure the present in conscious and unconscious ways, and that is often projected into the future?
- How can we develop the stamina and the intellectual, affective, and relational capacities to confront our individual and institutional complicity in higher education's foundational violence over the long haul, and accept the responsibilities that derive from this complicity without becoming overwhelmed or seeking redemption or immediate solutions?
- What does the "public good" mean in the context of a capitalist nation-state whose existence rests on stolen lands and lives (genocide), environmental degradation

(ecocide), and repressed knowledges (epistemicide)?
How can we challenge current efforts to privatize higher
education without romanticizing dominant imaginaries of
the public good?

- What do we need, apart from more knowledge and information, in order to shift enduring investments in individual
exceptionalism, American exceptionalism, and the exceptionalism of higher education itself? How can we offer
critiques without asserting our own exceptionalism?

- How do we acknowledge the complexities and heterogene-
ities of communities that have been harmed and marginalized
by the modern/colonial system, including acknowledging
that some of the futures imagined by those in these communities may also be shaped by colonial desires?

- Is it possible to imagine a future for higher education that
does not implicitly presume the continuity of systems
premised on violence? In the face of intensifying social
and ecological crises, can we afford not to at least consider
the possibility of such a future?

- How can we engage in strategic institutional efforts to
mitigate immediate harm without forgetting the limits of
those efforts and the full extent of those harms?

- How can we make more space in colleges and universities
for people (especially white people) to sit with the
implications of growing calls for the restitution of stolen
lives and land and of what these calls ask of them?

- How can we gesture toward possible decolonial futures
without projecting colonial desires onto them? How can
we remain aware of and accountable for the new and old
mistakes that we will inevitably make in the process of
trying to imagine higher education otherwise?

- If we disinvested from the continuity of "higher education
as we know it," what else might become possible?

- What if another form of higher education is not imaginable until our existing one becomes impossible—and, if this is the case, how might we prepare for this possibility?

No one can say in advance what might come from honestly confronting the colonial foundations of US higher education and considering the possible end of higher education as we know it. But perhaps people would be more willing to undertake this work if we remembered that current crises are nothing new in the United States—that is, if we understand ongoing settler colonialism, anti-Black violence, global imperialism, and ecological destruction as ongoing crises that are constitutive of our current systems and institutions. This, in turn, might allow us to reframe how we approach these crises: not as new problems to be solved in an attempt to restore business as usual but as the product of ongoing colonial conditions that need to be denaturalized, interrupted, and unraveled (Whyte, 2020a, 2020b). As the Out of the Woods Collective (2020) put it, "When we understand 'disaster as condition,' it means we have to be in it for the long haul. There is no single technology, no revolutionary moment (and certainly no election) that is going to fix it for us. Instead, we have to do it carefully and do it right: that's the responsibility to relations with others that we're hoping to remember, rather than forget."

An Invitation to Learn from Failure

As noted earlier, failure is an inevitable part of decolonizing work. This book itself as an example of a "failed" decolonial experiment. I am certain that in the process of writing this book, I have repeated many colonial patterns, including many of those that I critique.

Rather than assuming we can ever fully transcend colonial habits and behaviors such as the CIRCULAR patterns outlined in chapter 5, those engaged in decolonizing work can likely commit only to identifying, interrupting, and grappling with them over the long term. While we remain accountable for re-dressing the negative impacts of our mistakes, failure can also be an important site of learning from those mistakes if it is treated "as an educational moment and learning opportunity" (Arshad-Ayaz et al., 2020, p. 1). In fact, often the deepest learn-ing is possible when we fail. Generative failure requires strategies for honesty and self-reflexivity about where we really are in the learning process (we are often less advanced than we would like to think); clearer discernment of the true extent of the chal-lenges we face (we tend to underestimate their scope and scale); and accountability to those who pay the highest cost for our fail-ures (while failure may be inevitable, it often happens at the expense of already marginalized communities).

The following questions are based on a pedagogical resource we created in the Gesturing Towards Decolonial Futures arts and research collective (GTDF, 2021; see also Andreotti, 2021), in an effort to invite people to reframe failure as a "gift." These questions can encourage hyper-self-reflexive inquiry in order to support deepened discernment about where we really are in our process of unlearning investments in the modern/colonial system in general, and the true extent of our investments in the modern/colonial promises of higher education specifically. The questions invite us to recognize how and why we might have failed and to accept responsibility for the impact of those failures on others and ourselves. They also prompt us to ask how these failures relate to harmful systemic patterns and habits that we might critique intellectually, but still reproduce unconsciously.

To examine these patterns and learn from our failures so as not to continue repeating them requires a level of unfiltered honesty with ourselves when we are doing this work internally, and a level of deep trust in others when we are doing this work collectively. Cultivating this type of hyper-self-reflexivity, honesty, humility, and trust also takes considerable practice—and contains its own moments of failure. However, engaging with questions such as these can support deeper, more accountable engagements in decolonizing work in higher education contexts, and beyond:

- To what extent are you reproducing what you critique?
- To what extent are you avoiding looking at your own complicities and denials, and at whose expense? How might you be making more work for other people without realizing it?
- What is your theory of change; in other words, what description-prescription formula might you be mobilizing? What do you expect from this formula? What would you like your work to move in the world?
- Who are you accountable to? Who is benefiting most from your work? Who and what is this work really about? In what ways could your work be read as self-serving or self-congratulatory?
- What unconscious attachments, presumed entitlements, and desires may be directing your thinking, actions, and relationships? How do these affect you and your relationships?
- How wide is the gap between where you think you are and where you actually are? What truths are you still not ready, willing, or able to speak or to hear?
- What colonial habits of knowing, being, and relating do you continue to embody, and what social tensions are you failing to recognize?
- How can being overwhelmed, disillusioned, and uncertain about the future and how to move forward be generative?

- Who is your imagined audience? What do you expect from this audience? What compromises have you had to make in order for your work to be intelligible and relatable to this audience? To what extent can these compromises compromise the work itself? Who are you choosing not to upset and why? How does integrity manifest in your work?
- Who would legitimately roll their eyes at what you are doing? To what extent are you aware of how you are being "read" by different communities, especially marginalized communities?
- How can you respond with humility, honesty, and hyper-self-reflexivity when your work or self-image are challenged?
- Who would be able to help you be more honest in formulating your answers to the above questions? Would you be able to listen if they told you?
- Where are you stuck? What is keeping you there? How can you better learn to discern between escapist distractions and the work that needs to be done? What would you have to give up or let go of in order to go deeper?

Last Words

In this book, I mobilize decolonial critiques to historicize and contextualize the form of higher education that we currently inhabit, while also considering the risks and potential circularities that might result from efforts to imagine higher education otherwise that do not adequately problematize and recognize accountability for the coloniality of Western ways of knowing, being, and relating. I have also sought to gesture toward different possible horizons of higher education without romanticizing any particular alternative as the "solution" to the problems that we have created. Yet many questions remain about how we might unlearn colonial habits of being that we might not even realize we are embodying, and about how to relearn how to be in and responsible to the world in ways that could enable radically different higher education futures that are unfathomable from where we currently stand in the deeply colonial present.

Opening oneself up to what is viable but unimaginable is a difficult but not impossible task. If we are conditioned to imagine something or know the possible outcomes of something before we do it, can we compel ourselves to move toward something that we can't yet imagine, and for which there is no blueprint? This process is also likely to be uncomfortable, painful, and disorienting for many of us, as it requires the conditioning of muscles that have atrophied within modern/colonial systems, as well as the deflation of those muscles that have been overdeveloped. In fact, this task is so challenging that we generally avoid it, even if this avoidance contradicts our intellectual analyses or our stated ethical and political commitments. It might be that people will be willing to do this work only once they have calculated that the cost or risk of not doing it is higher than doing it. Many of us are not there yet, and some may never get there.

Perhaps the shifting conditions of our social and ecological context will make it increasingly challenging for us to avoid this work. This may be especially the case for younger generations that are no longer afforded the same securities, certainties, and continuities that were promised to previous generations (Bauman, 2011). Maybe it is only by being faced with the possible end of higher education as we know it that we can open up the precarious possibilities of higher education otherwise. Still, an "otherwise" is not possible if we do not do the work of disinvesting from the promises and perceived entitlements that are offered (if rarely delivered) by the form of higher education that we currently have, and the violent and unsustainable system in which it is embedded. In the face of a future

that is inhospitable to the perpetuation of our existing institutions, and perhaps even the perpetuation of humanity itself,
this task feels less and less optional. As we face a growing storm,
the floodwaters are rising. Some of us can continue wading
for now, or perhaps seeking out a temporary platform in order
to escape from the rising waters. However, at a certain point
the water level may rise to the point that we have no choice
but to learn how to swim. Perhaps that will be the point at
which we finally want to ask what beginnings might become
possible at the end of higher education as we know it.

Acknowledgments

Academic books are meant to be original works by the author. In the formal sense, this book is indeed an original work. It is composed of my writing and my ideas, as well as my mistakes. In another sense, I cannot claim sole authorship of the product of a process of thinking, learning, and unlearning that has been in many ways collective.

On the question of authorship, Fred Moten once said, "To the extent that I said anything or that I have something to say, that's because a whole bunch of people, a whole bunch of history, a whole bunch of things sent me to say it." I am inclined to agree with Moten: although I wrote this book, a whole bunch of people, history, and things "sent me to say it."

While it would be impossible to fully account for the many intellectual, affective, and physical labors and layers that went into this text, it is necessary to at least try. The book contains one account of these labors through its citational trail. Here, I provide another.

Thanks must go to the Musqueam Nation, on whose lands the bulk of this book was written. This beautiful place, its multiple histories, and its living stories have deeply informed my work, but I have never had the permission of its Indigenous caretakers to be here. Although the debt that I owe is unpayable, I thank them, nonetheless, and the land itself, for hosting me, and I affirm my support for their struggles to have their lands returned to them.

I would like to thank my many collaborators for their wisdom, intellectual generosity, humor, and razor-sharp critiques. This especially includes those who are part of the Gesturing Towards Decolonial Futures Collective, including Vanessa Andreotti, Cash Ahenakew, Rene Suša, Sarah Amsler, Dani D'Emilia, Will Valley, Camilla Cardoso, Dino Siwek, Azul (Carolina) Duque, Shawn Van Sluys, Tereza Cajkova, Elwood Jimmy, Dallas Hunt, Bill Calhoun, Lisa Taylor, Lynn Mario de Souza, Sonali Balajee, Tania Ramalho, and Kyra Fay.

I am also deeply thankful for the insights that I have gained through conversations with many other colleagues across the globe, including Sereana Naepi, Sheeva Sabati, Kumari Beck, Roopa Trilokekar, Lisa Brunner, Karen Pashby, Roxana Chiappa, Dale McCartney, Su-ming Khoo, Andre Keet, Dina Belluigi, Jhuliane Silva, Elizabeth Buckner, Gerardo Blanco, Dan McCarthy, Santiago Castiello-Gutiérrez, rosalind hampton, Juliana Martinez, and Kristi Carey. Many thanks are owed to Abbie Boggs, Nick Mitchell, Eli Meyerhoff, and Zach Schwartz-Weinstein for inviting me to be part of their abolitionist university studies crew, even though I never felt quite "radical" enough.

This book would not exist were it not for an invitation from Jeffrey Williams and Chris Newfield to be part of their Critical University Studies series, and the support of Johns Hopkins University Press's editorial director, Greg Britton. Thank you for shepherding me through the publishing process.

I am also extremely grateful to those who read and commented on drafts of this work, including Vanessa Andreotti, Michalinos Zembylas, Sarah Amsler, Don Fisher, Dale McCartney, Samantha Clarkson, Evan Bowness, Corrina Sparrow, Dallas Hunt, Jeffrey Williams, Neil McLaughlin, Eva Crowson, two anonymous peer reviewers, and an exceptional copyeditor, Steven Baker.

Finally, I want to thank my parents for having me and then making it possible for me to find my own way in the world; Rachel, for your steadfast sisterhood; Buddy, for being my greatest supporter; Deborah, for teaching me patience; Mary Ann and Jen, for being academic guides; my nephews, Kai and Jax, for prompting me to ask what kind of education we need from day one in order to support different possible futures; Attie, for your indefatigable emotional support; and Sami, for being the best and funniest friend a person could ask for.

Parts of chapter 3 previously appeared in "A colonial history of the higher education present: Rethinking land-grant institutions through processes of accumulation and relations of conquest," published in *Critical Studies in Education* © (2020), copyright Taylor & Francis, available online: https://doi.org/10.1080/17508487.2017.1409646. Parts of chapter 4 previously appeared in "Confronting the racial-colonial foundations of US higher education," published in *Journal for the Study of Postsecondary and Tertiary Education* (2018), available online: https://doi.org/10.28945/4105.

Works Cited

Introduction

Ahenakew, C. (2016). Grafting Indigenous ways of knowing onto non-Indigenous ways of being: The (underestimated) challenges of a decolonial imagination. *International Review of Qualitative Research, 9*(3), 323–340.

Ahenakew, C. (2019). *Towards scarring our collective soul wound.* Musagetes Foundation.

Ahmed, S. (2012). *On being included: Racism and diversity in institutional life.* Durham, NC: Duke University Press.

Ahmed, S. (2019). A complaint biography. *Biography, 42*(3), 514–523.

Andreotti, V., Jimmy, E., & Calhoun, B. (2021). Gift contract. *Gesturing towards Decolonial Futures*, February 24. https://decolonialfutures.net/2021/02/15/gift-contract/.

Andreotti, V., & Ahenakew, C. (2013). Educating. In S. Matthewman, C. West-Newman, and B. Curtis (eds.). *Being sociological*, 3rd ed. (pp. 233–250). New York: Palgrave MacMillan.

Andreotti, V. D. O., Stein, S., Ahenakew, C., & Hunt, D. (2015). Mapping interpretations of decolonization in the context of higher education. *Decolonization: Indigeneity, Education & Society, 4*(1), 21–40.

Baccher, J. S., & Sherman, R. (2019). Opinion: UC investments are going fossil free but not exactly for the reasons you think. *Los Angeles Times*, September 17. https://www.latimes.com/opinion/story/2019-09-16/divestment-fossil-fuel-university-of-california-climate-change.

Barnett, R. (ed.). (2012). *The future university: Ideas and possibilities.* Routledge.

Barnett, R. (2014). *Thinking about higher education.* Springer.

Belcourt, B. (2018). Material for worldbuilding. *Articulation Magazine*, April 7. http://www.articulationmagazine.com/material-for-worldbuilding/.

Boggs, A., & Mitchell, N. (2018). Critical University Studies and the Crisis Consensus. *Feminist Studies, 44*(2), 432–463.

Boggs, A., Meyerhoff, E., Mitchell, N., & Schwartz-Weinstein, Z (2019). *Abolitionist University Studies: An invitation.* Abolition University. https://abolition.university/wp-content/uploads/2019/08/Abolitionist-University-Studies_-An-Invitation-Release-1-version.pdf.

Boidin, C., Cohen, J., & Grosfoguel, R. (2012). Introduction: From university to pluriversity; a decolonial approach to the present crisis of western universities. *Human Architecture: Journal of the Sociology of Self-Knowledge, 10*(1), 2.

Bruyneel, K. (2013). The American liberal colonial tradition. *Settler Colonial Studies, 3*(3–4), 311–321.

Bruyneel, K. (2017). Creolizing collective memory: Refusing the settler memory of the Reconstruction Era. *Journal of French and Francophone Philosophy, 25*(2), 36–44.

Business in Vancouver (2016). UBC's billion-dollar trust fund baby. https://biv.com/article/2016/08/ubcs-billion-dollar-trust-fund-baby.

Byrd, J. A. (2011). *The transit of empire: Indigenous critiques of colonialism.* University of Minnesota Press.

Calderon, D. (2014). Uncovering settler grammars in curriculum. *Educational Studies, 50*(4), 313–338.

Carlson, K. T. (2005). Rethinking dialogue and history: The King's Promise and the 1906 Aboriginal Delegation to London. *Native Studies Review, 16*(2), 1–38.

Chatterjee, P., & Maira, S. (eds.). (2014). *The imperial university: Academic repression and scholarly dissent.* University of Minnesota Press.

Clark, B. R. (1972). The organizational saga in higher education. *Administrative Science Quarterly, 17*(2), 178–184.

Coloma, R. S. (2013). Empire: An analytical category for educational research. *Educational Theory, 63*(6), 639–658.

Cornum, L (2019). Burial ground acknowledgements. *New Inquiry*, October 14. https://thenewinquiry.com/burial-ground-acknowledgements.

Daigle, M. (2019). The spectacle of reconciliation: On (the) unsettling responsibilities to Indigenous peoples in the academy. *Environment and Planning D: Society and Space.*

Davenport, D. (2015). Presentism: The dangerous virus spreading across college campuses. *Forbes*, December 1. https://www.forbes.com/sites/daviddavenport/2015/12/01/presentism-the-dangerous-virus-spreading-across-college-campuses/#1294cf012dcb.

Davis, H., & Todd, Z. (2017). On the importance of a date, or decolonizing the Anthropocene. *ACME: An International E-Journal for Critical Geographies, 16*(4).

Day, I. (2015). Being or nothingness: Indigeneity, antiblackness, and settler colonial critique. *Critical Ethnic Studies, 1*(2), 102–121.

Diabo, G. K. I. (2019). Bad feelings, feeling bad: The affects of Asian-Indigenous coalition. *Inter-Asia Cultural Studies, 20*(2), 257–270.

Farrell, J., Burow, P. B., McConnell, K., Bayham, J., Whyte, K., & Koss, G. (2021). Effects of land dispossession and forced migration on Indigenous peoples in North America. *Science, 374*(6567).

Grande, S. (2004). *Red pedagogy: Native American social and political thought*. Rowman & Littlefield.

Grande, S. (2018). Refusing the university. In E. Tuck & K. W. Yang (eds.), *Toward what justice?* (pp. 47–65). Routledge.

Grant, L. (2018). A Musqueam view of the UBC campus. *UBC Campus and Community Planning Newsletter*, April 1. https://planning.ubc.ca/news/musqueam-view-ubc-campus.

Grosfoguel, R. (2013). The structure of knowledge in westernised universities: Epistemic racism/sexism and the four genocides/epistemicides. *Human Architecture: Journal of the Sociology of Self-Knowledge, 1*, 73–90.

Hailu, M., & Tachine, A. (2021). Black and Indigenous theoretical considerations for higher education sustainability. *Journal of Comparative & International Higher Education, 13*(Summer), 20–42.

hampton, r. (2020). *Black racialization and resistance at an elite university*. University of Toronto Press.

Hartman, S. V., & Wilderson, F. B. (2003). The position of the unthought. *Qui Parle, 13*(2), 183–201.

Hunt, D. (2018). "In search of our better selves": Totem transfer narratives and Indigenous futurities. *American Indian Culture and Research Journal, 42*(1), 71–90.

Hunt, S. (2014). Ontologies of Indigeneity: The politics of embodying a concept. *Cultural geographies, 21*(1), 27–32.

Jefferess, D. (2012). The "Me to We" social enterprise: Global education as lifestyle brand. *Critical Literacy: Theories and Practices, 6*(1), 18–30.

Jimmy, E., Andreotti, V., & Stein, S. (2019). Foreword. In C. Ahenakew, *Towards scarring our collective soul wound* (pp. 5–12). Musagetes Foundation.

Kapoor, I. (2004). Hyper-self-reflexive development? Spivak on representing the Third World "Other." *Third World Quarterly, 25*(4), 627–647.

Kapoor, I. (2014). Psychoanalysis and development: Contributions, examples, limits. *Third World Quarterly, 35*(7), 1120–1143.

Kelley, R. D. G., & Moten, F. (2017). Robin D. G. Kelley and Fred Moten in conversation. *YouTube.com*, uploaded https://www.youtube.com/watch?v=fP-2F9MXjRE.

King, T. L. (2019). *The Black shoals: Offshore formations of Black and Native Studies*. Duke University Press.

Kuokkanen, R. J. (2004). Toward the hospitality of the academy: The (im)possible gift of Indigenous epistemes. Doctoral dissertation, University of British Columbia, Vancouver.

La Paperson. (2017). *A third university is possible*. University of Minnesota Press.

Labaree, D. F. (2016). An affair to remember: America's brief fling with the university as a public good. *Journal of Philosophy of Education, 50*(1), 20–36.

MacKenzie, N. A. M. (1958). *The president's report, 1957–58*. University of British Columbia. https://www.library.ubc.ca/archives/pdfs/presidents/1958.pdf.

Mabry, S. M. (2019). The higher education decolonisation project: Negotiating cognitive dissonance. *Transformation: Critical Perspectives on Southern Africa, 100*(1), 179–189.

Marginson, S. (2016). *The dream is over*. University of California Press.

Marker, M. (2011). Sacred mountains and ivory towers: Indigenous pedagogies of place and invasions from modernity. In G. J. S. Dei (ed.), *Indigenous philosophies and critical education: A reader* (pp. 197–211). Peter Lang.

Marker, M. (2019). Indigenous knowledges, universities, and alluvial zones of paradigm change. *Discourse: Studies in the Cultural Politics of Education, 40*(4), 500–513.

Melamed, J. (2006). The spirit of neoliberalism: From racial liberalism to neoliberal multiculturalism. *Social Text, 24* (4 [89]), 1–24.

Metcalfe, A. S. (2012). Imag(in)ing the university: Visual sociology and higher education. *Review of Higher Education, 35*(4), 517–534.

Metcalfe, A. S. (2019). Witnessing Indigenous dispossession and academic arboricide: Visual auto-ethnography as anti-colonial dialectic. *Visual Arts Research, 45*(2), 80–90.

Meyerhoff, E. (2019). *Beyond education: Radical studying for another world*. University of Minnesota Press.

Minthorn, R. S. Z., & Nelson, C. A. (2018). Colonized and racist Indigenous campus tour. *Journal of Critical Scholarship on Higher Education and Student Affairs, 4*(1), 4.

Minthorn, R. S. Z., & Shotton, H. (2018). *Reclaiming Indigenous research in higher education*. Rutgers University Press.

Mitchell, N. (2015). (Critical ethnic studies) intellectual. *Critical Ethnic Studies, 1*(1), 86–94.

Mustaffa, J. B. (2017). Mapping violence, naming life: A history of anti-Black oppression in the higher education system. *International Journal of Qualitative Studies in Education, 30*(8), 711–727.

Patel, L. (2015). *Decolonizing educational research: From ownership to answerability*. Routledge.

Patel, L. (2021). *No study without struggle: Confronting the legacy of settler colonialism in higher education*. Beacon Press.

Patel, S. (2016). Complicating the tale of "Two Indians": Mapping "South Asian" complicity in white settler colonialism along the axis of caste and anti-Blackness. *Theory and Event, 19*(4).

Perkin, H. (2007). History of universities. In *International handbook of higher education* (pp. 159–205). Springer.

Phruksachart, M. (2020). The literature of white liberalism. *Boston Review*, August 21. http://bostonreview.net/race/melissa-phruksachart-literature -white-liberalism.

Pietsch, T. (2016). Between the local and the universal: Academic worlds and the long history of the university. In M. H. Chou, I. Kamola, & T. Pietsch (eds.), *Transnational politics of higher education: Contesting the global/ transforming the local*. Routledge.

Rodríguez, D. (2012). Racial/colonial genocide and the "neoliberal academy": In excess of a problematic. *American Quarterly*, 64(4), 809–813.

Ryan, D. (2019). UBC turns land into a river of gold. *Vancouver Sun*, March 29. https://vancouversun.com/news/local-news/0323-ubc-vision-1000-acres -1000-years.

Scott, D. (2004). *Conscripts of modernity: The tragedy of colonial enlightenment*. Duke University Press.

Shaker, P. (2010). Preserving Canadian exceptionalism: An educator's context. *EdCan Network*, August 5. https://www.edcan.ca/articles/preserving -canadian-exceptionalism-an-educators-context/.

Shotwell, A. (2016). *Against purity: Living ethically in compromised times*. University of Minnesota Press.

Simpson, L. B. (2016). Indigenous resurgence and co-resistance. *Critical Ethnic Studies*, 2(2), 19–34.

Smith, L.T. (2012). *Decolonizing methodologies: Research and indigenous peoples*. Zed Books.

Snelgrove, C., Dhamoon, R., & Corntassel, J. (2014). Unsettling settler colonialism: The discourse and politics of settlers, and solidarity with Indigenous nations. *Decolonization: Indigeneity, Education & Society*, 3(2).

Sorber, N. M., & Geiger, R. L. (2014). The welding of opposite views: Land-grant historiography at 150 years. In *Higher education: Handbook of theory and research* (pp. 385–422). Springer Netherlands.

Spivak, G. C. (1988). Can the subaltern speak? In C. Nelson & L. Grossberg (eds.), *Marxism and the interpretation of culture* (pp. 24–28). University of Illinois Press.

Spivak, G. C. (2004). Righting wrongs. *South Atlantic Quarterly*, 103(2–3), 523–581.

Stanley, T. (2009). The banality of colonialism: Encountering artifacts of genocide and white supremacy in Vancouver today. In S. R. Steinberg (ed.), *Diversity and multiculturalism: A reader* (pp. 143–159). Peter Lang.

Stein, S. (2019). Beyond higher education as we know it: Gesturing towards decolonial horizons of possibility. *Studies in Philosophy & Education*, 38(2), 143–161.

Stein, S. (2020). "Truth before reconciliation": The difficulties of transform- ing higher education in settler colonial contexts. *Higher Education Research and Development*, 39(1), 156–170.

Stein, S. (2021). What can decolonial and abolitionist critiques teach the field of higher education? *The Review of Higher Education, 44*(3), 387–414.

Stein, S., & Andreotti, V. D. O. (2017). Higher education and the modern/colonial global imaginary. *Cultural Studies ↔ Critical Methodologies, 17*(3), 173–181.

Stein, S., Andreotti, V., Hunt, D., & Ahenakew, C. (2021). Complexities and challenges of decolonizing higher education: Lessons from Canada. In S. H. Kumalo (ed.), *Decolonisation as democratisation: Global insights into the South Africa experience.* UKZN Press.

Stein, S., et al. (2020). Gesturing towards decolonial futures: Reflections on our learnings thus far. *Nordic Journal of Comparative and International Education (NJCIE), 4*(1), 43–65.

Stewart-Ambo, T., & Yang, K. W. (2021). Beyond land acknowledgment in settler institutions. *Social Text, 39*(1), 21–46.

Stonechild, B. (2006). *The new buffalo: The struggle for Aboriginal post-secondary education in Canada.* University of Manitoba Press.

TallBear, K. (2019). Caretaking relations, not American dreaming. *Kalfou, 6*(1), 24–41.

Thelin, J. R. (2004). *A history of American higher education.* Johns Hopkins University Press.

Thobani, S. (2007). *Exalted subjects: Studies in the making of race and nation in Canada.* University of Toronto Press.

Thobani, S. (2018). Neoliberal multiculturalism and western exceptionalism: The cultural politics of the West. *Fudan Journal of the Humanities and Social Sciences, 11*(2), 161–174.

Truth and Reconciliation Commission of Canada. (2015). *Honouring the truth, reconciling for the future: Summary of the final report of the Truth and Reconciliation Commission of Canada.* Available at http://nctr.ca/assets /reports/Final%20Reports/Executive_Summary_English_Web.pdf.

Tuck, E., & Yang, K. W. (2012). Decolonization is not a metaphor. *Decolonization: Indigeneity, Education, and Society, 1*(1), 1–40.

UBC (University of British Columbia). (n.d.). UBC-Aboriginal timeline. https://timeandplace.ubc.ca/timeline/

UBC (University of British Columbia). (2020). *Indigenous strategic plan.* Indigenous Portal, University of British Columbia. https://aboriginal-2018 .sites.olt.ubc.ca/files/2021/06/UBC.ISP_StrategicPlan2020-SPREAD -Borderless-REDUCED.pdf.

University News (2019). UBC raises Musqueam Band flag permanently at UBC Campus. February 25. https://news.ubc.ca/2019/02/25/ubc-raises -musqueam-indian-band-flag-permanently-at-vancouver-campus/.

Vowel, C. (2016). Beyond territorial acknowledgements. *Apihtawikosisan,* September 23. https://apihtawikosisan.com/2016/09/beyond-territorial -acknowledgments/.

Walcott, R. (2019). The end of diversity. *Public culture*, 31(2), 393–408.

Walia, H. (2013). *Undoing border imperialism*. AK Press.

Wark, J. (2021). Land acknowledgements in the academy: Refusing the settler myth. *Curriculum Inquiry*, 51(2), 191–209.

Wilder, C. S. (2013). *Ebony and ivy: Race, slavery, and the troubled history of America's universities*. Bloomsbury.

Whyte, K. (2020). Too late for indigenous climate justice: Ecological and relational tipping points. *Wiley Interdisciplinary Reviews: Climate Change*, 11(1), e603.

Wright, B. (1991). The "untameable savage spirit": American Indians in colonial colleges. *Review of Higher Education*, 14(4), 429–452.

Chapter 1. A Colonial History of the Higher Education Present

Adams, J. T. (2017). *The epic of America*. Routledge.

Ahenakew, C. (2016). Grafting Indigenous ways of knowing onto non-Indigenous ways of being: The (underestimated) challenges of a decolonial imagination. *International Review of Qualitative Research*, 9(3), 323–340.

Ahenakew, C. (2019). *Towards scarring our collective soul wound*. Musagetes Foundation.

Ahenakew, C., Andreotti, V., Cooper, G., & Hireme, H. (2014). Beyond epistemic provincialism: De-provincializing Indigenous resistance. *AlterNative: An International Journal of Indigenous Peoples*, 10(3), 216.

Ahmed, S. (2012). *On being included: Racism and diversity in institutional life*. Duke University Press.

Aikau, H. K. (2015). Following the Alaloa Kīpapa of our ancestors: A trans-indigenous futurity without the state (United States or otherwise). *American Quarterly*, 67(3), 653–661.

Alexander, M. J. (2005). *Pedagogies of crossing: Meditations on feminism, sexual politics, memory, and the sacred*. Duke University Press.

Arvin, M., Tuck, E., & Morrill, A. (2013). Decolonizing feminism: Challenging connections between settler colonialism and heteropatriarchy. *Feminist Formations*, 25(1), 8–34.

Benson, M. T., & Boyd, H. R. (2015). The public university: Recalling higher education's democratic purpose. *Thought & Action*, 31, 69–84.

Boggs, A., & Mitchell, N. (2018). Critical university studies and the crisis consensus. *Feminist Studies*, 44(2), 432–463.

Boggs, A., Meyerhoff, E., Mitchell, N., & Schwartz-Weinstein, Z (2019). *Abolitionist university studies: An invitation*. Abolition University. https://abolition.university/wp-content/uploads/2019/08/Abolitionist-University-Studies_-An-Invitation-Release-1-version.pdf.

Boidin, C., Cohen, J., & Grosfoguel, R. (2012). Introduction: From university to pluriversity; a decolonial approach to the present crisis of western universities. *Human Architecture: Journal of the Sociology of Self-Knowledge*, *10*(1), 2.

Bruyneel, K. (2013). The American liberal colonial tradition. *Settler Colonial Studies*, *3*(3–4), 311–321.

Byrd, J. A. (2011). *The transit of empire: Indigenous critiques of colonialism*. University of Minnesota Press.

Chambers, C. R., & Freeman, S., Jr. (2017). From margin to center: Rethinking the cannon in higher education programs. *Journal for the Study of Postsecondary and Tertiary Education*, *2*, 115–119.

Chatterjee, P., & Maira, S. (2014). *The imperial university*. University of Minnesota Press.

Cohen, A. M., & Kisker, C. B. (2009). *The shaping of American higher education: Emergence and growth of the contemporary system*. John Wiley & Sons.

Cole, E. R. (2020). *The campus color line: College presidents and the struggle for Black freedom*. Princeton University Press.

Coulthard, G. (2014). *Red skin, white masks: Rejecting the colonial politics of recognition*. University of Minnesota Press.

Clarke, M., & Fine, G. A. (2010). "A" for Apology: Slavery and the discourse of remonstrance in two American universities. *History and Memory*, *22*(1), 81–112.

Cullen, J. (2003). *The American dream: A short history of an idea that shaped a nation*. Oxford University Press.

Cusicanqui, S. R. (2012). Ch'ixinakax utxiwa: A reflection on the practices and discourses of decolonization. *South Atlantic Quarterly*, *111*(1), 95–109.

Davis, H., & Todd, Z. (2017). On the importance of a date, or, decolonizing the Anthropocene. *ACME: An International Journal for Critical Geographies*, *16*(4), 761–780.

DiAngelo, R. (2011). White fragility. *International Journal of Critical Pedagogy*, *3*(3), 54–70.

Ferguson, R. A. (2012). *The reorder of things: The university and its pedagogies of minority difference*. University of Minnesota Press.

Flowers, R. (2015). Refusal to forgive: Indigenous women's love and rage. *Decolonization: Indigeneity, Education & Society*, *4*(2), 32–49.

Geiger, R. L. (2014). *The history of American higher education: Learning and culture from the founding to World War II*. Princeton University Press.

Global Footprint Network (n.d.). https://www.footprintnetwork.org.

Goldrick-Rab, S. (2016). *Paying the price: College costs, financial aid, and the betrayal of the American dream*. University of Chicago Press.

Guinier, L. (2015). *The tyranny of the meritocracy: Democratizing higher education in America*. Beacon Press.

hampton, r. (2020). *Black racialization and resistance at an elite university*. University of Toronto Press.

Hartman, S. (2008). *Lose your mother: A journey along the Atlantic slave route.* Macmillan.

Hong, G. K. (2008). "The future of our worlds": Black feminism and the politics of knowledge in the university under globalization. *Meridians, 8*(2), 95–115.

Hong, G. K. (2014). Property. In B. Burgett & G. Helder (eds.), *Keywords for American Cultural Studies.* New York University Press. http://keywords .nyupress.org/american-cultural-studies/essay/property/.

Jimmy, E., Andreotti, V., and Stein, S. (2019). *Towards braiding.* Musagetes.

Kendi, I. X. (2012). *The Black campus movement: Black students and the racial reconstitution of higher education, 1965–1972.* Springer.

Kezar, A. J. (2004). Obtaining integrity? Reviewing and examining the charter between higher education and society. *Review of Higher Education, 27*(4), 429–459.

Kimball, E. W., & Ryder, A. J. (2014). Using history to promote reflection: A model for reframing student affairs practice. *Journal of Student Affairs Research and Practice, 51*(3), 298–310.

King, T. L. (2019). *The Black shoals: Offshore formations of Black and Native studies.* Duke University Press.

Kotef, H. (2020). Violent attachments. *Political Theory, 48*(1), 4–29.

La Paperson. (2017). *A third university is possible.* University of Minnesota Press.

Lee, R., & Ahtone, T. (2020). Land-grab universities: Expropriated Indigenous land is the foundation of the land-grant university. *High Country News,* April, pp. 32–45.

Leroy, J. (2016). Black history in occupied territory: On the entanglements of slavery and settler colonialism. *Theory & Event, 19*(4).

Lucas, C. J. (2006). *American higher education: A history.* St. Martin's Press.

Maldonado-Torres, N. (2007). On the coloniality of being: Contributions to the development of a concept. *Cultural Studies, 21*(2–3), 240–270.

Maldonado-Torres, N. (2011). Thinking through the decolonial turn: Post-continental interventions in theory, philosophy, and critique—An introduction. *Transmodernity: Journal of Peripheral Cultural Production of the Luso-Hispanic World, 1*(2).

Marginson, S. (2016). *The dream is over: The crisis of Clark Kerr's California idea of higher education.* University of California Press.

McNamee, S. J., & Miller, R. K. (2009). *The meritocracy myth.* Rowman & Littlefield.

Mettler, S. (2014). *Degrees of inequality: How the politics of higher education sabotaged the American Dream.* Basic Books.

Meyerhoff, E. (2019). *Beyond education: Radical studying for another world.* University of Minnesota Press.

Mignolo, W. D. (2007). Delinking: The rhetoric of modernity, the logic of coloniality, and the grammar of de-coloniality. *Cultural studies*, 21(2–3), 449–514.

Mills, C. W. (2015). Decolonizing Western political philosophy. *New Political Science*, 37(1), 1–24.

Minthorn, R. S. Z., & Shotton, H. (eds.) (2018). *Reclaiming Indigenous research in higher education.* Rutgers University Press.

Mitchell, N. (forthcoming). *Discipline and surplus: Black studies, women's studies, and the dawn of neoliberalism.* Duke University Press.

Moreton-Robinson, A. (2015). *The white possessive: Property, power, and indigenous sovereignty.* University of Minnesota Press.

Mustaffa, J. B. (2017). Mapping violence, naming life: A history of anti-Black oppression in the higher education system. *International Journal of Qualitative Studies in Education*, 30(8), 711–727.

Newfield, C. (2016). *The great mistake: How we wrecked public universities and how we can fix them.* Johns Hopkins University Press.

Nicolazzo, Z., & Marine, S. B. (2016). Teaching the history of US higher education: A critical duoethnography. *Journal for the Study of Postsecondary and Tertiary Education*, 1, 215.

Nidiffer, J. (1999). Poor historiography: The "poorest" in American higher education. *History of Education Quarterly*, 39(3), 321–336.

Nopper, T. (2011). The wages of non-Blackness: Contemporary immigrant rights and discourses of character, productivity, and value. *Tensions Journal*, (5), 1–25.

Paradies, Y. (2020). Unsettling truths: modernity, (de-)coloniality and Indigenous futures. *Postcolonial Studies*, 23(4), 438–456.

Patel, L. (2015). *Decolonizing educational research: From ownership to answer-ability.* Routledge.

Patel, L. (2021). *No study without struggle: Confronting the legacy of settler colonialism in higher education.* Beacon Press.

Patton, L. D. (2016). Disrupting postsecondary prose: Toward a critical race theory of higher education. *Urban Education*, 51(3), 315–342.

Pease, D. (2009). Re-thinking "American Studies after US exceptionalism." *American Literary History*, 21(1), 19–27.

Pusser, B. (2014). Forces in tension: The state, civil society and market in the future of the university. In P. Gibbs & R. Barnett (eds.), *Thinking about higher education* (pp. 71–89). Springer International Publishing.

Reber, S., & Sinclair, C. (2020). Opportunity engines: Middle-class mobility in higher education. Brookings Institution, May. https://www.brookings.edu/wp-content/uploads/2020/05/Opportunity-Engines_Final.pdf.

Robinson, C. J. (2000). *Black Marxism: The making of the Black radical tradition.* University of North Carolina Press.

Rudolph, F. (1962). *The American college and university: A history*. Alfred A. Knopf.

Santos, B. D. S. (2007). Beyond abyssal thinking: From global lines to ecologies of knowledges. *Review (Fernand Braudel Center)*, 30(1), 45–89.

Seamster, L., & Ray, V. (2018). Against teleology in the study of race: Toward the abolition of the progress paradigm. *Sociological Theory*, 36(4), 315–342.

Sharpe, C. (2016). *In the wake: On blackness and being*. Duke University Press.

Shotwell, A. (2016). *Against purity: Living ethically in compromised times*. University of Minnesota Press.

Silva, D. F.D. (2007). *Toward a global idea of race*. University of Minnesota Press.

Silva, D. F. D. (2014). Toward a Black feminist poethics: The quest(ion) of Blackness toward the end of the world. *Black Scholar*, 44(2), 81–97.

Silva, D. F. D. (2016). The racial limits of social justice: The ruse of equality of opportunity and the global affirmative action mandate. *Critical Ethnic Studies*, 2(2), 184–209.

Sirvent, R., & Haiphong, D. (2019). *American exceptionalism and American innocence: A people's history of fake news—From the Revolutionary War to the War on Terror*. Skyhorse.

Smith, L. T. (2012). *Decolonizing methodologies: Research and Indigenous peoples*. London: Zed Books.

Stein, S. (2018). Racialized frames of value in US university responses to the travel ban. *ACME: An International E-Journal for Critical Geographies*, 17(4), 893–919.

Stein, S. (2020). A colonial history of the higher education present: Rethinking land-grant institutions through processes of accumulation and relations of conquest. *Critical Studies in Education*, 61(2), 212–228.

Stoler, A. L. (2009). *Along the archival grain: Epistemic anxieties and colonial common sense*. Princeton University Press.

Stratton, B. J. (2017). Two universities examined a founder's role in the Sand Creek Massacre. *History News Network*. https://historynewsnetwork.org/article/166896.

TallBear, K. (2019). Caretaking relations, not American dreaming. *Kalfou*, 6(1), 24–41.

Taylor, L. K. (2013). Against the tide: Working with and against the affective flows of resistance in Social and Global Justice Learning. *Critical Literacy: Theories and Practices*, 7(2).

Taylor, M. L. (2020). Seminaries and slavery: An abolition struggle paradigm for research. *Theology Today*, 76(4), 308–321.

Thelin, J. R. (2004). *A history of American higher education*. Johns Hopkins University Press.

Trask, H. K. (2004). The color of violence. *Social Justice*, *31*(4 (98)), 8–16.

Trow, M. (2000). From mass higher education to universal access: The American advantage. *Minerva*, *37*(4), 303–328.

Tuck, E. (2009). Suspending damage: A letter to communities. *Harvard Educational Review*, *79*(3), 409–428.

Tuck, E., & Yang, K. W. (2012). Decolonization is not a metaphor. *Decolonization: Indigeneity, Education, and Society*, *1*(1), 1–40.

Veysey, L. (1965). *The emergence of the American university*. University of Chicago Press.

Walia, H. (2013). *Undoing border imperialism*. AK Press.

Walters, L. K. (2017). Slavery and the American university: Discourses of retrospective justice at Harvard and Brown. *Slavery & Abolition*, *38*(4), 719–744.

Whyte, K. P. (2018). On resilient parasitisms, or why I'm skeptical of Indigenous/settler reconciliation. *Journal of Global Ethics*, *14*(2), 277–289.

Whyte, K. P. (2020). Too late for indigenous climate justice: Ecological and relational tipping points. *Wiley Interdisciplinary Reviews: Climate Change*, *11*(1), e603.

Wilder, C. S. (2013). *Ebony and ivy: Race, slavery, and the troubled history of America's universities*. Bloomsbury.

Wilderson, F. (2010). *Red, white, and black: Cinema and the structure of U.S. antagonisms*. Duke University Press.

Willinsky, J. (1998). *Learning to divide the world: Education at empire's end*. University of Minnesota Press.

Wynter, S. (2003). Unsettling the coloniality of being/power/truth/freedom: Towards the human, after man, its overrepresentation—An argument. *CR: The New Centennial Review*, *3*(3), 257–337.

Chapter 2. The Violent Origins of US Higher Education

Ahenakew, C. (2016). Grafting Indigenous ways of knowing onto non-Indigenous ways of being: The (underestimated) challenges of a decolonial imagination. *International Review of Qualitative Research*, *9*(3), 323–340.

Arvin, M. (2019). Indigenous feminist notes on embodying alliance against settler colonialism. *Meridians*, *18*(2), 335–357.

Arvin, M., Tuck, E., & Morrill, A. (2013). Decolonizing feminism: Challenging connections between settler colonialism and heteropatriarchy. *Feminist Formations*, 8–34.

Baldwin, A. (1786). University of Georgia at Louisville, 1786, as described in a letter from Abraham Baldwin to Joel Barlow [June 12]. University of Georgia Libraries, updated May 30, 2017. https://www.libs.uga.edu/hargrett/archives/exhibit/baldwin1786/trans.html.

Battiste, M. (2017). *Decolonizing education: Nourishing the learning spirit.* University of British Columbia Press.

Boggs, A., & Mitchell, N. (2018). Critical university studies and the crisis consensus. *Feminist Studies, 44*(2), 432–463.

Boggs, A., Meyerhoff, E., Mitchell, N., & Schwartz-Weinstein, Z (2019). *Abolitionist University Studies: An invitation.* Abolition University. https://abolition.university/wp-content/uploads/2019/08/Abolitionist -University-Studies_-An-Invitation-Release-1-version.pdf.

Brophy, A. L. (2016). *University, court, and slave: Pro-slavery thought in southern colleges and courts and the coming of civil war.* Oxford University Press.

Brophy, A. L. (2018). Forum on slavery and universities: Introduction. *Slavery and Abolition, 39*(2), 229–235.

Brown University Steering Committee on Slavery and Justice. (2006). *Slavery and justice: Report of the Brown University Steering Committee on Slavery and Justice.* Brown University. http://brown.edu/Research/Slavery_Justice /documents/SlaveryAndJustice.pdf.

Bruce, P. A. (1920a). *History of the University of Virginia, 1819–1919: The Lengthened Shadow of One Man.* Vol. 1. Macmillan.

Bruce, P. A. (1920b) *History of the University of Virginia, 1819–1919: The Lengthened Shadow of One Man.* Vol. 2. Macmillan.

Bruyneel, K. (2013). The American liberal colonial tradition. *Settler Colonial Studies, 3*(3–4), 311–321.

Bruyneel, K. (2017). Creolizing collective memory: Refusing the settler memory of the Reconstruction Era. *Journal of French and Francophone Philosophy, 25*(2), 36–44.

Calloway, C. G. (2010). *The Indian history of an American institution: Native Americans and Dartmouth.* Dartmouth College Press.

Carney, C. M. (1999). *Native American higher education in the United States.* Transaction.

Carpenter, J. (2013). Thomas Jefferson and the ideology of democratic schooling. *Democracy and Education, 21*(2), 5.

Chakravartty, P., & Silva, D. F. D. (2012). Accumulation, dispossession, and debt: The racial logic of global capitalism—an introduction. *American Quarterly, 64*(3), 361–385.

Civil Society Leaders. (2014). Open letter to Harvard University President Drew Faust from Civil Society Leaders concerning Harvard's endowment investments in land and natural resources. Croatan Institute, April. https://croataninstitute.org/wp-content/uploads/2021/04/Harvard _Land_Letter_1.pdf:

Clarke, M., & Fine, G. A. (2010). "A" for Apology: Slavery and the discourse of remonstrance in two American universities. *History & Memory, 22*(1), 81–112.

Cohen, A. M., & Kisker, C. B. (2010). *The shaping of American higher education: Emergence and growth of the contemporary system.* John Wiley & Sons.

Daigle, M. (2019). The spectacle of reconciliation: On (the) unsettling responsibilities to Indigenous peoples in the academy. *Environment and Planning D: Society and Space, 37*(4), 703–721.

Dartmouth University. (n.d.). Undergraduate admissions: History and traditions. Accessed February 24, 2022. https://admissions.dartmouth.edu /about/history-traditions.

Davis, H., & Todd, Z. (2017). On the importance of a date, or decolonizing the Anthropocene. *ACME: An International E-Journal for Critical Geographies, 16*(4).

Dugdale, A., Fueser, J. J., & de Castro Alves, J. C. (2001). *Yale, slavery and abolition.* Amistad Committee. Available at: http://www.yaleslavery.org /YSA.pdf

Fairbairn, M., LaChance, J., De Master, K. T., & Ashwood, L. (2021). *In vino veritas, in aqua lucrum*: Farmland investment, environmental uncertainty, and groundwater access in California's Cuyama Valley. *Agriculture and Human Values, 38*(1), 285–299.

Faulkner, M. S. (2013). *Slavery at the University of Virginia: A catalogue of current and past initiatives.* University of Virginia Idea Fund. Division for Diversity, Equity, and Inclusion, University of Virginia, January. https:// dei.virginia.edu/sites/g/files/jsddwu511/files/inline-files/SlaveryatUVA _FAULKNER_001.pdf.

Fuentes, M. J., & White, D. G. (2016). *Scarlet and black: Slavery and dispossession in Rutgers history.* Rutgers University Press.

Geiger, R. L. (2014). *The history of American higher education: Learning and culture from the founding to World War II.* Princeton University Press.

Gordon, A. F. (2008). *Ghostly matters: Haunting and the sociological imagination.* University of Minnesota Press.

GRAIN & Rede Social de Justiça e Direitos Humanos. (2018). Harvard's billion–dollar farmland fiasco. GRAIN, September 6. https://grain.org /entries/6006-harvard-s-billion-dollar-farmland-fiasco.

Grosfoguel, R. (2013). The structure of knowledge in Westernized universities: Epistemic racism/sexism and the four genocides/epistemicides of the long 16th century. *Human Architecture: Journal of the Sociology of Self-Knowledge, 11*(1), 73–90.

Grande, S. (2018). Refusing the university. In E. Tuck & K. W. Yang (eds.), *Toward what justice?* (pp. 47–65). Routledge.

Harris, L. M., Campbell, J. T., & Brophy, A. L. (eds.). (2019). *Slavery and the university: Histories and legacies.* University of Georgia Press.

Hartman, S. (2008). *Lose your mother: A journey along the Atlantic slave route.* Macmillan.

Harvey, D. (2005). *The new imperialism*. Oxford University Press.

Jefferson, T. (1818). Report of the commissioners of the University of Virginia (The Rockfish Gap Report). Founding.com. https://founding.com /founders-library/government-documents/american-state-and-local -government-documents/report-to-the-commissioners-of-the-university -of-virginia-the-rockfish-gap-report-thomas-jefferson-1818/.

King, T. L. (2016). New world grammars: The "unthought" Black discourses of conquest. *Theory & Event*, 19(4).

Kish, Z., & Leroy, J. (2015). Bonded life: Technologies of racial finance from slave insurance to philanthrocapital. *Cultural Studies*, 29(5–6), 630–651.

Labaree, D. F. (2016). Learning to love the bomb: The cold war brings the best of times to American higher education. In P. Smeyers & M. Depaepe (eds.), *Educational research: Discourses of change and changes of discourse* (pp. 101–117). Springer.

Lewis, S. L., & Maslin, M. A. (2015). A transparent framework for defining the Anthropocene epoch. *Anthropocene Review*, 2(2), 128–146.

Lipe, K. (2018). Toward equity and equality: Transforming universities into Indigenous places of learning. In R. S. Minthorn & H. J. Shotton (eds.), *Reclaiming Indigenous research in higher education* (pp. 162–177). Rutgers University Press.

Longstreth, R. (2014). The parts and their whole: Conceptualizing a planning strategy for restoration at Thomas Jefferson's Academical Village. *Journal of Planning History*, 13(1), 3–23.

Lowe, L. (2015). *The intimacies of four continents*. Duke University Press.

Lucas, C. J. (2006). *American higher education: A history*. St. Martin's Press.

Mignolo, W. (2003). Globalization and the geopolitics of knowledge: The role of the humanities in the corporate university. *Nepantla: Views from South*, 4(1), 97–119.

Miller, R. J. (2005). The doctrine of discovery in American Indian law. *Idaho Law Review*, 42, 1.

Oast, J. B. (2009). Forgotten masters: Institutional slavery in Virginia, 1680–1860. PhD thesis, College of William and Mary, Williamsburg, VA.

Office of the Dean of Students. (2015). Students and traditions. University of Virginia, accessed February 2, 2022. https://odos.virginia.edu/students -traditions.

President's Commission on Slavery and the University (2018). Report to President Teresa A. Sullivan. University of Virginia. https://dei.virginia .edu/sites/g/files/jsddwu511/files/inline-files/PCSU%20Report%20 FINAL_July%202018.pdf.

Rodríguez, D. (2012). Racial/colonial genocide and the "neoliberal academy": In excess of a problematic. *American Quarterly*, 64(4), 809–813.

Santos, B. D. S. (2007). Beyond abyssal thinking: From global lines to ecologies of knowledges. *Binghamton University Review, 30*(1), 45–89.

Silva, D. F.D. (2007). *Toward a global idea of race*. University of Minnesota Press.

Simpson, L. B. (2014). Land as pedagogy: Nishnaabeg intelligence and rebellious transformation. *Decolonization: Indigeneity, Education, and Society, 3*(3).

Smith, L. T. (2012). *Decolonizing methodologies: Research and Indigenous peoples*. Zed Books.

Stanley, T. (2009). The banality of colonialism: Encountering artifacts of genocide and white supremacy in Vancouver today. In S. R. Steinberg (ed.), *Diversity and multiculturalism: A reader* (pp. 143–159). Peter Lang.

Stonechild, B. (2006). *The new buffalo: The struggle for Aboriginal post-secondary education in Canada*. University of Manitoba Press.

Thelin, J. R. (2004). *A history of American higher education*. Johns Hopkins University Press.

Tuck, E. (2009). Suspending damage: A letter to communities. *Harvard Educational Review, 79*(3), 409–428.

Tuck, E., & Yang, K. W. (2012). Decolonization is not a metaphor. *Decolonization: Indigeneity, Education, and Society, 1*(1), 1–40.

University of Georgia (1785). University of Georgia charter, 1785. University of Georgia Libraries, updated May 30, 2017. https://www.libs.uga.edu /hargrett/archives/exhibit/charter/chartertranscription.html.

Vimalassery, M., Pegues, J. H., & Goldstein, A. (2017). Colonial unknowing and relations of study. *Theory and Event, 20*(4), 1042–1054.

Whyte, K. (2018). Settler colonialism, ecology, and environmental injustice. *Environment and Society, 9*(1), 125–144.

Wilder, C. S. (2013). *Ebony and ivy: Race, slavery, and the troubled history of America's universities*. Bloomsbury.

Willinsky, J. (1998). *Learning to divide the world: Education at empire's end*. University of Minnesota Press.

Wolfe, B. (2013). Unearthing slavery at the University of Virginia. *University of Virginia Magazine*, Spring. uvamagazine.org.

Wolfe, B. (2020). Slavery at the University of Virginia. In *Encyclopedia Virginia*, December 14. https://encyclopediavirginia.org/entries/slavery-at-the -university-of-virginia/.

Wright, B. (1988). "For the children of the infidels"?: American Indian education in the colonial colleges. *American Indian Culture and Research Journal, 12*(3), 1–14.

Wright, B. (1991). The "untameable savage spirit": American Indians in colonial colleges. *Review of Higher Education, 14*(4), 429–452.

Chapter 3. Dispossession at the Roots of "Democracy's Colleges"

Acemoglu, D., Egorov, G., & Sonin, K. (2016). *Social mobility and stability of democracy: Re-evaluating de Tocqueville.* National Bureau of Economic Research.

Adams, D. W. (1988). Fundamental considerations: The deep meaning of Native American schooling, 1880–1900. *Harvard Educational Review, 58*(1), 1–29.

Ahenakew, C., Andreotti, V., Cooper, G., & Hireme, H. (2014). Beyond epistemic provincialism: De-provincializing Indigenous resistance. *AlterNative: An International Journal of Indigenous Peoples, 10*(3), 216.

AIHEC (American Indian Higher Education Consortium). (2014). Statement of the AIHEC to the United States Senate Committee on Appropriations, Subcommittee on Agriculture, Rural Development, Food and Drug Administration, and Related Agencies. April 3. http://www.aihec.org/what-we-do/docs/FY15/AIHEC_FY2015_Agric%20Stmt_(S)_4-3-2014.pdf.

APLU (Association of Public and Land-Grant Universities). (2012). *The Land-grant tradition.* Washington, DC. https://www.aplu.org/library/the-land-grant-tradition.

Arvin, M., Tuck, E., & Morrill, A. (2013). Decolonizing feminism: Challenging connections between settler colonialism and heteropatriarchy. *Feminist Formations,* 8–34.

Barker, J. (2015). The corporation and the tribe. *American Indian Quarterly, 39*(3), 243–270.

Barker, J. (2016). The new Indian removal. *Tequila Sovereign.* Accessed August 5, 2017. https://tequilasovereign.wordpress.com/2016/05/31/the-new-indian-removal/.

Barrow, C. W. (1990). *Universities and the capitalist state: Corporate liberalism and the reconstruction of American higher education, 1894–1928.* University of Wisconsin Press.

Battiste, M. (2017). *Decolonizing education: Nourishing the learning spirit.* University of British Columbia Press.

Behle, J. G. (2013). Educating the toiling peoples: Students at the Illinois Industrial University, Spring 1868. In R. L. Geiger & N. M. Sorber (eds.), *The land-grant colleges and the reshaping of American higher education* (pp. 73–93). Transaction.

Bledstein, B. (1976). *The culture of professionalism: The middle class and the development of higher education in America.* New York.

Boggs, A., Meyerhoff, E., Mitchell, N., & Schwartz-Weinstein, Z (2019). *Abolitionist university studies: An invitation.* Abolition University. https://abolition.university/wp-content/uploads/2019/08/Abolitionist-University-Studies_-An-Invitation-Release-1-version.pdf.

Bowles, S., & Gintis, H. (1976). *Schooling in capitalist America: Educational reform and the contradictions of economic life.* Haymarket Books.

Brayboy, B. M. J. (2005). Toward a tribal critical race theory in education. *Urban Review, 37*(5), 425–446.

Brint, S. G., & Karabel, J. (1989). *The diverted dream: Community colleges and the promise of educational opportunity in America, 1900–1985.* Oxford University Press.

Brown, D. M. (2003). Hegemony and the discourse of the land grant movement: Historicizing as a point of departure. *Journal of Advanced Composition, 23*(2), 319–349.

Byrd, J. A. (2011). *The transit of empire: Indigenous critiques of colonialism.* University of Minnesota Press.

Chang, D. A. (2011). Enclosures of land and sovereignty: The allotment of American Indian lands. *Radical History Review, 2011*(109), 108–119.

Chaput, C. (2004). Democracy, capitalism, and the ambivalence of Willa Cather's frontier rhetorics: Uncertain foundations of the US public University system. *College English, 66*(3), 310–334.

Coulthard, G. (2014). *Red skin, white masks: Rejecting the colonial politics of recognition.* University of Minnesota Press.

Cross, C. F. (2012). Democracy, the West, and land-grant colleges. In D. M. Fogel & E. Malson-Huddle, *Precipice or crossroads? Where America's great public universities stand and where they are going midway through their second century* (pp. 1–15). State University of New York Press.

Crow, M. M., & Dabaras, W. B. (2012). University-based R&D and economic development: The Morrill Act and the emergence of the American research university. In D. M. Fogel, D. Mark, & E. Malson-Huddle (eds.), *Precipice or crossroads? Where America's great public universities stand and where they are going midway through their second century* (pp. 119–158). State University of New York Press.

Davis, J. (2001). American Indian boarding school experiences: Recent studies from Native perspectives. *OAH Magazine of History, 15*(2), 20–22.

Dahl, A. J. (2014). Empire of the people: The ideology of democratic empire in the antebellum United States. Doctoral dissertation. University of Minnesota.

Deloria, V. (1996). Reserving to themselves: Treaties and the powers of Indian tribes. *Arizona Law Review, 38*, 963–980.

Dunbar-Ortiz, R. (2014). *An Indigenous peoples' history of the United States.* Beacon Press.

Eddy, E., Jr. (1957). *Colleges for our land and time: The land-grant idea in American education.* Harper & Brothers.

Ferguson, R. A. (2012). *The reorder of things: The university and its pedagogies of minority difference.* University of Minnesota Press.

Folbre, N. (2010). *Saving State U: Fixing public higher education.* New Press.

Frymer, P. (2014). "A rush and a push and the land is ours": Territorial expansion, land policy, and US state formation. *Perspectives on Politics, 12*(1), 119.

Gates, P. W. (1976). An overview of American land policy. *Agricultural History*, *50*(1), 213–229.

Gee, G. (2012). The modern public university. In D. M. Fogel & E. Malson-Huddle (eds.), *Precipice or crossroads? Where America's great public universities stand and where they are going midway through their second century*. State University of New York Press.

Geiger, R. L. (2014). *The history of American higher education: Learning and culture from the founding to World War II*. Princeton University Press.

Goldstein, A. (2008). Where the nation takes place: Proprietary regimes, antistatism, and US settler colonialism. *South Atlantic Quarterly*, *107*(4), 833–861.

Goldstein, A. (2014). Finance and foreclosure in the colonial present. *Radical History Review*, *2014*(118), 42–63.

Goodchild, L. F., & Wrobel, D. M. (2014). Western college expansion: Churches and evangelization, states and boosterism, 1818–1945. In L. F. Goodchild, R. Jonsen, P. Limerick, & D. Longanecker (eds.), *Higher education in the American West: Regional history and state contexts* (pp. 3–37). Palgrave MacMillan.

Greenstone, M., Looney, A., Patashnik, H., & Yu, M. (2013). *Thirteen economic facts about social mobility and the role of education*. The Hamilton Project, Brookings Institution. https://www.brookings.edu/wp-content/uploads/2016/06/THP_13EconFacts_FINAL.pdf.

Harvey, D. (2005). *The new imperialism*. Oxford University Press.

Johnson, E. L. (1981). Misconceptions about the early land-grant colleges. *Journal of Higher Education*, *52*(4), 333–351.

Karuka, M. (2019). *Empire's tracks: Indigenous nations, Chinese workers, and the transcontinental railroad*. University of California Press.

Kerr, C. (1991). *The great transformation in higher education, 1960–1980*. State University of New York Press.

Key, S. (1996). Economics or education: The establishment of American land-grant universities. *Journal of Higher Education*, *67*(2), 196–220.

King, T. L. (2016). New World grammars: The 'unthought' Black discourses of conquest. *Theory and Event*, *19*(4).

Labaree, D. F. (2016). An affair to remember: America's brief fling with the university as a public good. *Journal of Philosophy of Education*, *50*(1), 20–36.

La Paperson. (2017). *A third university is possible*. University of Minnesota Press.

Launius, S., & Boyce, G. A. (2021). More than metaphor: Settler colonialism, frontier logic, and the continuities of racialized dispossession in a southwest US city. *Annals of the American Association of Geographers*, *111*(1), 157–174.

Lee, J. M., & Keys, S.W. (2013). Land-grant but unequal: State one-to-one match funding for 1890 land-grant universities. APLU Office of Access and

Success, Publication 3000-PB1. Washington, DC: Association of Public and Land-Grant Universities. https://www.aplu.org/library/land-grant -but-unequal-state-one-to-one-match-funding-for-1890-land-grant -universities/file.

Lee, R., & Ahtone, T. (2020). Land-grab universities: Expropriated Indigenous land is the foundation of the land-grant university. *High Country News*, April: 32–45.

Levine, D. O. (1988). *The American college and the culture of aspiration, 1915–1940*. Cornell University Press.

Lloyd, D., & Wolfe, P. (2016). Settler colonial logics and the neoliberal regime. *Settler Colonial Studies, 6*(2), 109–118.

Macoun, A., & Strakosch, E. (2013). The ethical demands of settler colonial theory. *Settler Colonial Studies, 3*(3–4), 426–443.

McNamee, S. J., & Miller, R. K. (2004). *The meritocracy myth*. Rowman & Littlefield.

Miller, R. J. (2005). The Doctrine of Discovery in American Indian law. *Idaho Law Review, 42*.

Miller, R. J. (2006). *Native America, discovered and conquered: Thomas Jefferson, Lewis & Clark, and manifest destiny*. Greenwood.

Miller, R. J. (2011). American Indians, the Doctrine of Discovery, and manifest destiny. *Wyoming Law Review, 11*(2), 329–349.

Nash, M. A. (2019). Entangled pasts: Land-grant colleges and American Indian dispossession. *History of Education Quarterly, 59*(4), 437–467.

Nevins, A. (1962). *The state universities and democracy*. Iowa State University Press.

Nichols, R. (2017). Theft is property! The recursive logic of dispossession. *Political Theory, 46*(1).

Paschall, M. R. (2016). The failure of reform: A history of higher education in the United States. Doctoral dissertation. University of California, Santa Cruz.

Peters, S. J. (2013). Storying and restorying the land-grant system. In R. L. Geiger & N. M. Sorber (eds.), *The land-grant colleges and the reshaping of American higher education* (pp. 335–353). Transaction.

Pommersheim, F. (2009). *Broken landscape: Indians, Indian tribes, and the Constitution*. Oxford University Press.

Rifkin, M. (2013). Settler common sense. *Settler Colonial Studies, 3*(3–4), 322–340.

Rodríguez, D. (2012). Racial/colonial genocide and the "neoliberal academy": In excess of a problematic. *American Quarterly, 64*(4), 809–813.

Ross, E. D. (1942). *Democracy's college: The land-grant movement in the formative stage*. Iowa State College Press.

Sauder, R. A., & Sauder, R. M. (1987). The Morrill Act's influence on public land disposal after 1870. *Agricultural History, 61*(2), 34.

Silva, D. F.D. (2007). *Toward a global idea of race.* University of Minnesota Press.

Simon, L. A. K. (2009). Affirming the Morrill Act for a twenty-first century global society. Available at Office of Faculty and Academic Staff Development, Michigan State University. https://ofasd.msu.edu/wp-content/uploads/2017/09/monograph.pdf

Slaughter, S., & Rhoades, G. (2004). *Academic capitalism and the new economy: Markets, state, and higher education.* Johns Hopkins University Press.

Sorber, N. M. (2011). Farmers, scientists, and officers of industry: The formation and reformation of land-grant colleges in the northeastern United States, 1862–1906. Doctoral dissertation, Pennsylvania State University.

Sorber, N. M., & Geiger, R. L. (2014). The welding of opposite views: Land-grant historiography at 150 years. In M. B. Paulsen (ed.), *Higher Education: Handbook of Theory and Research* 29 (pp. 385–422). Springer.

Snelgrove, C., Dhamoon, R., & Corntassel, J. (2014). Unsettling settler colonialism: The discourse and politics of settlers, and solidarity with Indigenous nations. *Decolonization: Indigeneity, Education, and Society* 3(2).

Thelin, J. R. (2004). *A history of American higher education.* Johns Hopkins University Press.

Trask, H. K. (2004). The color of violence. *Social Justice, 31*(4), 8–16.

Tuck, E., & McKenzie, M. (2014). *Place in research: Theory, methodology, and methods.* Routledge.

Turner, F. J. (1910). Commencement address: Pioneer ideals and the state university. *Indiana University Bulletin, 8*(6), 6–29.

Turner, F. J. (1920). *The frontier in history.* Dover.

Wheatle, K. I. (2019). Neither just nor equitable: Race in the congressional debate of the second Morrill Act of 1890. *American Educational History Journal, 46*(2), 1–20.

Whyte, K. (2018). Settler colonialism, ecology, and environmental injustice. *Environment and Society, 9*(1), 125–144.

Williams, R. L. (1991). *The origins of federal support for higher education: George W. Atherton and the land-grant college movement.* Pennsylvania State University Press.

Wolfe, P. (2006). Settler colonialism and the elimination of the native. *Journal of Genocide Research, 8*(4), 387–409.

Wolfe, P. (2012). Against the intentional fallacy: Legocentrism and continuity in the rhetoric of Indian dispossession. *American Indian Culture and Research Journal, 36*(1), 3–45.

Chapter 4. The "Golden Age" of Higher Education

Ahmed, S. (2012). *On being included: Racism and diversity in institutional life.* Duke University Press.

Baez, B. (2006) Merit and difference. *Teachers College Record, 108*(6), 996–1016.

Barkan, J. (2013). *Corporate sovereignty: Law and government under capitalism.* University of Minnesota Press.

Beach, J. M. (2007). The ideology of the American dream: Two competing philosophies in education, 1776–2006. *Educational Studies, 41*(2), 148–164.

Bell, D. A., Jr. (1980). *Brown v. Board of Education* and the interest-convergence dilemma. *Harvard Law Review, 93*(3), 518–533.

Berlant, L. G. (2011). *Cruel optimism.* Duke University Press.

Boggs, A. H. (2013). Prospective students, potential threats: The figure of the international student in US higher education. Doctoral dissertation. University of California, Davis.

Boggs, A., & Mitchell, N. (2018). Critical university studies and the crisis consensus. *Feminist Studies, 44*(2), 432–463.

Boggs, A., Meyerhoff, E., Mitchell, N., & Schwartz-Weinstein, Z (2019). *Abolitionist university studies: An invitation.* Abolition University. https://abolition.university/wp-content/uploads/2019/08/Abolitionist-University-Studies_-An-Invitation-Release-1-version.pdf.

Brasuell, J. (2019). Infographic: The cumulative carbon emissions of every country since 1750. *Planetizen*, December 5. https://www.planetizen.com/news/2019/12/107509-infographic-cumulative-carbon-emissions-every-country-1750.

Brint, S. G., & Karabel, J. (1989). *The diverted dream: Community colleges and the promise of educational opportunity in America, 1900–1985.* Oxford University Press.

Brown, P., & Tannock, S. (2009). Education, meritocracy, and the global war for talent. *Journal of Education Policy, 24*(4), 377–392.

Brown, P., Lauder, H., & Ashton, D. (2010). *The global auction: The broken promises of education, jobs, and incomes.* Oxford University Press.

Burden-Stelley, C. (2020). Modern U.S. racial capitalism. *Monthly Review*, July 1. https://monthlyreview.org/2020/07/01/modern-u-s-racial-capitalism/.

Byrd, J. A. (2011). *The transit of empire: Indigenous critiques of colonialism.* University of Minnesota Press.

Campbell, H., & Murrey, A. (2014). Culture-centric pre-emptive counterinsurgency and US Africa Command: Assessing the role of the US social sciences in US military engagements in Africa. *Third World Quarterly, 35*(8), 1457–1475.

Chatterjee, P., & Maira, S. (2014). *The imperial university.* University of Minnesota Press.

Chun, E. B., & Feagin, J. R. (2021). *Who killed higher education? Maintaining white dominance in a desegregating era.* Routledge.

Cohen, A. M., & Kisker, C. B. (2010). *The shaping of American higher education: Emergence and growth of the contemporary system*. John Wiley & Sons.

Cornum, L. (2018). The irradiated international. *Data and Society*, June. https://datasociety.net/wp-content/uploads/2018/06/ii-web.pdf.

Cullen, J. (2003). *The American dream: A short history of an idea that shaped a nation*. Oxford University Press.

Cumings, B. (1997). Boundary displacement: Area studies and international studies during and after the Cold War. *Bulletin of Concerned Asian Scholars, 29*(1), 6–26.

Davis, H., & Todd, Z. (2017). On the importance of a date, or decolonizing the Anthropocene. *ACME: An International E-Journal for Critical Geographies, 16*(4).

De Wit, H. (2002). *Internationalization of higher education in the United States of America and Europe: A historical, comparative, and conceptual analysis*. Greenwood.

Dudziak, M. L. (2011). *Cold War civil rights: Race and the image of American democracy* Politics and Society in Twentieth Century America 73. Princeton University Press.

Dunbar-Ortiz, R. (2014). *An Indigenous peoples' history of the United States*. Beacon Press.

Ferguson, R. A. (2012). *The reorder of things: The university and its pedagogies of minority difference*. University of Minnesota Press.

Fischer, K. (2019). The barriers to mobility: Why higher ed's promise remains unfulfilled. *Chronicle of Higher Education*, December 31. https://www.chronicle.com/interactives/20191231-barriers-to-mobility.

Fulbright, W. J. (1972). The war and its effects: The Military-Industrial-Academic Complex. In H. I. Schiller & J. D. Phillips, *Super-state: Readings in the Military-Industrial-Complex* (pp. 173–177). University of Illinois Press.

Gilmore, R. W. (2007). *Golden gulag: Prisons, surplus, crisis, and opposition in globalizing California*. University of California Press.

Gindin, S., & Panitch, L. (2012). *The making of global capitalism*. Verso Books.

Goldrick-Rab, S. (2016). *Paying the price: College costs, financial aid, and the betrayal of the American dream*. University of Chicago Press.

Gonzalez, G. (1982). Imperial reform in the neo-colonies: The University of California's basic plan for higher education in Colombia. *Journal of Education*, 330–350.

Grossman, Z. (n.d.). From Wounded Knee to Syria: U.S. military interventions since 1890. Evergreen State College. Accessed February 12, 2022. https://sites.evergreen.edu/zoltan/interventions/.

Guinier, L. (2015). *The tyranny of the meritocracy: Democratizing higher education in America*. Beacon Press.

Harvey, D. (1990). *The condition of postmodernity: An enquiry into the origins of cultural change*. Blackwell.

Heller, H. (2016). *The capitalist university: The transformations of higher education in the United States (1945–2016)*. Pluto Press.

Hickel, J. (2019). Degrowth: A theory of radical abundance. *real-world economics review* (87).

Johnston, M. (2018). MSU and Vietnam: A dark chapter in the school's history. *Spartan Newsroom* (Michigan State University School of Journalism), May 1. https://news.jrn.msu.edu/2018/05/msu-and-vietnam -a-dark-chapter-of-the-schools-history/.

Joseph, M. (2015). Investing in the cruel entrepreneurial university. *South Atlantic Quarterly*, 114(3), 491–511.

Kamola, I. (2014). US universities and the production of the global imaginary. *British Journal of Politics and International Relations*, 16(3), 515–533.

Kapoor, I. (2014). Psychoanalysis and development: Contributions, examples, limits. *Third World Quarterly*, 35(7), 1120–1143.

Karuka, M. (2019). *Empire's tracks: Indigenous nations, Chinese workers, and the transcontinental railroad*. University of California Press.

Kerr, C. (1978). Higher education: Paradise lost? *Higher Education*, 7(3), 261–278.

Kim, D., & Rury, J. L. (2007). The changing profile of college access: The Truman Commission and enrollment patterns in the postwar era. *History of Education Quarterly*, 47(3), 302–327.

King, T. L. (2016). New World grammars: The "unthought" Black discourses of conquest. *Theory and Event*, 19(4).

Kramer, P. A. (2009). Is the world our campus? International students and US global power in the long twentieth century. *Diplomatic History*, 33(5), 775–806.

Kramer, P. A. (2016). Embedding capital: Political-economic history, the United States, and the world. *Journal of the Gilded Age and Progressive Era*, 15(3), 331–362.

Kuzmarov, J. (2009). Modernizing repression: Police training, political violence, and nation-building in the "American century." *Diplomatic History*, 33(2), 191–221.

Labaree, D. F. (2016). Learning to love the bomb: The cold war brings the best of times to American higher education. In P. Smeyers & M. Depaepe (eds.), *Educational research: Discourses of change and changes of discourse* (pp. 101–117). Springer.

Liu, A. (2011). Unraveling the myth of meritocracy within the context of US higher education. *Higher Education*, 62(4), 383–397.

Lucas, C. J. (2006). *American higher education: A history*. St. Martin's Press.

Mahmud, T. (2012). Debt and discipline. *American Quarterly*, 64(3), 469–494.

Marez, C. (2014). Seeing in the red: Looking at student debt. *American Quarterly*, 66(2), 261–281.

Marginson, S. (2016). *The dream is over*. University of California Press.

McClanahan, A. J. (2017). Becoming non-economic: Human capital theory and Wendy Brown's *Undoing the Demos. Theory and Event*, 20(2), 510–519.

McMillan Cottom, T. (2017). *Lower ed: The troubling rise of for-profit colleges in the new economy*. The New Press.

McNamee, S. J., & Miller, R. K. (2009). *The meritocracy myth*. Rowman & Littlefield.

Melamed, J. (2006). The spirit of neoliberalism: From racial liberalism to neoliberal multiculturalism. *Social Text*, 24(4 (89)), 1–24.

Michigan State University Vietnam Group Archive. (n.d.). About the project. Michigan State University. http://vietnamproject.archives.msu.edu/about .php.

Mitchell, N. (2011). Disciplinary matters: Black studies and the politics of institutionalization. Doctoral dissertation, University of California, Santa Cruz.

Mitchell, N. (2015). (Critical ethnic studies) intellectual. *Critical Ethnic Studies*, 1(1), 86–94.

Mitchell, N. (2016). The fantasy and fate of ethnic studies in an age of uprisings: An interview with Nick Mitchell. *Undercommoning*, July 13. http://undercommoning.org/nick-mitchell-interview/.

Morgensen, S. L. (2011). The biopolitics of settler colonialism: Right here, right now. *Settler Colonial Studies*, 1(1), 52–76.

Moten, F. (2015). Untitled presentation at "The university in theory; Or, the future of (fugitive) study." Plenary session at annual meeting of Cultural Studies Association, Riverside, CA, May.

Mustaffa, J. B. (2017). Mapping violence, naming life: a history of anti-Black oppression in the higher education system. *International Journal of Qualitative Studies in Education*, 30(8), 711–727.

Newfield, C. (2008). *Unmaking the public university: The forty-year assault on the middle class*. Harvard University Press.

Newfield, C. (2016). *The great mistake: How we wrecked public universities and how we can fix them*. Johns Hopkins University Press.

Paik, A. N. (2013). Education and empire, old and new: HR 3077 and the resurgence of the US university. *Cultural Dynamics*, 25(1), 3–28.

President's Commission on Higher Education (1947). *Higher Education for American democracy*. Government Printing Office. Available on Google Books, https://www.google.com/books/edition/Higher_Education_for _American_Democracy/.

Rostow, W. W. (1960). *The stages of growth: A non-communist manifesto.* Cambridge University Press.

Santos, B. S. (ed.). (2006). *Another production is possible: Beyond the capitalist canon.* Verso.

Shotwell, A. (2016). *Against purity: Living ethically in compromised times.* University of Minnesota Press.

Silva, D. F. D. (2001). Towards a critique of the socio-logos of justice: The analytics of raciality and the production of universality. *Social Identities, 7*(3), 421–454.

Silva, D. F. D. (2011). Notes for a critique of the "metaphysics of race." *Theory, Culture, and Society, 28*(1), 138–148.

Silva, D. F. D. (2014). Toward a Black feminist poethics: The quest(ion) of Blackness toward the end of the world. *Black Scholar, 44*(2), 81–97.

Silva, D. F. D. (2015). Globality. *Critical Ethnic Studies, 1*(1), 33–38.

Silva, D. F. D (2016). The racial limits of social justice: The ruse of equality of opportunity and the global affirmative action mandate. *Critical Ethnic Studies, 2*(2), 184–209.

Slaughter, S., & Rhoades, G. (2004). *Academic capitalism and the new economy: Markets, state, and higher education.* Johns Hopkins University Press.

Soederberg, S. (2014). Student loans, debtfare, and the commodification of debt: The securitization and displacement of risk. *Critical Sociology, 40*(5), 689–709.

Souto-Otero, M. (2010). Education, meritocracy, and redistribution. *Journal of Education Policy, 25*(3), 397–413.

Steffen, W., Grinevald, J., Crutzen, P., & McNeill, J. (2011). The Anthropocene: Conceptual and historical perspectives. *Philosophical Transactions of the Royal Society A: Mathematical, Physical and Engineering Sciences, 369*(1938), 842–867.

Steffen, W., Broadgate, W., Deutsch, L., Gaffney, O., & Ludwig, C. (2015). The trajectory of the Anthropocene: The great acceleration. *Anthropocene Review, 2*(1), 81–98.

Stein, S., et al. (2020). Gesturing towards decolonial futures: Reflections on our learnings thus far. *Nordic Journal of Comparative and International Education (NJCIE), 4*(1), 43–65.

Stein, S., Hunt, D., Suša, R., & Andreotti, V. D. O. (2017). The educational challenge of unraveling the fantasies of ontological security. *Diaspora, Indigenous, and Minority Education, 11*(2), 69–79.

Stein, D. P. (2016). "This nation has never honestly dealt with the question of a peacetime economy": Coretta Scott King and the struggle for a nonviolent economy in the 1970s. *Souls, 18*(1), 80–105.

TallBear, K. (2019). Caretaking relations, not American dreaming. *Kalfou, 6*(1), 24–41.

Thelin, J. R. (2004). *A history of American higher education*. Johns Hopkins University Press.

Trow, M. (2000). From mass higher education to universal access: The American advantage. *Minerva*, 37(4), 303–328.

United Nations (2017). *World economic and social survey: Reflecting on seventy years of development policy analysis.* Available at https://www.un.org /development/desa/dpad/wp-content/uploads/sites/45/publication /WESS_2017-FullReport.pdf.

Vandenberg-Daves, J. (2003). "A look at the total knowledge of the world": The University of Minnesota, the land-grant ideal, and the politics of US public higher education, 1950–1990. *History of Education*, 32(1), 57–79.

Wellmon, C. (2021). The crushing contradictions of the American University. *The Chronicle of Higher Education*, April 22.

Williams, J. (2006). The pedagogy of debt. *College Literature*, 33(4), 155–169.

Willinsky, J. (1998). *Learning to divide the world: Education at empire's end.* University of Minnesota Press.

Whyte, K. (2019). Way beyond the lifeboat: An Indigenous allegory of climate justice. In D. Munshi, K. Bhavnani, J. Foran, & P. Kurian (eds.), *Climate futures: Reimagining global climate justice.* University of California Press.

Wynter, S. (2003). Unsettling the coloniality of being/power/truth/freedom: Towards the human, after man, its overrepresentation—An argument. *CR: The New Centennial Review*, 3(3), 257–337.

Wynter, S., & McKittrick, K. (2015). Unparalleled catastrophe for our species? Or, to give humanness a different future—Conversations. In K. McKittrick (ed.), *Sylvia Wynter: On being human as praxis* (pp. 9–89). Duke University Press.

Young, M. (1958). *The rise of the meritocracy, 1870–2033: An essay on education and society.* Thames and Hudson.

Chapter 5. Inclusion Is Not Reparation

Adorno, T. W. (2009). Questions on intellectual emigration. *Social Text*, 27(2), 159–164.

Ahmed, S. (2004). Declarations of whiteness: The non-performativity of anti-racism. *borderlands*, 3(2). Archived at *Trove*. https://webarchive.nla .gov.au/awa/20050616083826/http://www.borderlandsjournal.adelaide .edu.au/vol3no2_2004/ahmed_declarations.htm.

Ahmed, S. (2012). *On being included: Racism and diversity in institutional life.* Duke University Press.

Al-Kassim, D. (2008) Archiving resistance: Women's testimony at the threshold of the state. *Cultural Dynamics*, 20(2), 167–192.

Alcoff, L. M. (2007). Epistemologies of ignorance: Three types. In S. Sullivan & N. Tuana (eds.), *Race and epistemologies of ignorance* (pp. 39–58). State University of New York Press.

Amsler, S. (2019). Gesturing towards radical futurity in education for alternative futures. *Sustainability Science, 14*(4), 925–930.

Andreotti, V. D. O., Stein, S., Ahenakew, C., & Hunt, D. (2015). Mapping interpretations of decolonization in the context of higher education. *Decolonization: Indigeneity, Education, & Society, 4*(1), 21–40.

Ballantyne, E. F. (2014). Dechinta Bush University: Mobilizing a knowledge economy of reciprocity, resurgence, and decolonization. *Decolonization: Indigeneity, Education, and Society 3*(3), 67–85.

Boggs, A., & Mitchell, N. (2018). Critical university studies and the crisis consensus. *Feminist Studies, 44*(2), 432–463.

Boggs, A., Meyerhoff, E., Mitchell, N., & Schwartz-Weinstein, Z (2019). *Abolitionist university studies: An invitation.* Abolition University. https:// abolition.university/wp-content/uploads/2019/08/Abolitionist -University-Studies_-An-Invitation-Release-1-version.pdf.

Brophy, A. L. (2008). Considering William and Mary's history with slavery: The case of President Thomas Roderick Dew. *William & Mary Bill of Rights Journal, 16*(4), 1091–1139.

Brophy, A. L. (2018). Forum on slavery and universities: Introduction. *Slavery & Abolition, 39*(2), 229–235.

Clarke, M., & Fine, G. A. (2010). "A" for Apology: Slavery and the discourse of remonstrance in two American universities. *History & Memory, 22*(1), 81–112.

Cole, E. R., & Harper, S. R. (2017). Race and rhetoric: An analysis of college presidents' statements on campus racial incidents. *Journal of Diversity in Higher Education, 10*(4).

Cornum, L (2019). Burial ground acknowledgements. *New Inquiry*, October 14. https://thenewinquiry.com/burial-ground-acknowledgements.

Coulthard, G. S. (2014). *Red skin, white masks: Rejecting the colonial politics of recognition.* University of Minnesota Press.

Daigle, M. (2019). The spectacle of reconciliation: On (the) unsettling responsibilities to Indigenous peoples in the academy. *Environment and Planning D: Society and Space, 37*(4), 703–721.

Davis, S., & Harris, J. C. (2015). But we didn't mean it like that: A critical race analysis of campus responses to racial incidents. *Journal of Critical Scholarship on Higher Education and Student Affairs, 2*(1).

Desai, S. (2019). The first reparations attempt at an American college comes from its students. *Atlantic*, April 18. https://www.theatlantic.com /education/archive/2019/04/why-are-georgetown-students-paying -reparations/587443/.

Dugdale, A., Fueser, J. J., & de Castro Alves, J. C. (2001). *Yale, slavery, and abolition*. Amistad Committee. http://www.yaleslavery.org/YSA.pdf.

Duster, C. R., & Kwak, B. (2017). Georgetown apologizes, renames halls after slaves. *NBC News*, April 18. https://www.nbcnews.com/news/nbcblk /georgetown-apologizes-renames-halls-after-slaves-n747976.

Edwards, R. L. (2016). Foreword. In M. J. Fuentes & D. G. White, *Scarlet and black*, Volume 1: *Slavery and dispossession in Rutgers history* (pp. vii–ix). Rutgers University Press.

Faulkner, M. S. (2013) *Slavery at the University of Virginia: A catalogue of current and past initiatives*. University of Virginia Idea Fund. Division for Diversity, Equity, and Inclusion, University of Virginia, January. https:// dei.virginia.edu/sites/g/files/jsddwu511/files/inline-files/SlaveryatUVA _FAULKNER_001.pdf.

Flowers, R. (2015). Refusal to forgive: Indigenous women's love and rage. *Decolonization: Indigeneity, Education, and Society, 4*(2), 32–49.

Fuentes, M. J., & White, D. G. (eds.). (2016). *Scarlet and black*, Volume 1: *Slavery and dispossession in Rutgers history*. Rutgers University Press.

Gaudry, A., & Lorenz, D. (2018). Indigenization as inclusion, reconciliation, and decolonization: Navigating the different visions for Indigenizing the Canadian academy. *AlterNative: An International Journal of Indigenous Peoples, 14*(3), 218–227.

Gaztambide-Fernández, R. A. (2012). Decolonization and the pedagogy of solidarity. *Decolonization: Indigeneity, Education, and Society, 1*(1).

Grande, S. (2018). Refusing the university. In E. Tuck & K. W. Yang (eds.), *Toward what justice?* (pp. 47–65). Routledge.

Graves, L. (2012). In the age of slavery. *University of Virginia Magazine*, January 12. http://uvamagazine.org/articles/in_the_age_of_slavery/.

Grosfoguel, R. (2013). The structure of knowledge in westernized universities: Epistemic racism/sexism and the four genocides/epistemicides of the long 16th century. *Human Architecture, 11*(1).

Harris, L. M., Campbell, J. T., & Brophy, A. L. (eds.). (2019). *Slavery and the university: Histories and legacies*. University of Georgia Press.

Hunt, D. (2018). "In search of our better selves": Totem transfer narratives and Indigenous futurities. *American Indian Culture and Research Journal, 42*(1), 71–90.

Kelley, R. D. G. (2016). Black study, Black struggle. *Boston Review*, March 1. https://bostonreview.net/forum/robin-d-g-kelley-black-study-black -struggle.

Lee, R., & Ahtone, T. (2020). Land-grab universities: Expropriated Indigenous land is the foundation of the land-grant university. *High Country News*, April: 32–45.

Lowe, L. (2015). *The intimacies of four continents*. Duke University Press.

McElhinny, B. (2016). Reparations and racism, discourse and diversity: Neoliberal multiculturalism and the Canadian age of apologies. *Language and Communication, 51*, 50–68.

McMillan Cottom, T. M. (2016). Georgetown's slavery announcement is remarkable, but it's not reparations. *Vox*, September 2. https://www.vox .com/2016/9/2/12773110/georgetown-slavery-admission-reparations.

McMillan Cottom, T. M., & Tuchman, G. (2015). Rationalization of higher education. *Emerging trends in the social and behavioral sciences: An interdisciplinary, searchable, and linkable resource*, 1–17.

Mills, C. (2007). White ignorance. In S. Sullivan & N. Tuana (eds.), *Race and epistemologies of ignorance* (pp. 26–31). State University New York Press.

Mitchell, N. (2015). (Critical ethnic studies) intellectual. *Critical Ethnic Studies, 1*(1), 86–94.

Mitchell, N. (2016). The fantasy and fate of ethnic studies in an age of uprisings: An interview with Nick Mitchell. *Undercommoning*, July 13. https://undercommoning.org/nick-mitchell-interview/.

Moten, F., & Harney, S. (2004). The university and the undercommons: Seven theses. *Social Text, 22*(2), 101–115.

Mustaffa, J. B. (2017). Mapping violence, naming life: A history of anti-Black oppression in the higher education system. *International Journal of Qualitative Studies in Education, 30*(8), 711–727.

Patton, L. D. (2016). Disrupting postsecondary prose: Toward a critical race theory of higher education. *Urban Education, 51*(3), 315–342.

Pietsch, T. (2016). Between the local and the universal: Academic worlds and the long history of the university. In M. H. Chou, I. Kamola, & T. Pietsch (eds.), *Transnational politics of higher education: Contesting the global / transforming the local*. Routledge.

Povinelli, E. A. (2002). *The cunning of recognition: Indigenous alterities and the making of Australian multiculturalism*. Duke University Press.

Redden, E. (2021). Paying reparations. *InsideHigherEd*, June 15. https://www .insidehighered.com/news/2021/06/15/virginia-theological-seminary -issues-first-reparations-checks.

Red Shirt–Shaw, M. (2020). Beyond the land acknowledgement: College "LAND BACK" or free tuition for Indigenous students. *Hack the Gates: Policy and Practice Briefs*. https://hackthegates.org/wp-content/uploads /2020/08/Redshirt-Shaw_Landback_HTGreport.pdf.

Richardson, R. (2021). Undergraduates at Brown vote for university to offer reparations. *NBC News*, March 29. https://www.nbcnews.com/news /nbcblk/undergraduates-brown-vote-university-offer-reparations -n1262413.

Santos, B. D. S. (2007). Beyond abyssal thinking: From global lines to ecologies of knowledges. *Binghamton University Review, 30*(1), 45–89.

Sharpe, C. (2014a). Black studies: In the wake. *Black Scholar, 44*(2), 59–69.

Sharpe, C. (2014b). The lie at the center of everything. *Black Studies Papers, 1*(1), 189–214.

Shotwell, A. (2016). *Against purity: Living ethically in compromised times.* University of Minnesota Press.

Silva, D. F. D. (2007). *Toward a global idea of race.* University of Minnesota Press.

Simpson, L. (2011). *Dancing on our turtle's back: Stories of Nishnaabeg re-creation, resurgence, and a new emergence.* Arbeiter Ring.

Simpson, L., & Coulthard, G. (2014). Dechinta Bush University, Indigenous land-based education, and embodied resurgence. *Decolonization: Indigeneity, Society, and Education,* November 26. https://decolonization.wordpress.com /2014/11/26/leanne-simpson-and-glen-coulthard-on-dechinta-bush -university-indigenous-land-based-education-and-embodied-resurgence.

Somani, A. (2011). The apology and its aftermath: National atonement or the management of minorities? *Postcolonial Text, 6*(1), 1–18.

Squire, D., Nicolazzo, Z., & Perez, R. J. (2019). Institutional response as non-performative: What university communications (don't) say about movements toward justice. *Review of Higher Education, 42*(5), 109–133.

Stein, S. (2016). Universities, slavery, and the unthought of anti-Blackness. *Cultural Dynamics, 28*(2), 169–187.

Stein, S. (2018). Racialized frames of value in US university responses to the travel ban. *ACME: An International E-Journal for Critical Geographies, 17*(4), 893–919.

Stein, S. (2020). "Truth before reconciliation": The difficulties of transform-ing higher education in settler colonial contexts. *Higher Education Research and Development, 39*(1), 156–170.

Stein, S., et al. (2020). Gesturing towards decolonial futures: Reflections on our learnings thus far. *Nordic Journal of Comparative and International Education (NJCIE), 4*(1), 27–27.

Stewart-Ambo, T., & Yang, K. W. (2021). Beyond land acknowledgment in settler institutions. *Social Text, 39*(1), 21–46.

Swarns, R. L. (2019). Is Georgetown's $400,000-a-year plan to aid slave descendants enough? *New York Times,* October 30. https://www.nytimes .com/2019/10/30/us/georgetown-slavery-reparations.html.

Taylor, M. L. (2020). Seminaries and slavery: An abolition struggle paradigm for research. *Theology Today, 76*(4), 308–321.

Toope, S. J. (2019). Legacies of enslavement. Vice Chancellor's Office, University of Cambridge. Retrieved from: https://www.v-c.admin.cam.ac .uk/projects/legacies-of-enslavement.

Tuck, E. (2009). Suspending damage: A letter to communities. *Harvard Educational Review, 79*(3), 409–428.

Tuck, E., & Yang, K. W. (2012). Decolonization is not a metaphor. *Decolonization: Indigeneity, Education, and Society, 1*(1), 1–40.

UCARE (University and Community Action for Racial Equity). (2012). Call for reflection and action: Addressing the University of Virginia's legacy of slavery, segregation and discrimination by seeking truth, understanding, repair, and relationship. Available at University of Mississippi Slavery Research Group. https://slaveryresearchgroup.olemiss.edu/wp-content /uploads/sites/145/2017/01/UCARE-report.pdf.

University of Virginia. (2013). *Slavery at the University of Virginia: Visitor's guide.* http://vpdiversity.virginia.edu/sites/vpdiversity.virginia.edu/files /documents/Slaveryat.UVaBrochure_FINAL.pdf.

Vimalassery, M., Pegues, J. H., & Goldstein, A. (2016). Introduction: On colonial unknowing. *Theory & Event, 19*(4).

Von Daacke, Kirt (2013). Universities Studying Slavery (USS)—The birth of a movement. President's Commission on Slavery and the University, University of Virginia. https://slavery.virginia.edu/universities-studying -slavery-uss-the-birth-of-a-movement/.

Vowel, C. (2016). Beyond territorial acknowledgements. *Apihtawikosisan,* September 23. https://apihtawikosisan.com/2016/09/beyond-territorial -acknowledgments/.

Walcott, R. (2011). Into the ranks of man: Vicious modernism and the politics of reconciliation. In A. Mathur, J. Dewar, and M. DeGagne (eds.), *Cultivating Canada: Reconciliation through the lens of cultural diversity* (pp. 341–349). Aboriginal Healing Foundation.

Wark, J. (2021). Land acknowledgements in the academy: Refusing the settler myth. *Curriculum Inquiry, 51*(2), 191–209.

Wilder, C. S. (2013). *Ebony and ivy: Race, slavery, and the troubled history of America's universities.* Bloomsbury.

White, D. (2016). Scarlet and black: A reconciliation. In M. J. Fuentes & D. G. White, *Scarlet and black,* Volume 1: *Slavery and dispossession in Rutgers history* (pp. 1–5). Rutgers University Press.

Wolfe, E. (2013) Unearthing slavery at the University of Virginia. *University of Virginia Magazine* (Spring). http://uvamagazine.org/articles/unearthing _slavery_at_the_university_of_virginia.

Wynter, S. (1994). No humans involved: An open letter to my colleagues. *Forum NHI: Knowledge for the 21st Century, 1*(1), 42–73.

Wynter, S. (2003). Unsettling the coloniality of being/power/truth/freedom: Towards the human, after man, its overrepresentation—An argument. *CR: The New Centennial Review, 3*(3), 257–337.

Yellowhead Institute (2019). *Land back: A Yellowhead Institute Red Paper.* https://redpaper.yellowheadinstitute.org/wp-content/uploads/2019/10/red-paper-report-final.pdf.

Chapter 6. Imagining Higher Education Otherwise

Agathangelou, A. M., Olwan, D. M., Spira, T. L., & Turcotte, H. M. (2015). Sexual divestments from empire: Women's studies, institutional feelings, and the "odious" machine. *Feminist Formations, 27*(3), 139–167.

Andreotti, V. (2021). *Hospicing modernity: Facing humanity's wrongs and implications for social activism.* North Atlantic Books.

Andreotti, V., Stein, S., Sutherland, A., Pashby, K., Suša, R., & Amsler, S. (2018). Mobilising different conversations about global justice in education: Toward alternative futures in uncertain times. *Policy & Practice: A Development Education Review, 26.*

Aronowitz, S. (2000). *The knowledge factory: Dismantling the corporate university and creating true higher learning.* Beacon Press.

Arshad-Ayaz, A., Naseem, M. A., & Mohamad, D. (2020). Engineering and humanitarian intervention: learning from failure. *Journal of International Humanitarian Action, 5*(1), 1–14.

Barnett, R. (2014). *Thinking about higher education.* Springer.

Bauman, Z. (2001). *The individualized society.* Polity Press.

Bauman, Z. (2011). *Liquid modern challenges to education.* Padova University Press.

Beverungen, A., Hoedemaekers, C., & Veldman, J. (2014). Charity and finance in the university. *Critical Perspectives on Accounting, 25*(1), 58–66.

Biesta, G. (2020). Trying to be at home in the world: New parameters for art education. *Artlink,* September 1. https://www.artlink.com.au/articles/4781/trying-to-be-at-home-in-the-world-new-parameters-f/.

Boggs, A., & Mitchell, N. (2018). Critical university studies and the crisis consensus. *Feminist Studies, 44*(2), 432–463.

Boggs, A., Meyerhoff, E., Mitchell, N., & Schwartz-Weinstein, Z (2019). *Abolitionist university studies: An invitation.* Abolition University. https://abolition.university/wp-content/uploads/2019/08/Abolitionist-University-Studies_-An-Invitation-Release-1-version.pdf.

Bok, D. (2003). *Universities in the marketplace: The commercialization of higher education.* Princeton University Press.

Bousquet, M. (2008). *How the university works: Higher education and the low-wage nation.* New York University.

Burman, A. (2012). Places to think with, books to think about: Words, experience and the decolonization of knowledge in the Bolivian Andes. *Human Architecture, 10*(1).

Chan, A. S., & Fisher, D. (2009). Introduction. In A. S. Chan & D. Fisher (eds.), *The exchange university: Corporatization of academic culture* (pp. 1–18). University of British Columbia Press.

Fisher, D. (1992). Privatization and education: Some reflections on Canada. In L. Gordon & J. Codd (eds.), *Education policy and the changing role of the state* (pp. 45–60). Massey University.

GTDF (Gesturing Towards Decolonial Futures) (2021). The gifts of failure. https://decolonialfutures.net/portfolio/the-gifts-of-failure/.

Haraway, D. J. (2016). *Staying with the trouble: Making kin in the Chthulucene.* Duke University Press.

Harkavy, I. (2006). The role of universities in advancing citizenship and social justice in the 21st century. *Education, Citizenship, and Social Justice, 1,* 5–37.

Jimmy, E. (2019). [Untitled commentary about We Are the Weather]. Lisa Hirmer. http://www.lisahirmer.ca/wp-content/uploads/2019/04/elwood-jimmy-text.pdf.

Jimmy, E., Andreotti, V., and Stein, S. (2019). *Towards braiding.* Musagetes Foundation.

Kahn, S., Huelsman, M. & Mishory, J. (2019). *Bridging progressive policy debates: How student debt and the racial wealth gap reinforce each other.* Roosevelt Institute. September. Available at https://production-tcf.imgix.net/app/uploads/2019/09/06161443/RI_Student-Debt-and-RWG-201908.pdf

Kamola, I., & Meyerhoff, E. (2009). Creating commons: Divided governance, participatory management, and struggles against enclosure in the university. *Polygraph, 21,* 15–37.

Lea, D. (2009). The managerial university and the decline of modern thought. *Educational Philosophy and Theory 43*(8), 816–837.

Lloyd, D., & Wolfe, P. (2016). Settler colonial logics and the neoliberal regime. *Settler Colonial Studies, 6*(2), 109–118.

Marez, C. (2014). Seeing in the red: Looking at student debt. *American Quarterly, 66*(2), 261–281.

Martínez-Alemán, A. M. (2014). Managerialism as the "new" discursive masculinity in the university. *Feminist Formations, 26*(2), 107–134.

McMillan Cottom, T. (2017). *Lower ed: How for-profit colleges deepen inequality in America.* The New Press.

McMillan Cottom, T., & Tuchman, G. (2015). Rationalization of higher education. In R. Scott & S. Kosslyn (eds.), *Emerging trends in the social and behavioral sciences: An interdisciplinary, searchable, and linkable resource* (pp. 1–17). John Wiley & Sons. https://tressiemc.com/wp-content/uploads/2015/05/cottom-tuchman-rationalization-in-highered-final.pdf.

Melamed, J. (2015). Racial capitalism. *Critical Ethnic Studies, 1*(1), 76–85.

Metcalfe, A. S. (2010). Revisiting academic capitalism in Canada: No longer the exception. *Journal of Higher Education, 81*(4), 489–514.

Metcalfe, A. S., & Slaughter, S. (2008). The differential effects of academic capitalism on women in the academy. In J. Glazer-Raymo (ed.), *Unfinished agendas: New and continuing gender challenges in higher education* (pp. 80–111). Johns Hopkins University Press.

Newfield, C. (2008). *Unmaking the public university: The forty-year assault on the middle class.* Harvard University Press.

Newson, J., Polster, C., & Woodhouse, H. (2012). Toward an alternative future for Canada's corporatized universities. *ESC: English Studies in Canada, 38*(1), 51–70.

Olssen, M., & Peters, M. A. (2005). Neoliberalism, higher education, and the knowledge economy: From the free market to knowledge capitalism. *Journal of Education Policy, 20*(3), 313–345.

Out of the Woods Collective. (2020). An interview with Out of the Woods. *Journal of Aesthetics & Protest, 11.* http://www.joaap.org/issue11/OutoftheWoods.html.

Posecznick, A. (2014). On theorising and humanising academic complicity in the neoliberal university. *Learning and Teaching, 7*(1), 1–11

Preston, S., & Aslett, J. (2014). Resisting neoliberalism from within the academy: Subversion through an activist pedagogy. *Social Work Education, 33*(4), 502–518.

Pusser, B. (2014). Forces in tension: The state, civil society, and market in the future of the university. In P. Gibbs & R. Barnett (eds.), *Thinking about higher education* (pp. 71–89). Springer International.

Rhoads, R. A., & Rhoades, G. (2005). Graduate employee unionization as symbol of and challenge to the corporatization of U.S. research universities. *Journal of Higher Education, 76*(3), 243–275.

Robin, C. (2020). The pandemic is the time to resurrect the public university. *New Yorker,* May 7. https://www.newyorker.com/culture/cultural-comment/the-pandemic-is-the-time-to-resurrect-the-public-university

Shotwell, A. (2016). *Against purity: Living ethically in compromised times.* University of Minnesota Press.

Silva, D. F.D. (2014). Toward a Black feminist poethics: The quest(ion) of Blackness toward the end of the world. *Black Scholar, 44*(2), 81–97.

Slaughter, S., & Rhoades, G. (2004). *Academic capitalism and the new economy: Markets, state, and higher education.* Johns Hopkins University Press.

Soederberg, S. (2014). Student loans, debtfare, and the commodification of debt: The securitization and displacement of risk. *Critical Sociology, 40*(5), 689–709.

Spivak, G. C. (2004). Righting wrongs. *South Atlantic Quarterly, 103*(2–3), 523–581.

Stein, S. (2019). Beyond higher education as we know it: Gesturing towards decolonial horizons of possibility. *Studies in Philosophy and Education, 38*(2), 143–161.

Stein, S., et al. (2020). Gesturing towards decolonial futures: Reflections on our learnings thus far. *Nordic Journal of Comparative and International Education (NJCIE)*, 4(1), 43–65.

Stein, S., Andreotti, V., Suša, R., & Cajkova, T. (2022). From "education for sustainable development" to "education for the end of the world as we know it." *Educational Philosophy and Theory*, 54(3), 274–287.

Sumner, J. (2009). Keeping the commons in academic culture: Protecting the knowledge commons from the enclosure of the knowledge economy. In A. S. Chan & D. Fisher (eds.), *The exchange university: Corporatization of academic culture* (pp. 188–202). University of British Columbia Press.

Suspitsyna, T. (2010). Accountability in American education as a rhetoric and a technology of governmentality. *Journal of Education Policy*, 25(5), 567–586.

Thorkelson, E. (2015). What does the American university stand for? In C. Soulié and C. Charle (eds.), *La Dérégulation Académique: la Construction étatisée des Marchés Universitaires Dans le Monde*. Syllepse.

Tuck, E., & Yang, K. W. (2012). Decolonization is not a metaphor. *Decolonization: Indigeneity Education & Society*, 1(1), 1–40.

Ty, M. (2011). Introduction: Higher education on its knees. *Qui Parle: Critical Humanities and Social Sciences*, 20(1), 3–32.

Van der Zwan, N. (2014). Making sense of financialization. *Socio-economic Review*, 12(1), 99–129.

Whyte, K. (2020a). Against crisis epistemology. In B. Hokowhitu, A. Moreton-Robinson, L. Tuhiwai-Smith, S. Larkin, & C. Andersen (eds.), *Handbook of Critical Indigenous Studies* (pp. 52–64). Routledge.

Whyte, K. (2020b). Too late for Indigenous climate justice: Ecological and relational tipping points. *Wiley Interdisciplinary Reviews: Climate Change*, 11(1), e603.

Williams, J. (2006). The pedagogy of debt. *College Literature*, 33(4), 155–169.

Index

complicity: in colonization, 98–104; in harm, 28–34; institutional, in slavery, 110–20

conditional inclusion, 136, 168, 174–77, 182–85, 218–19, 220

continuous progress, promises of, 5, 76–78, 87, 177–81, 193–94

COVID-19 pandemic, 261

critical approaches to justice, 234–37, 242

Crutzen, P., 198

Cullen, Jim, 164

Dahl, Adam, 154

Daigle, Michelle, 23, 24

Dartmouth College, 91, 104–10

Dartmouth College v. Woodward (1819), 87

Davis, Heather, 16, 94–95

Dawes Act (1887), 150–51

Dechinta Centre for Research and Learning, 237–38, 267–68

decolonial framework: characterized, 2, 6–8, 50–51; addressing settler memory, 8–9; CIRCULAR patterns, 247–49, *248*; decolonial critiques, 57–63, *59*; decolonial futures, gesturing toward, 266–71; decolonial historiography, 56–57; of land-grant history, 125–26, 142–43; possible responses to, 34–41. *See also* higher education, colonial history of; higher education, imagined otherwise; reparation

Degrees of Inequality (Mettler), 74

Deloria, Vine, 149

democracy: colonial concept of liberty and, 97–98; economic opportunity and, 139–42; expansionism and, 154–55; as justification for colonial violence, 132, 159–60; Turner's "frontier thesis," 156

Democracy's College (Ross), 142

description-prescription formula, 256–60

Diné (Navajo) peoples, 193

Discipline and Surplus (Mitchell), 68

disinvestment, 249–50, 261–66

dispossession. *See* land dispossession; land-grant institutions

diversity, equity, and inclusion (DEI) efforts, 185, 267

divestment vs. disinvestment, 262–63

Doctrine of Discovery, 143–45, 146–47, 157

Du Bois, W.E.B., 62

Dunbar-Ortiz, Roxanne, 126, 150, 176–77

Ebony and Ivy (Wilder), 111

ecological violence: as condition of possibility, 50–51; costs of economic growth, 196–99; in land dispossession, 93–98, 114–15, 131–32; racial-colonial violence and, 10

economics: democracy and economic growth, 139–42; ecological costs of growth, 196–99; interest convergence and, 174–77; land-grant system and, 133–35; post-War promises of progress, 171–74; post-War US hegemony, 187–89, 194–95. *See also* capitalism

The Emergence of the American University (Veysey), 63

The Epic of America (Adams), 74

equality. *See* social mobility

Evans, John, 53

exceptionalism: American, 72–75, 122, 155–56, 187–89; Canadian, 11; reproduction of in higher education, 229–33; white, 71–76

failure, learning from, 271–74

Farrell, Justin, 16

Ferguson, Roderick, 68, 135, 163, 175, 177, 182–83, 185

Fine, Alan, 112, 222

Fischer, Karin, 166

the Five E's, 39–41, 260

Florida ex Rel. Hawkins v. Board of Control (1956), 170

Flowers, Rachel, 231

Folbre, Nancy, 141, 143

frontier concept, 127, 143–45, 155–59

"Frontier Thesis" (Turner), 155–56

Frymer, Paul, 148

Fuentes, Marisa J., 111, 213–14, 215

Fulbright, William, 189